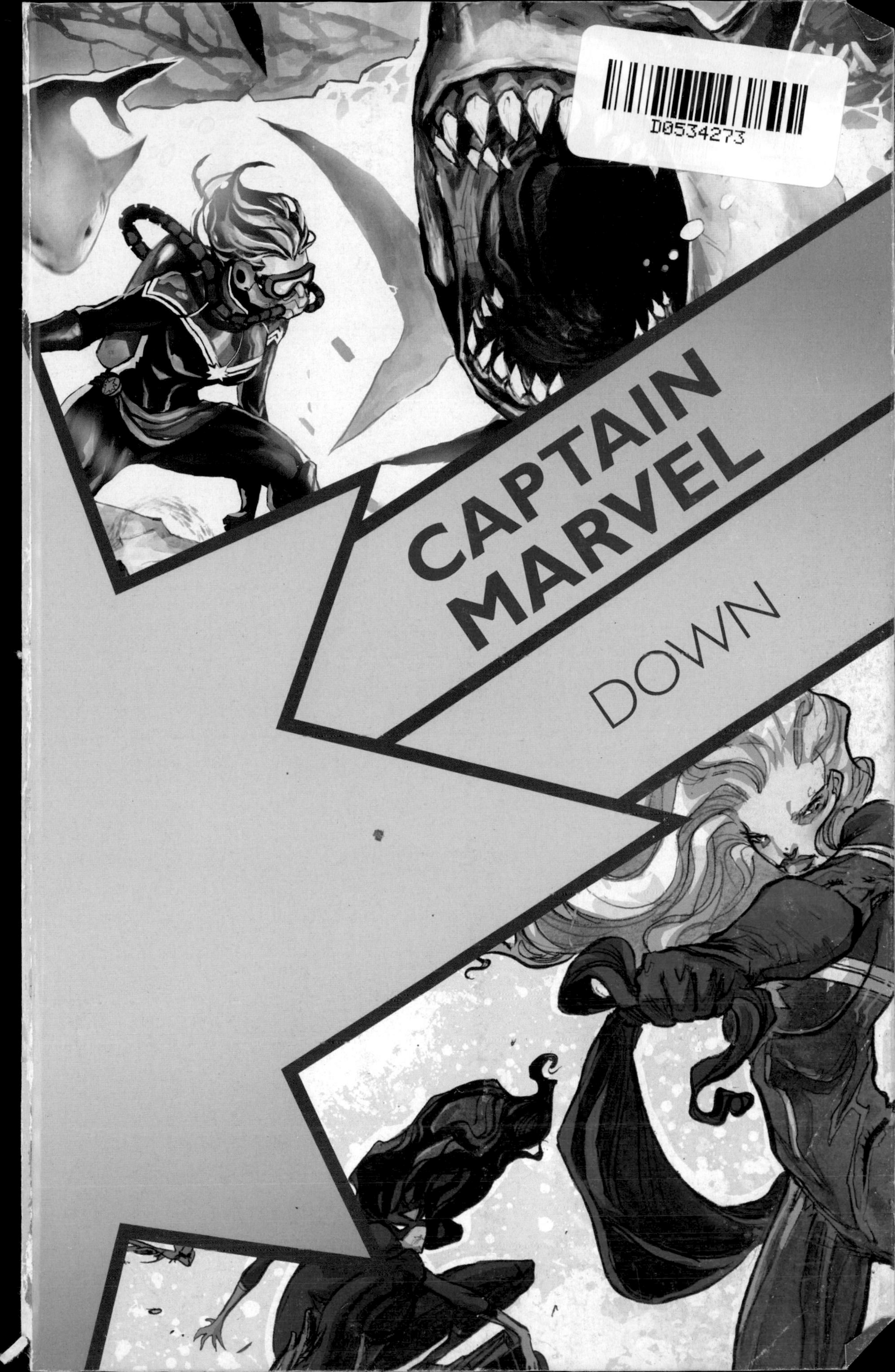
CAPTAIN
MARVEL
DOWN

WRITERS KELLY SUE DeCONNICK (#7-12)

& CHRISTOPHER SEBELA (#7-8 & #10-12)

ARTISTS DEXTER SOY (#7-8)

& FILIPE ANDRADE (#9-12)

COLOR ARTISTS DEXTER SOY (#7),

VERONICA GANDINI (#8)

& JORDIE BELLAIRE (#9-12)

LETTERER VC'S JOE CARAMAGNA

COVER ART JAMIE McKELVIE & JORDIE BELLAIRE (#7 & #9),

DEXTER SOY (#8) AND JOE QUINONES (#10-12)

EDITOR SANA AMANAT

SENIOR EDITOR STEPHEN WACKER

COLLECTION EDITOR: CORY LEVINE
ASSISTANT EDITORS: ALEX STARBUCK & NELSON RIBEIRO
EDITORS, SPECIAL PROJECTS: JENNIFER GRÜNWALD & MARK D. BEAZLEY
SENIOR EDITOR, SPECIAL PROJECTS: JEFF YOUNGQUIST
SVP OF PRINT & DIGITAL PUBLISHING SALES: DAVID GABRIEL
BOOK DESIGN: JEFF POWELL & CORY LEVINE

EDITOR IN CHIEF: AXEL ALONSO
CHIEF CREATIVE OFFICER: JOE QUESADA
PUBLISHER: DAN BUCKLEY
EXECUTIVE PRODUCER: ALAN FINE

CAPTAIN MARVEL VOL. 2: DOWN. Contains material originally published in magazine form as CAPTAIN MARVEL #7-12. First printing 2013. ISBN# 978-0-7851-6550-7. Published by MARVEL WORLDWIDE, INC., a subsidiary of MARVEL ENTERTAINMENT, LLC. OFFICE OF PUBLICATION: 135 West 50th Street, New York, NY 10020. Copyright © 2012 and 2013 Marvel Characters, Inc. All rights reserved. All characters featured in this issue and the distinctive names and likenesses thereof, and all related indicia are trademarks of Marvel Characters, Inc. No similarity between any of the names, characters, persons, and/or institutions in this magazine with those of any living or dead person or institution is intended, and any such similarity which may exist is purely coincidental. **Printed in the U.S.A.** ALAN FINE, EVP - Office of the President, Marvel Worldwide, Inc. and EVP & CMO Marvel Characters B.V.; DAN BUCKLEY, Publisher & President - Print, Animation & Digital Divisions; JOE QUESADA, Chief Creative Officer; TOM BREVOORT, SVP of Publishing; DAVID BOGART, SVP of Operations & Procurement, Publishing; C.B. CEBULSKI, SVP of Creator & Content Development; DAVID GABRIEL, SVP of Print & Digital Publishing Sales; JIM O'KEEFE, VP of Operations & Logistics; DAN CARR, Executive Director of Publishing Technology; SUSAN CRESPI, Editorial Operations Manager; ALEX MORALES, Publishing Operations Manager; STAN LEE, Chairman Emeritus. For information regarding advertising in Marvel Comics or on Marvel.com, please contact Niza Disla, Director of Marvel Partnerships, at ndisla@marvel.com. For Marvel subscription inquiries, please call 800-217-9158. **Manufactured between 3/28/2013 and 4/30/2013 by QUAD/GRAPHICS, VERSAILLES, KY, USA.**

10 9 8 7 6 5 4 3 2 1

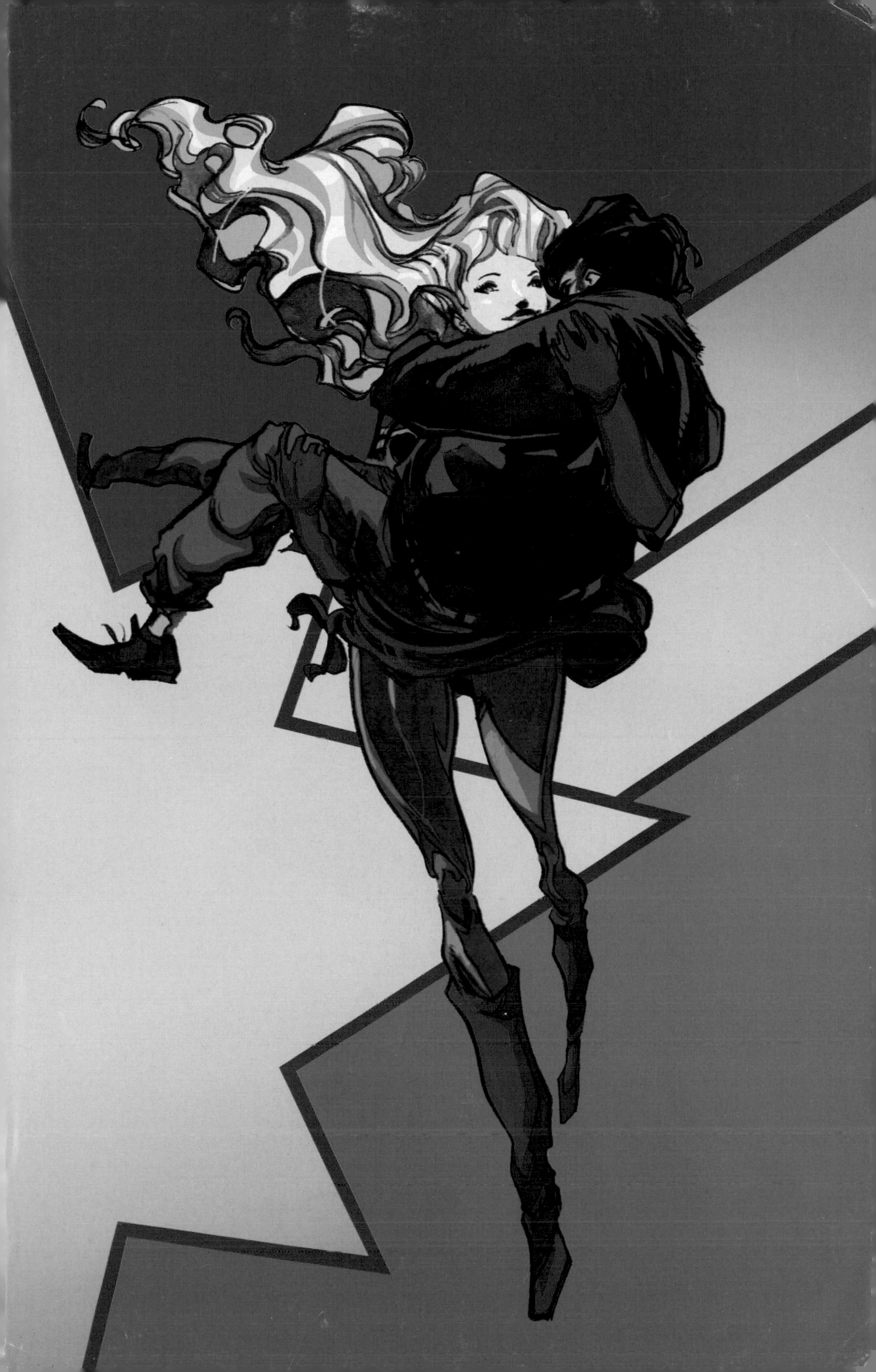

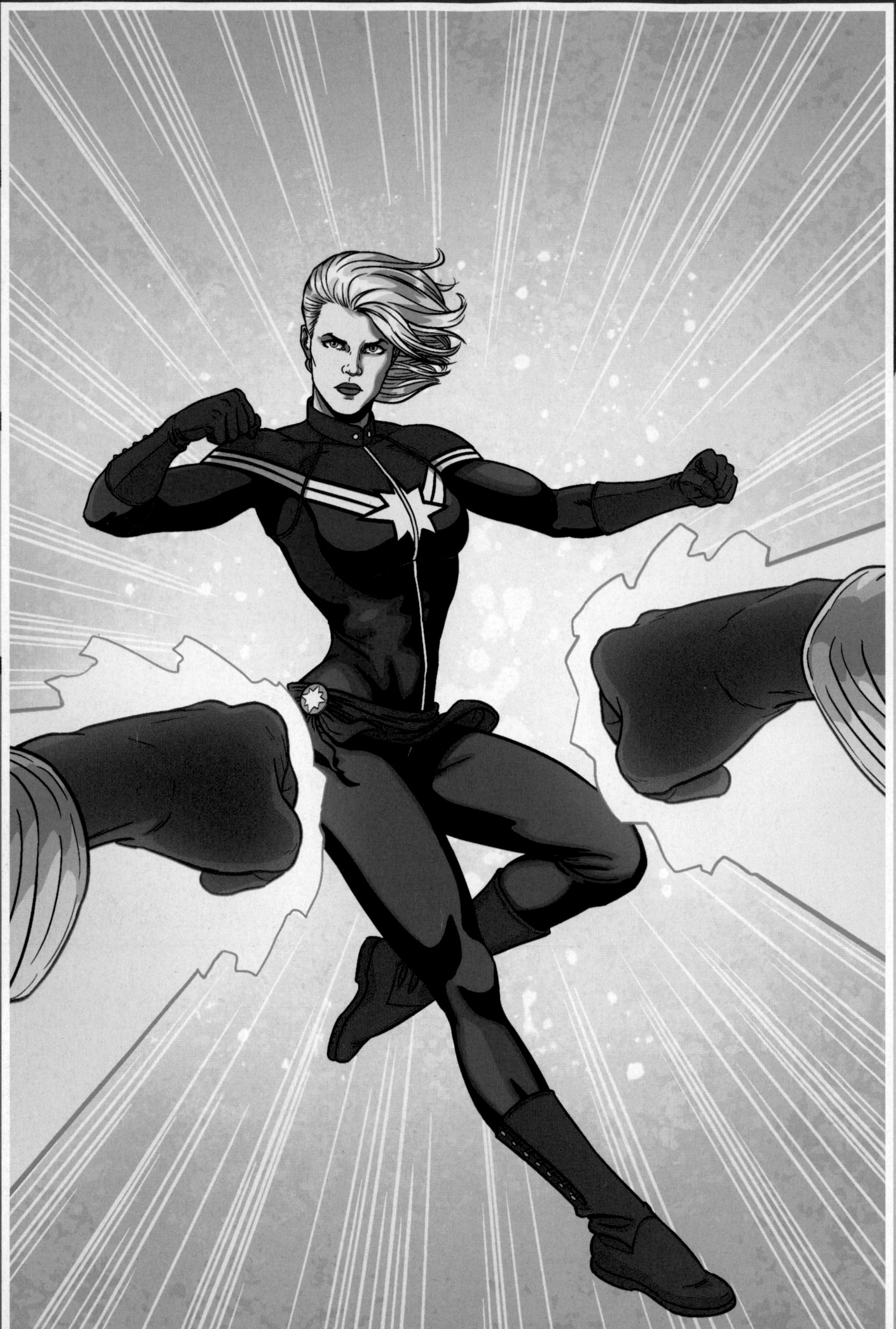

SEVEN

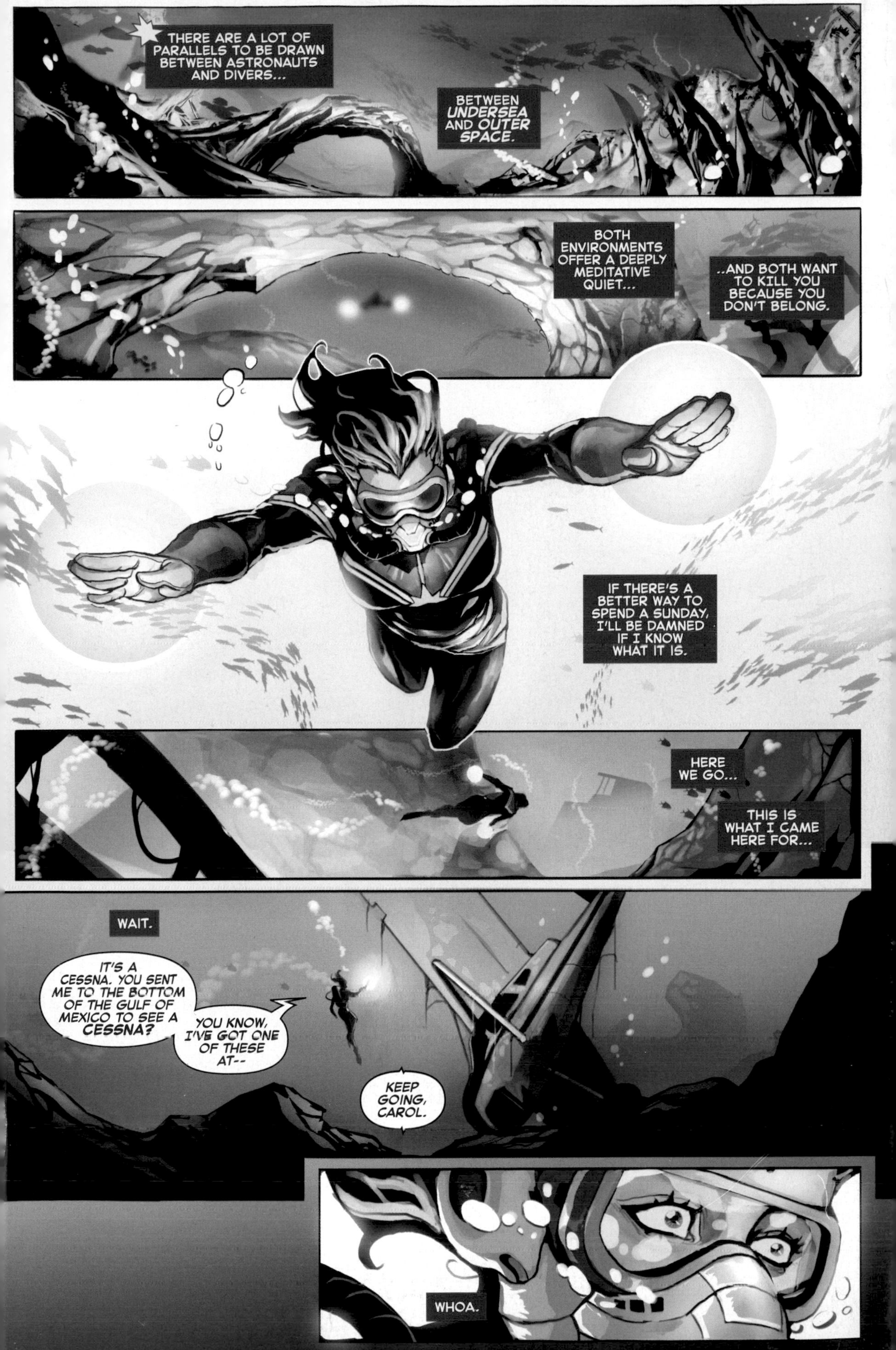
THERE ARE A LOT OF PARALLELS TO BE DRAWN BETWEEN ASTRONAUTS AND DIVERS...
BETWEEN UNDERSEA AND OUTER SPACE.
BOTH ENVIRONMENTS OFFER A DEEPLY MEDITATIVE QUIET...
..AND BOTH WANT TO KILL YOU BECAUSE YOU DON'T BELONG.
IF THERE'S A BETTER WAY TO SPEND A SUNDAY, I'LL BE DAMNED IF I KNOW WHAT IT IS.
HERE WE GO...
THIS IS WHAT I CAME HERE FOR...
WAIT.
IT'S A CESSNA. YOU SENT ME TO THE BOTTOM OF THE GULF OF MEXICO TO SEE A CESSNA?
YOU KNOW, I'VE GOT ONE OF THESE AT--
KEEP GOING, CAROL.
WHOA.

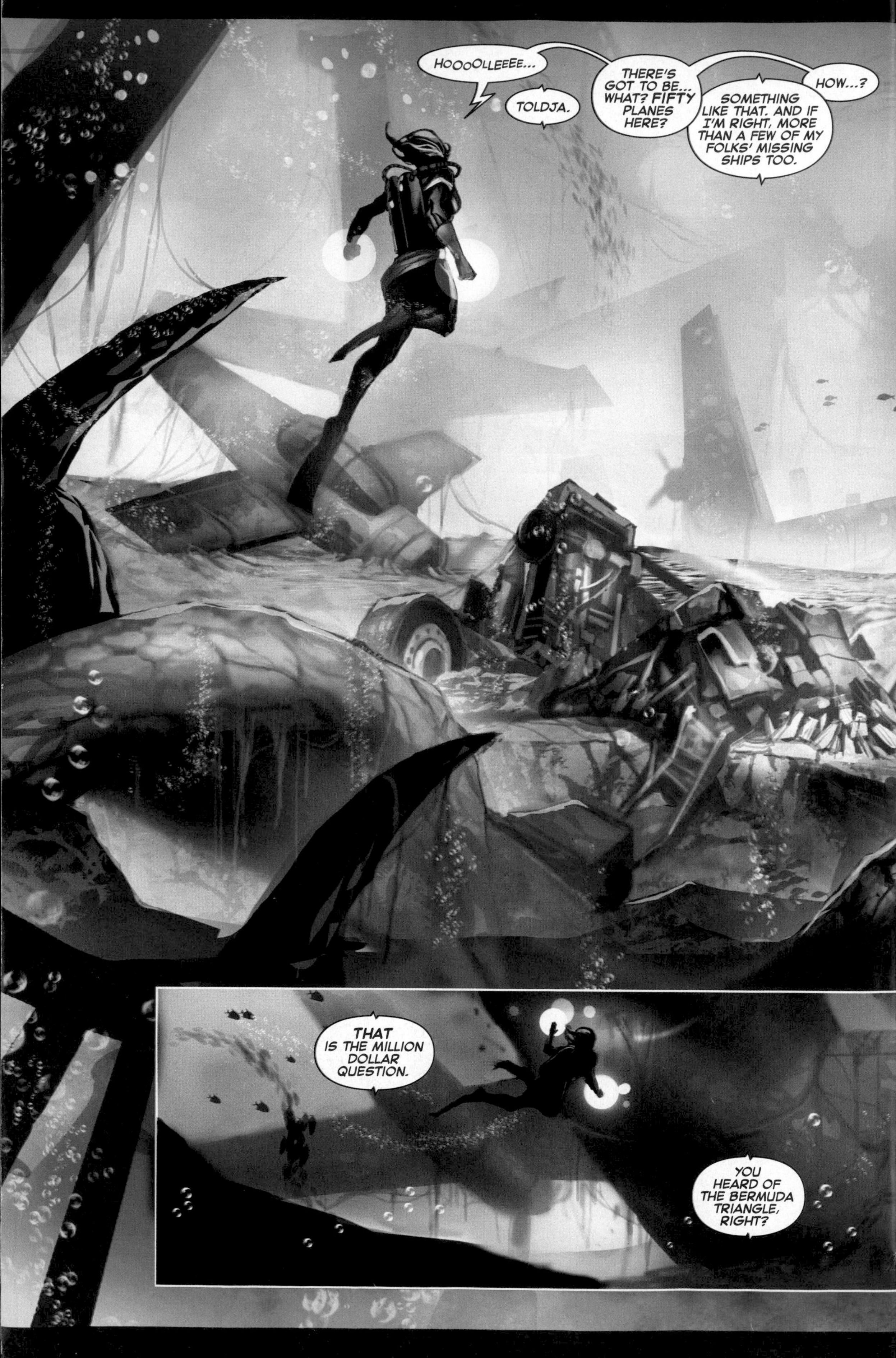
HOOOOLLEEEE...
TOLDJA.
THERE'S GOT TO BE... WHAT? FIFTY PLANES HERE?
HOW...?
SOMETHING LIKE THAT. AND IF I'M RIGHT, MORE THAN A FEW OF MY FOLKS' MISSING SHIPS TOO.
THAT IS THE MILLION DOLLAR QUESTION.
YOU HEARD OF THE BERMUDA TRIANGLE, RIGHT?

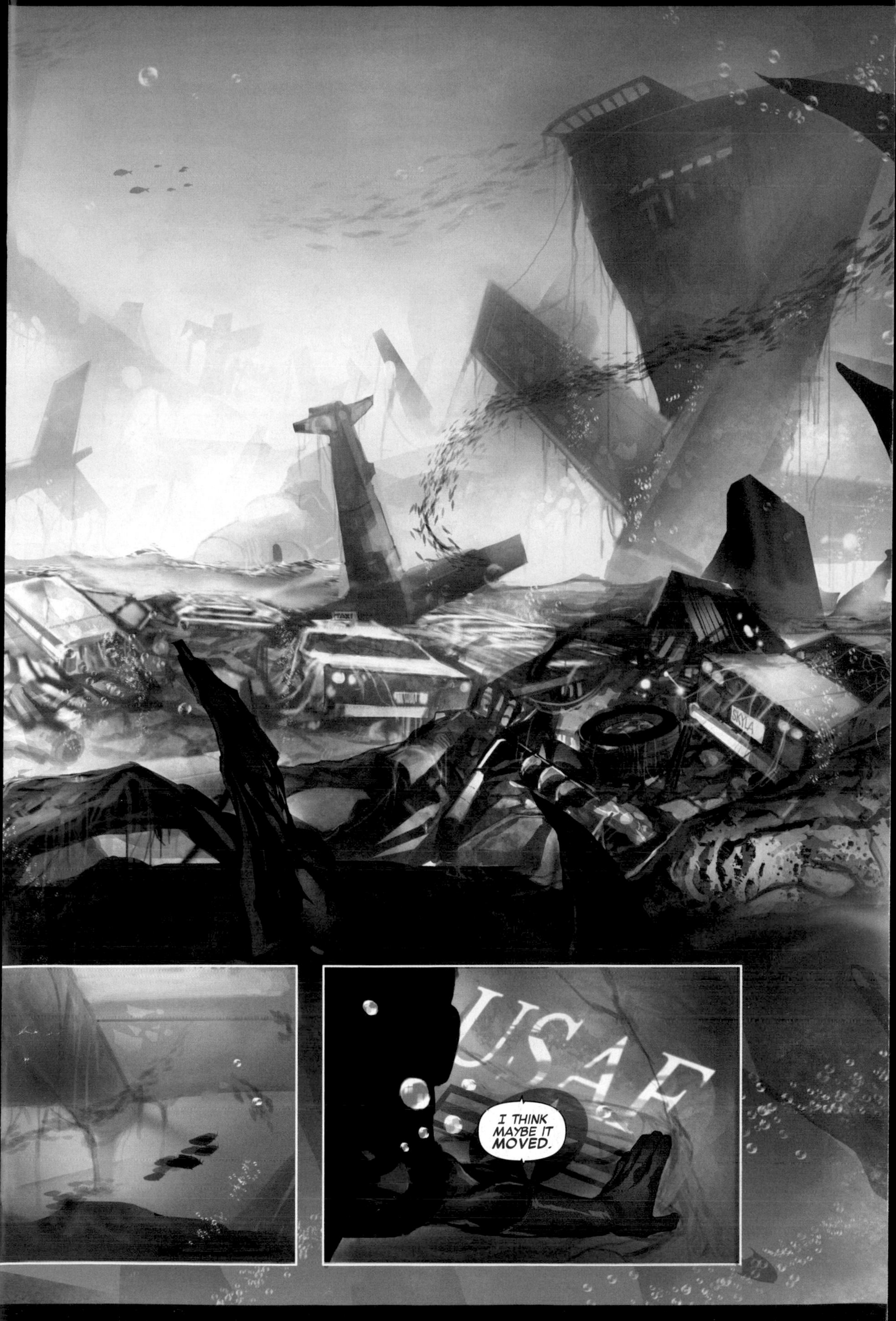
SKYLA
USAF
I THINK MAYBE IT MOVED.

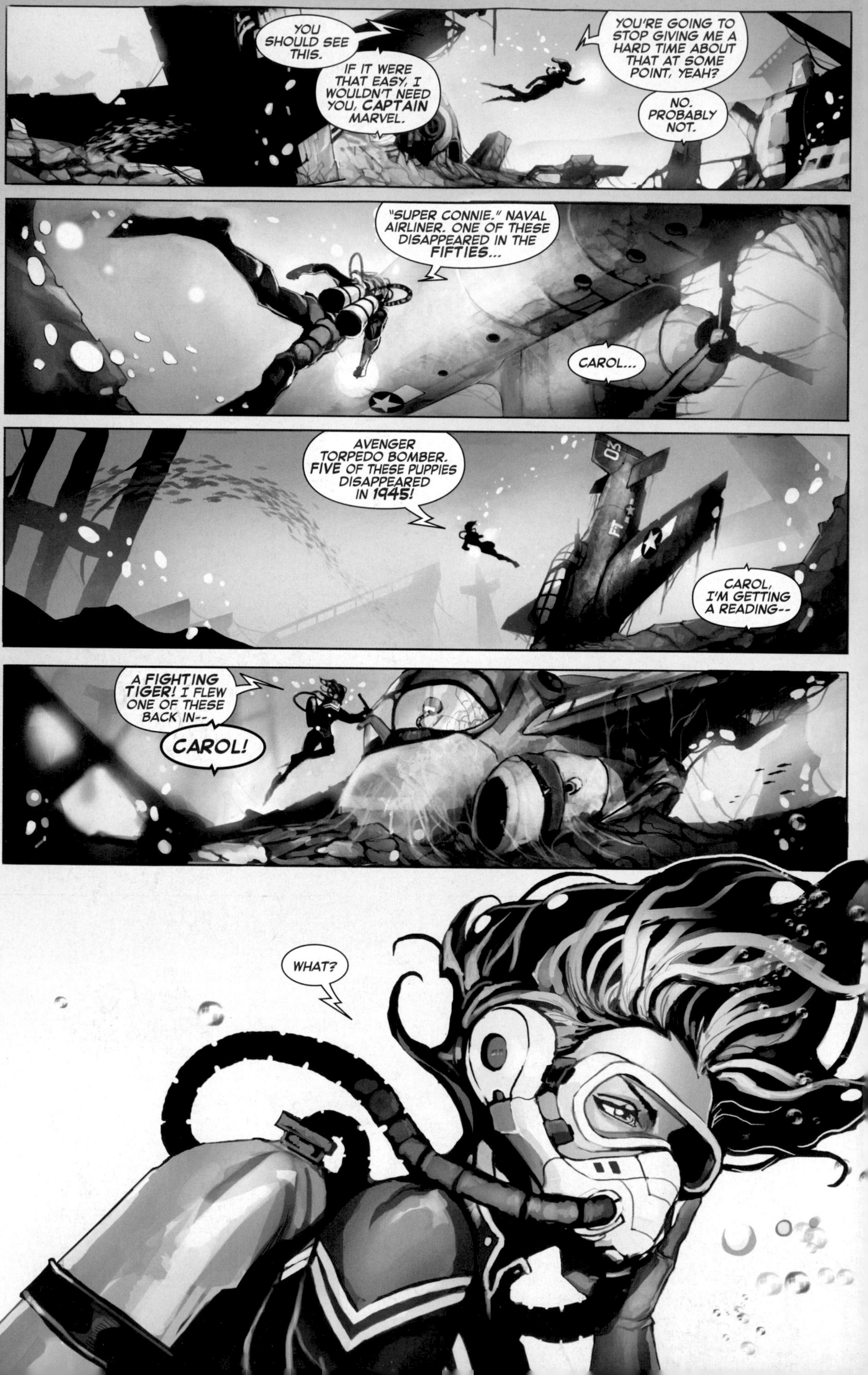
YOU SHOULD SEE THIS.
IF IT WERE THAT EASY, I WOULDN'T NEED YOU, CAPTAIN MARVEL.
YOU'RE GOING TO STOP GIVING ME A HARD TIME ABOUT THAT AT SOME POINT, YEAH?
NO. PROBABLY NOT.
"SUPER CONNIE." NAVAL AIRLINER. ONE OF THESE DISAPPEARED IN THE FIFTIES...
CAROL...
AVENGER TORPEDO BOMBER. FIVE OF THESE PUPPIES DISAPPEARED IN 1945!
CAROL, I'M GETTING A READING--
A FIGHTING TIGER! I FLEW ONE OF THESE BACK IN--
CAROL!
WHAT?

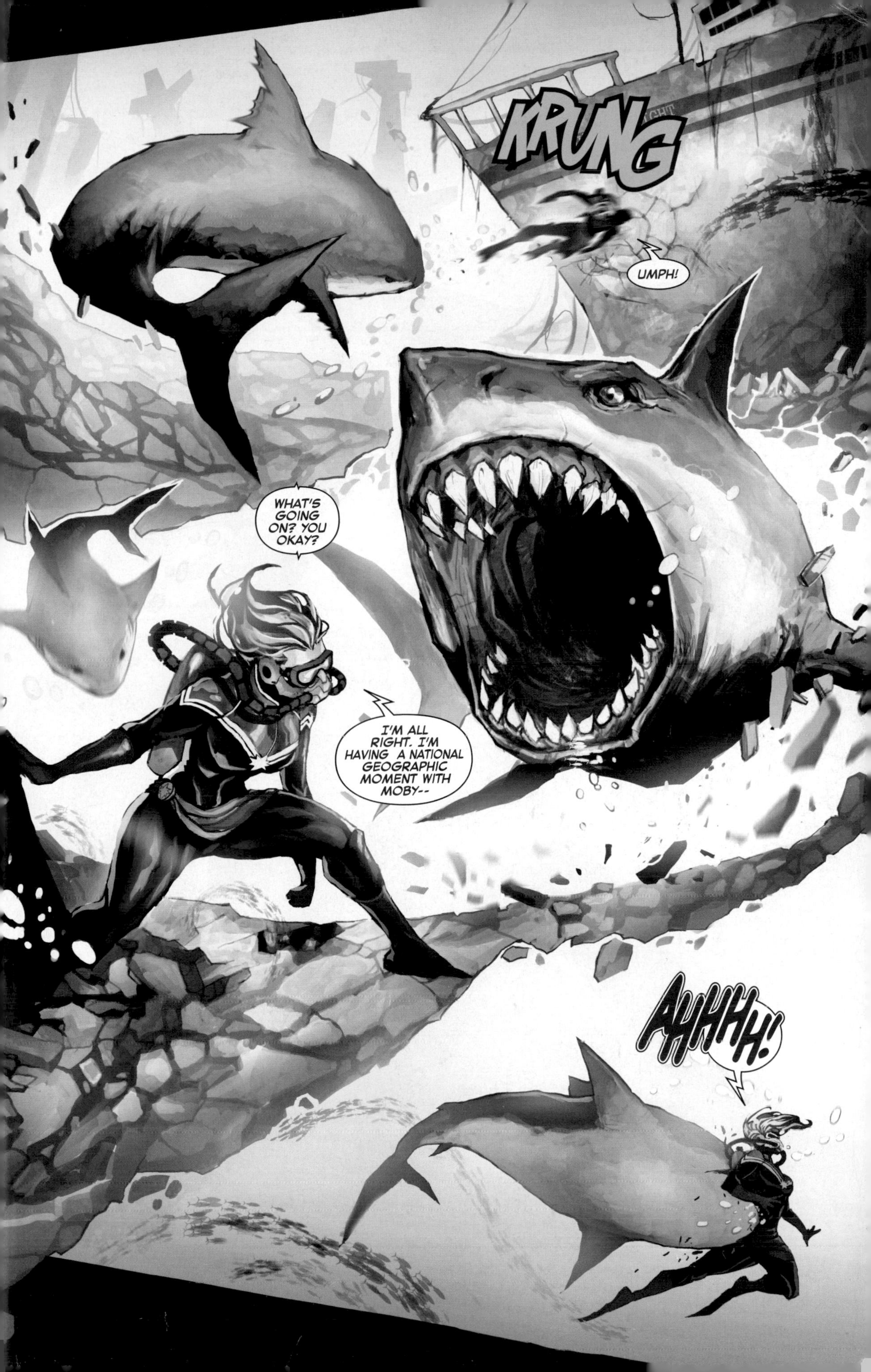
KRUNG
UMPH!
WHAT'S GOING ON? YOU OKAY?
I'M ALL RIGHT. I'M HAVING A NATIONAL GEOGRAPHIC MOMENT WITH MOBY--
AHHHH!

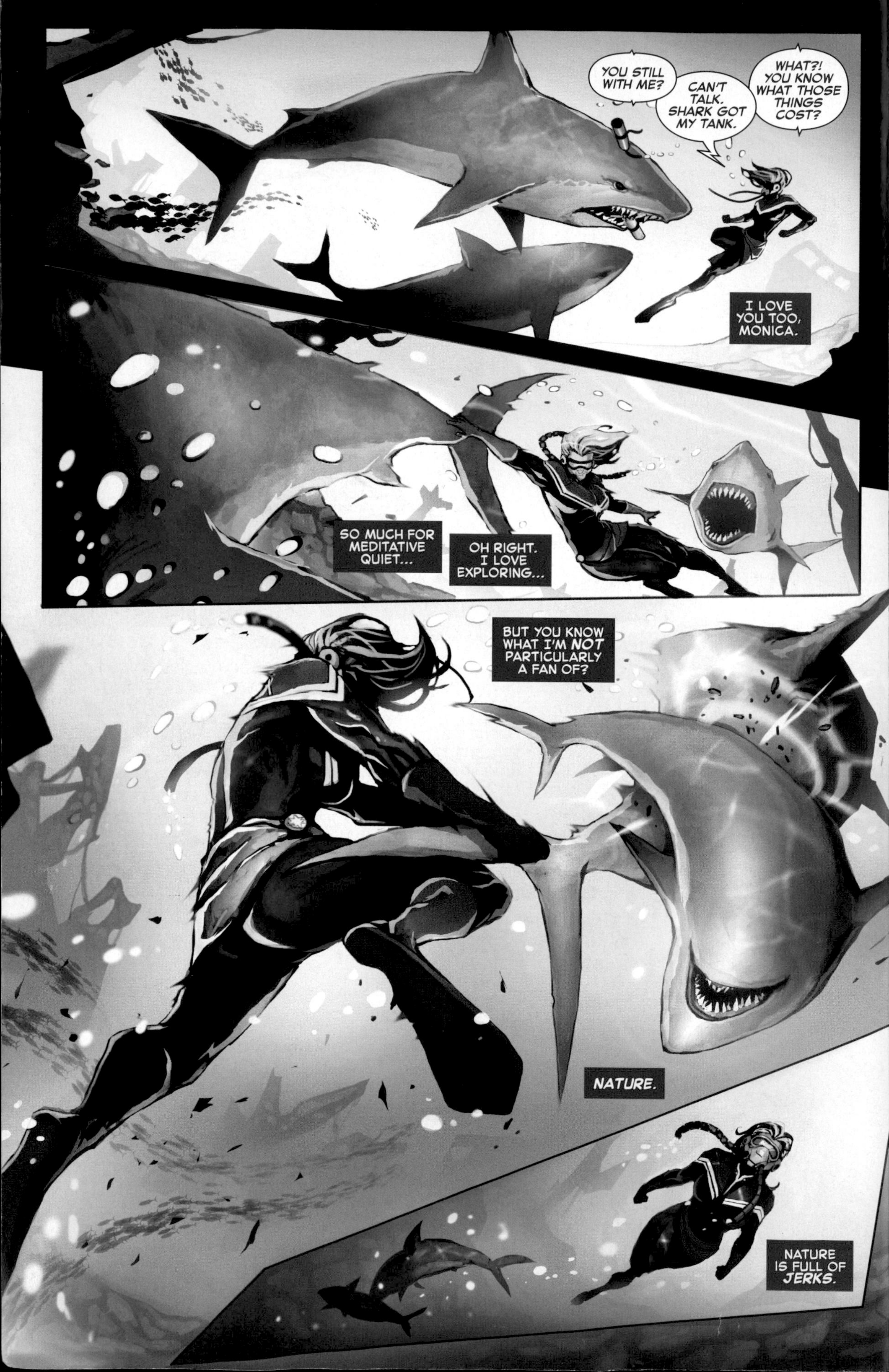
YOU STILL WITH ME?
CAN'T TALK. SHARK GOT MY TANK.
WHAT?! YOU KNOW WHAT THOSE THINGS COST?
I LOVE YOU TOO, MONICA.
SO MUCH FOR MEDITATIVE QUIET...
OH RIGHT. I LOVE EXPLORING...
BUT YOU KNOW WHAT I'M NOT PARTICULARLY A FAN OF?
NATURE.
NATURE IS FULL OF JERKS.

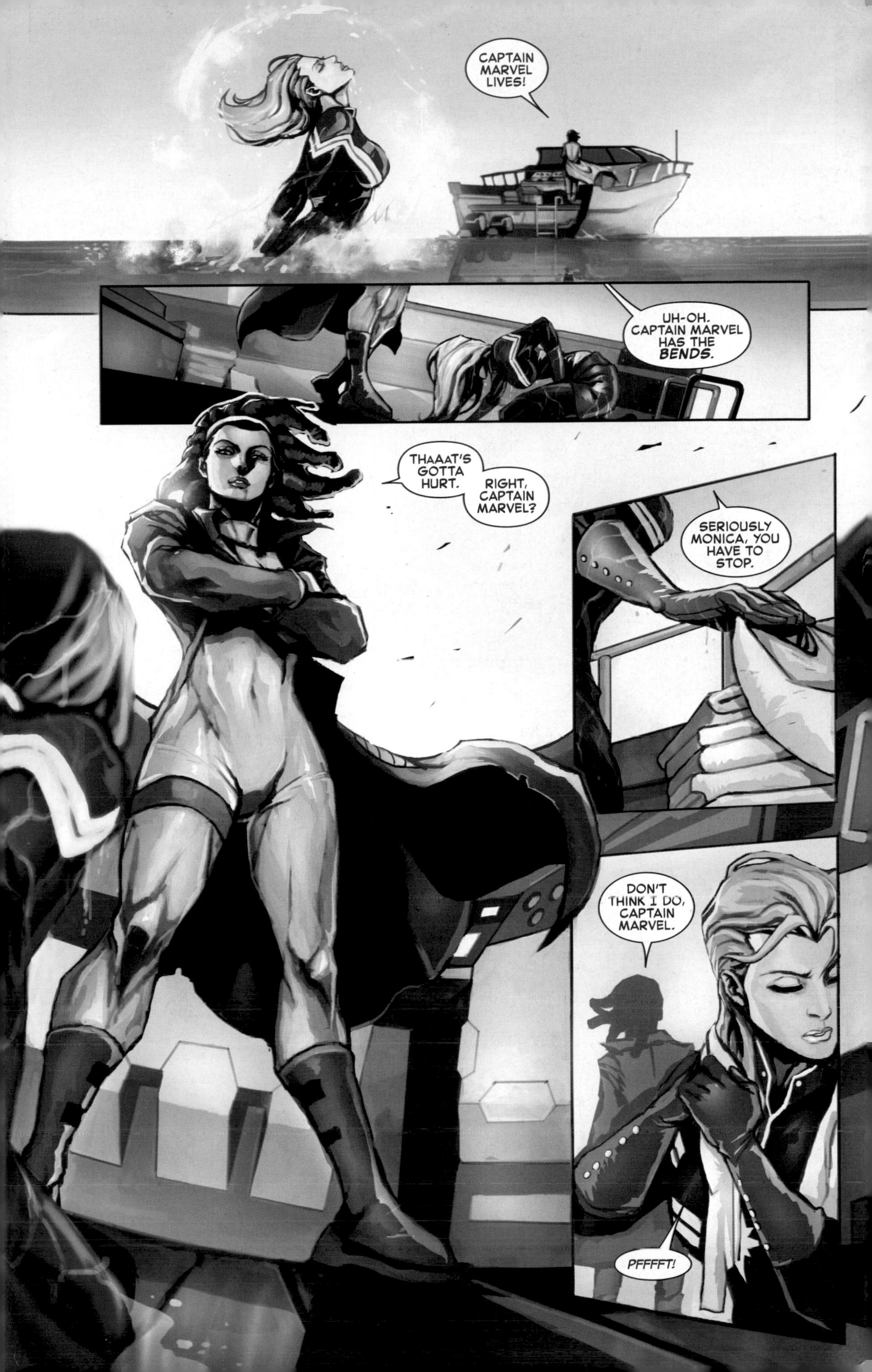
CAPTAIN MARVEL LIVES!
UH-OH. CAPTAIN MARVEL HAS THE BENDS.
THAAAT'S GOTTA HURT.
RIGHT, CAPTAIN MARVEL?
SERIOUSLY MONICA, YOU HAVE TO STOP.
DON'T THINK I DO, CAPTAIN MARVEL.
PFFFFT!

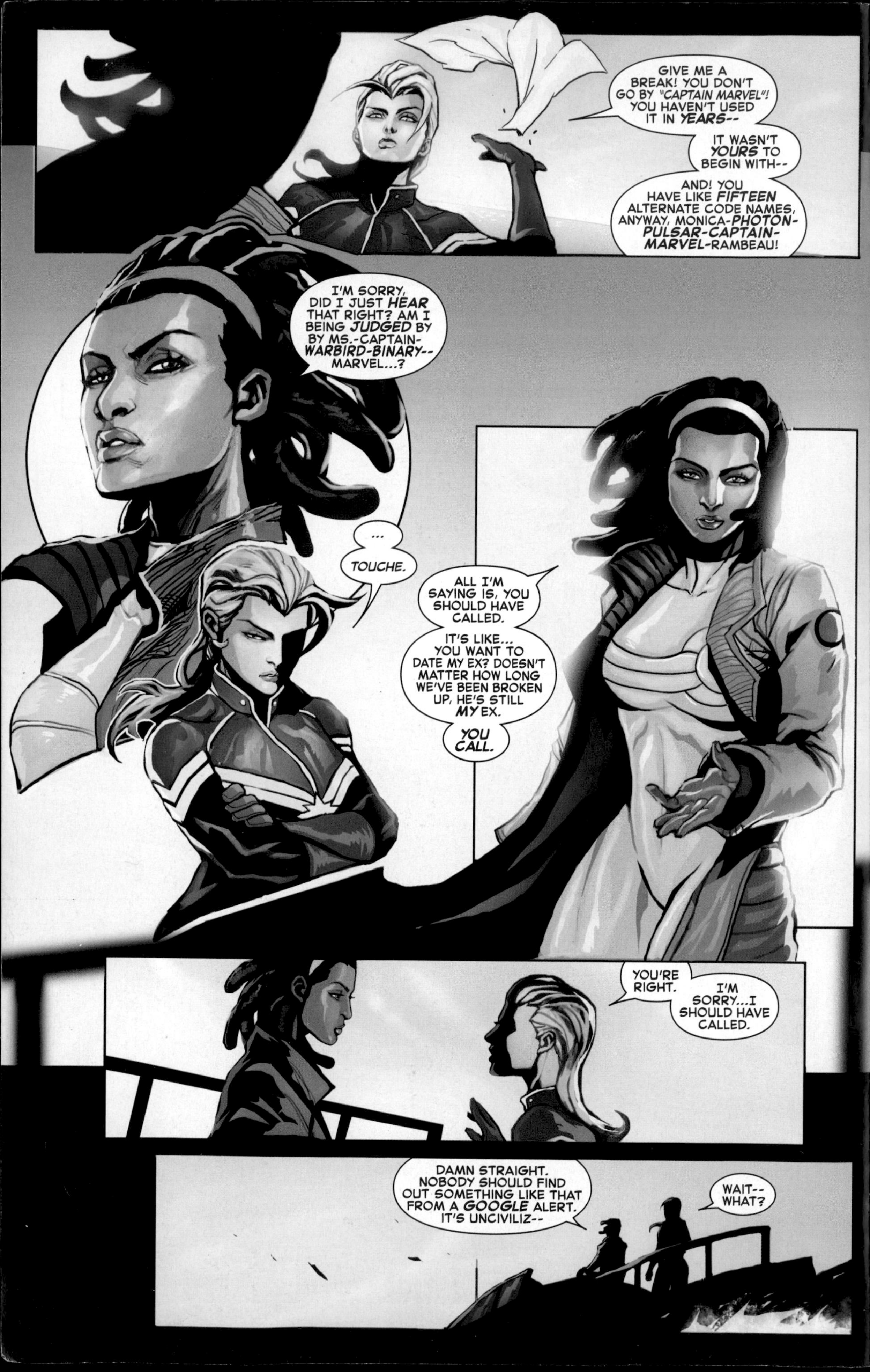
GIVE ME A BREAK! YOU DON'T GO BY "CAPTAIN MARVEL"! YOU HAVEN'T USED IT IN YEARS--
IT WASN'T YOURS TO BEGIN WITH--
AND! YOU HAVE LIKE FIFTEEN ALTERNATE CODE NAMES, ANYWAY, MONICA-PHOTON-PULSAR-CAPTAIN-MARVEL-RAMBEAU!
I'M SORRY, DID I JUST HEAR THAT RIGHT? AM I BEING JUDGED BY BY MS.-CAPTAIN-WARBIRD-BINARY--MARVEL...?
... TOUCHE.
ALL I'M SAYING IS, YOU SHOULD HAVE CALLED.
IT'S LIKE... YOU WANT TO DATE MY EX? DOESN'T MATTER HOW LONG WE'VE BEEN BROKEN UP, HE'S STILL MY EX.
YOU CALL.
YOU'RE RIGHT.
I'M SORRY...I SHOULD HAVE CALLED.
DAMN STRAIGHT. NOBODY SHOULD FIND OUT SOMETHING LIKE THAT FROM A GOOGLE ALERT. IT'S UNCIVILIZ--
WAIT-- WHAT?

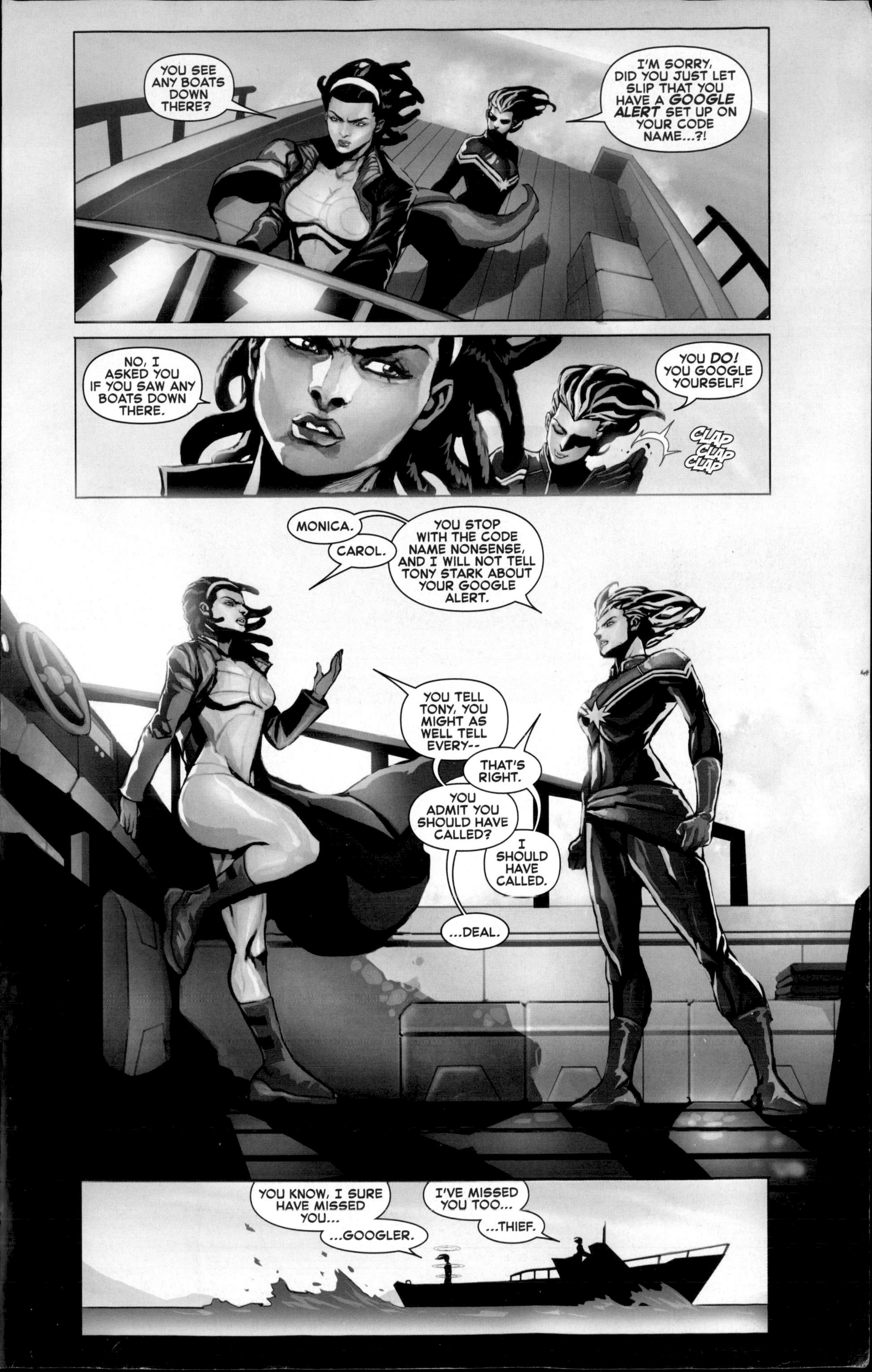
YOU SEE ANY BOATS DOWN THERE?
I'M SORRY, DID YOU JUST LET SLIP THAT YOU HAVE A *GOOGLE ALERT* SET UP ON YOUR CODE NAME...?!
NO, I ASKED YOU IF YOU SAW ANY BOATS DOWN THERE.
YOU *DO!* YOU GOOGLE YOURSELF!
CLAP CLAP CLAP
MONICA.
CAROL.
YOU STOP WITH THE CODE NAME NONSENSE, AND I WILL NOT TELL TONY STARK ABOUT YOUR GOOGLE ALERT.
YOU TELL TONY, YOU MIGHT AS WELL TELL EVERY--
THAT'S RIGHT.
YOU ADMIT YOU SHOULD HAVE CALLED?
I SHOULD HAVE CALLED.
...DEAL.
YOU KNOW, I SURE HAVE MISSED YOU...
...GOOGLER.
I'VE MISSED YOU TOO...
...THIEF.

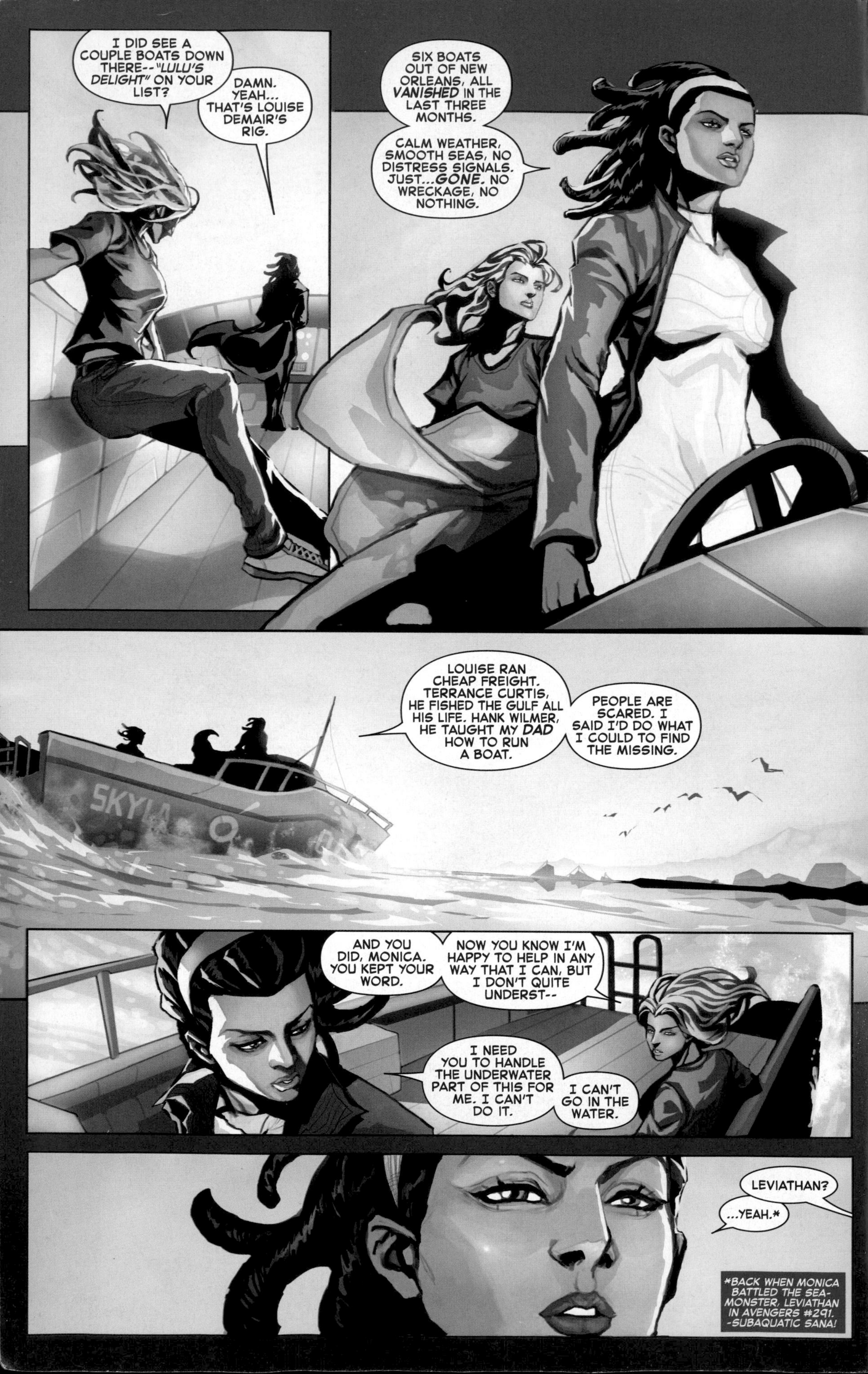
I DID SEE A COUPLE BOATS DOWN THERE-- "LULU'S DELIGHT" ON YOUR LIST?
DAMN. YEAH... THAT'S LOUISE DEMAIR'S RIG.
SIX BOATS OUT OF NEW ORLEANS, ALL VANISHED IN THE LAST THREE MONTHS.
CALM WEATHER, SMOOTH SEAS, NO DISTRESS SIGNALS. JUST... GONE. NO WRECKAGE, NO NOTHING.
LOUISE RAN CHEAP FREIGHT. TERRANCE CURTIS, HE FISHED THE GULF ALL HIS LIFE. HANK WILMER, HE TAUGHT MY DAD HOW TO RUN A BOAT.
PEOPLE ARE SCARED. I SAID I'D DO WHAT I COULD TO FIND THE MISSING.
SKYLA
AND YOU DID, MONICA. YOU KEPT YOUR WORD.
NOW YOU KNOW I'M HAPPY TO HELP IN ANY WAY THAT I CAN, BUT I DON'T QUITE UNDERST--
I NEED YOU TO HANDLE THE UNDERWATER PART OF THIS FOR ME. I CAN'T DO IT.
I CAN'T GO IN THE WATER.
LEVIATHAN?
...YEAH.*
*BACK WHEN MONICA BATTLED THE SEA-MONSTER, LEVIATHAN IN AVENGERS #291. -SUBAQUATIC SANA!

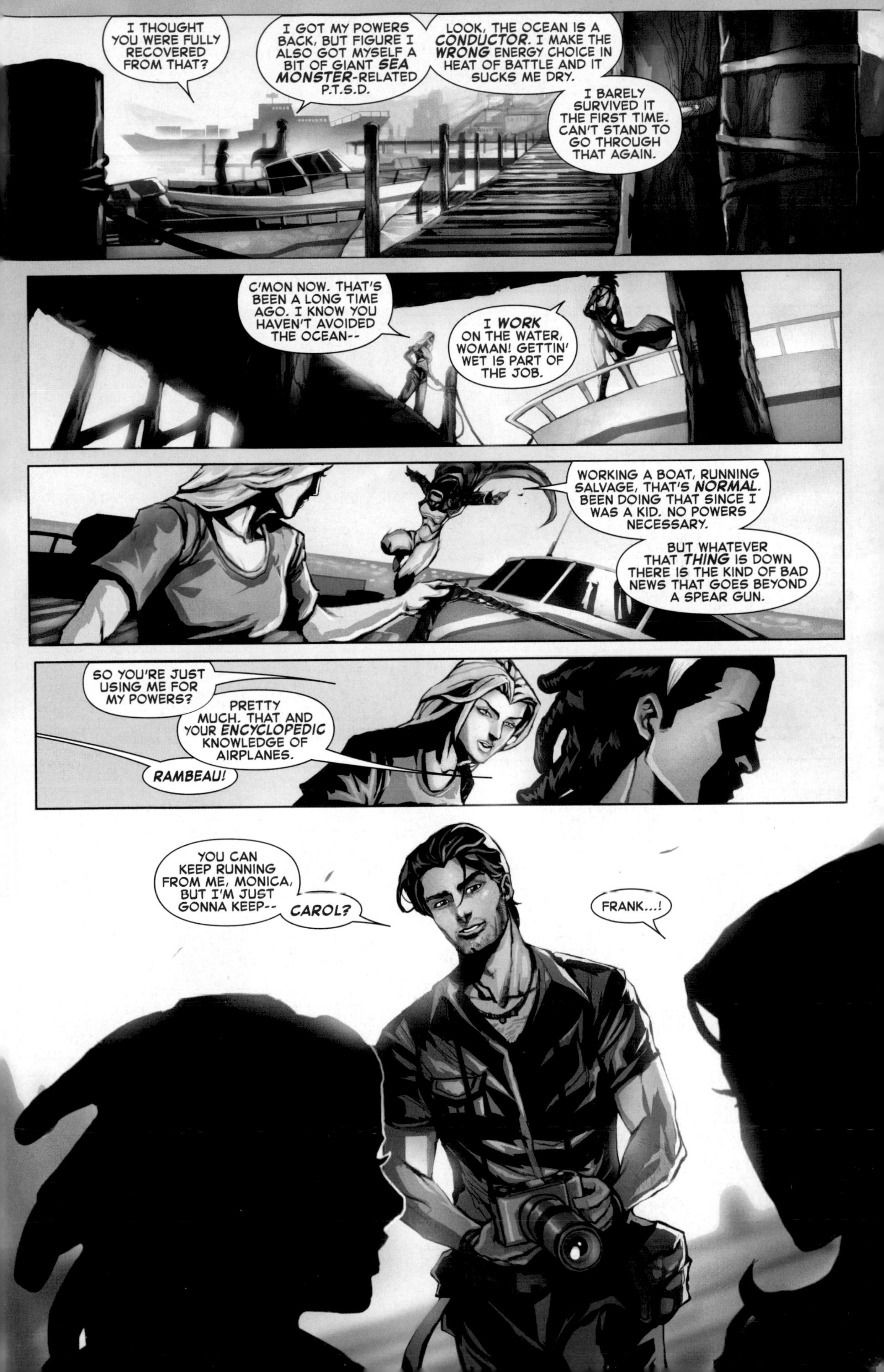
I THOUGHT YOU WERE FULLY RECOVERED FROM THAT?
I GOT MY POWERS BACK, BUT FIGURE I ALSO GOT MYSELF A BIT OF GIANT SEA MONSTER-RELATED P.T.S.D.
LOOK, THE OCEAN IS A CONDUCTOR. I MAKE THE WRONG ENERGY CHOICE IN HEAT OF BATTLE AND IT SUCKS ME DRY.
I BARELY SURVIVED IT THE FIRST TIME. CAN'T STAND TO GO THROUGH THAT AGAIN.
C'MON NOW. THAT'S BEEN A LONG TIME AGO. I KNOW YOU HAVEN'T AVOIDED THE OCEAN--
I WORK ON THE WATER, WOMAN! GETTIN' WET IS PART OF THE JOB.
WORKING A BOAT, RUNNING SALVAGE, THAT'S NORMAL. BEEN DOING THAT SINCE I WAS A KID. NO POWERS NECESSARY.
BUT WHATEVER THAT THING IS DOWN THERE IS THE KIND OF BAD NEWS THAT GOES BEYOND A SPEAR GUN.
SO YOU'RE JUST USING ME FOR MY POWERS?
PRETTY MUCH. THAT AND YOUR ENCYCLOPEDIC KNOWLEDGE OF AIRPLANES.
RAMBEAU!
YOU CAN KEEP RUNNING FROM ME, MONICA, BUT I'M JUST GONNA KEEP--
CAROL?
FRANK...!

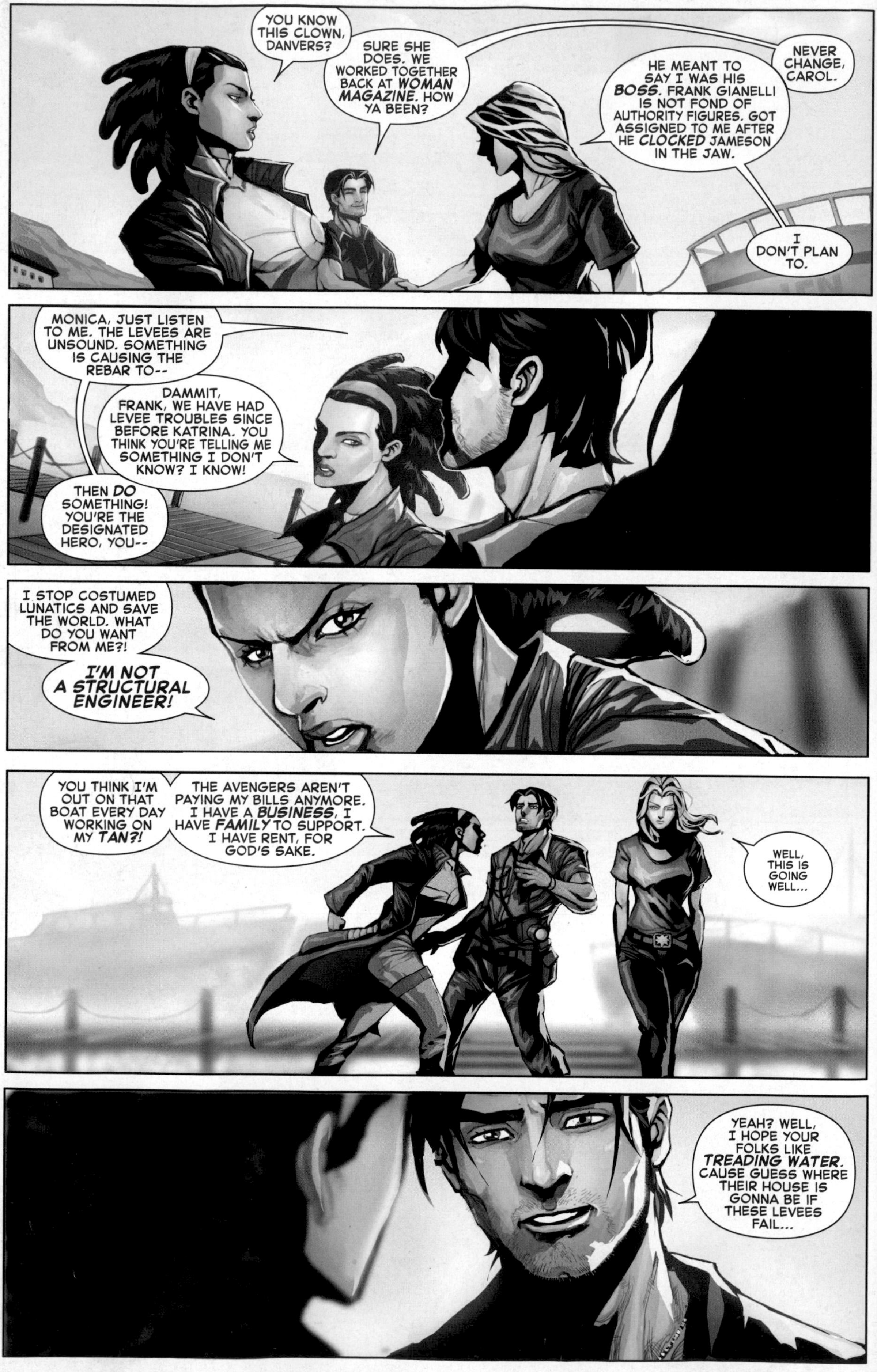
YOU KNOW THIS CLOWN, DANVERS?
SURE SHE DOES. WE WORKED TOGETHER BACK AT WOMAN MAGAZINE. HOW YA BEEN?
HE MEANT TO SAY I WAS HIS BOSS. FRANK GIANELLI IS NOT FOND OF AUTHORITY FIGURES. GOT ASSIGNED TO ME AFTER HE CLOCKED JAMESON IN THE JAW.
NEVER CHANGE, CAROL.
I DON'T PLAN TO.
MONICA, JUST LISTEN TO ME. THE LEVEES ARE UNSOUND. SOMETHING IS CAUSING THE REBAR TO--
DAMMIT, FRANK, WE HAVE HAD LEVEE TROUBLES SINCE BEFORE KATRINA. YOU THINK YOU'RE TELLING ME SOMETHING I DON'T KNOW? I KNOW!
THEN DO SOMETHING! YOU'RE THE DESIGNATED HERO, YOU--
I STOP COSTUMED LUNATICS AND SAVE THE WORLD. WHAT DO YOU WANT FROM ME?!
I'M NOT A STRUCTURAL ENGINEER!
YOU THINK I'M OUT ON THAT BOAT EVERY DAY WORKING ON MY TAN?!
THE AVENGERS AREN'T PAYING MY BILLS ANYMORE. I HAVE A BUSINESS, I HAVE FAMILY TO SUPPORT. I HAVE RENT, FOR GOD'S SAKE.
WELL, THIS IS GOING WELL...
YEAH? WELL, I HOPE YOUR FOLKS LIKE TREADING WATER. CAUSE GUESS WHERE THEIR HOUSE IS GONNA BE IF THESE LEVEES FAIL...

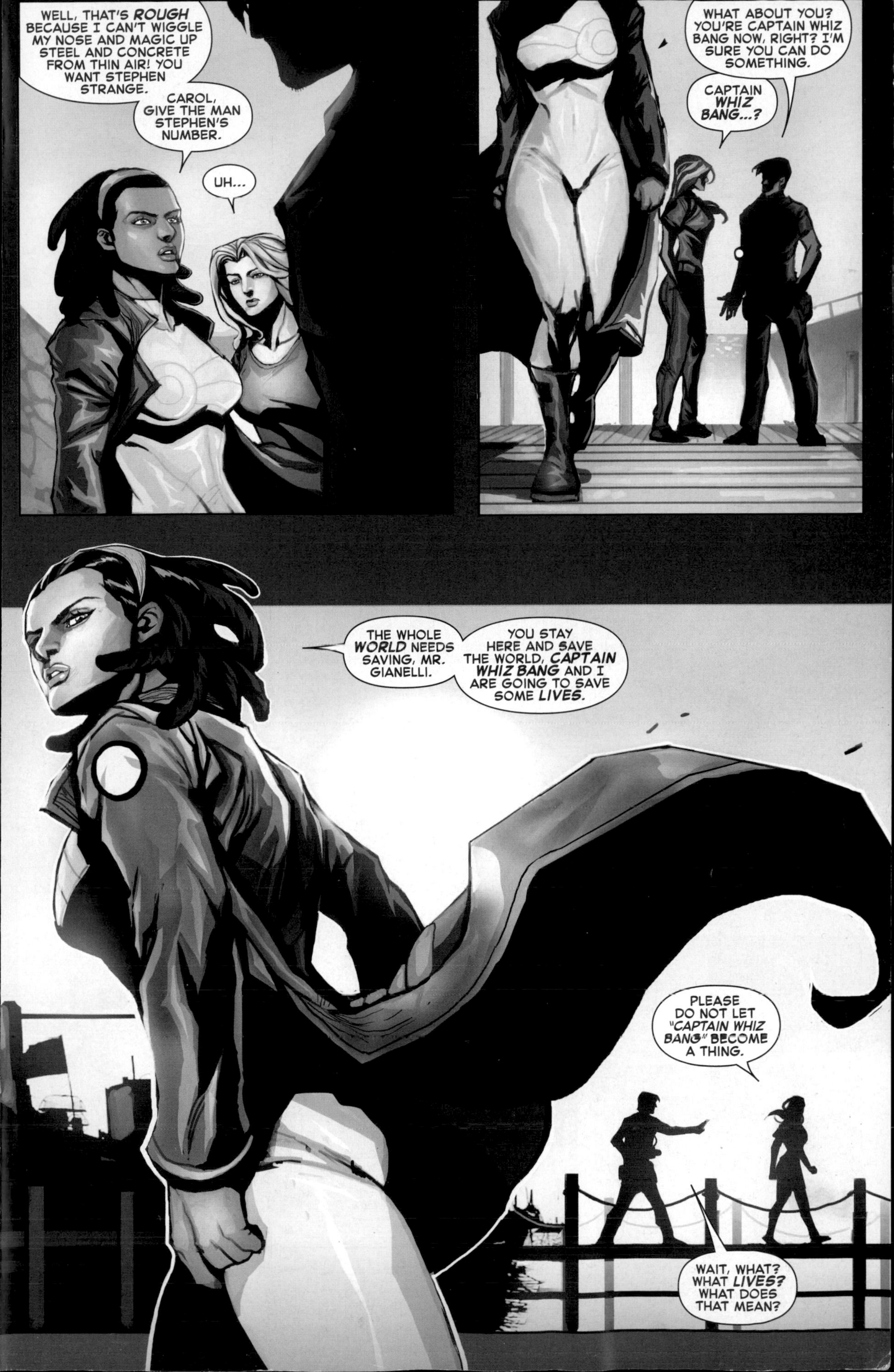
WELL, THAT'S ROUGH BECAUSE I CAN'T WIGGLE MY NOSE AND MAGIC UP STEEL AND CONCRETE FROM THIN AIR! YOU WANT STEPHEN STRANGE.
CAROL, GIVE THE MAN STEPHEN'S NUMBER.
UH...
WHAT ABOUT YOU? YOU'RE CAPTAIN WHIZ BANG NOW, RIGHT? I'M SURE YOU CAN DO SOMETHING.
CAPTAIN WHIZ BANG...?
THE WHOLE WORLD NEEDS SAVING, MR. GIANELLI.
YOU STAY HERE AND SAVE THE WORLD. CAPTAIN WHIZ BANG AND I ARE GOING TO SAVE SOME LIVES.
PLEASE DO NOT LET "CAPTAIN WHIZ BANG" BECOME A THING.
WAIT, WHAT? WHAT LIVES? WHAT DOES THAT MEAN?

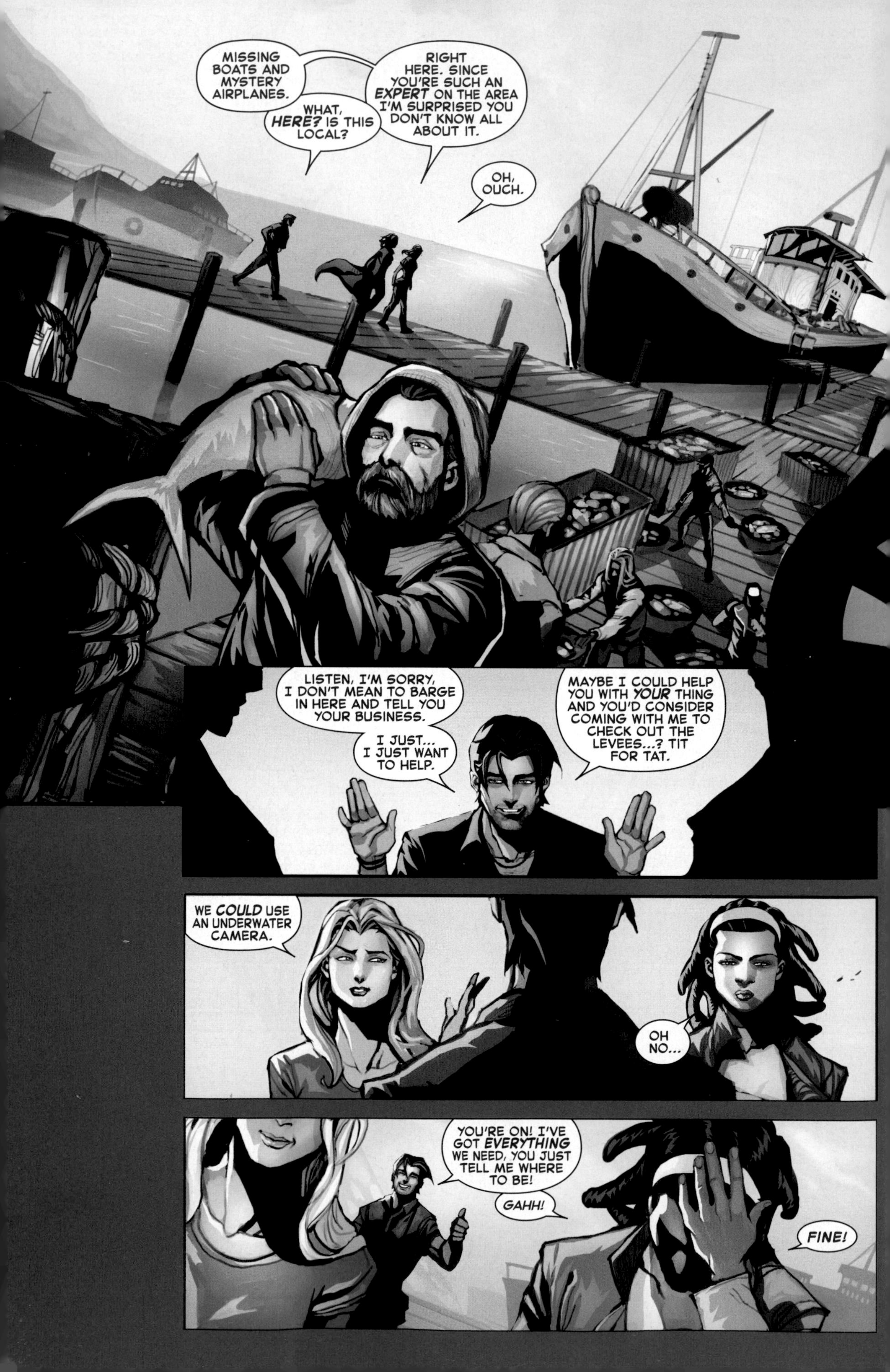
MISSING BOATS AND MYSTERY AIRPLANES.
WHAT, HERE? IS THIS LOCAL?
RIGHT HERE. SINCE YOU'RE SUCH AN EXPERT ON THE AREA I'M SURPRISED YOU DON'T KNOW ALL ABOUT IT.
OH, OUCH.
LISTEN, I'M SORRY, I DON'T MEAN TO BARGE IN HERE AND TELL YOU YOUR BUSINESS.
I JUST... I JUST WANT TO HELP.
MAYBE I COULD HELP YOU WITH YOUR THING AND YOU'D CONSIDER COMING WITH ME TO CHECK OUT THE LEVEES...? TIT FOR TAT.
WE COULD USE AN UNDERWATER CAMERA.
OH NO...
YOU'RE ON! I'VE GOT EVERYTHING WE NEED, YOU JUST TELL ME WHERE TO BE!
GAHH!
FINE!

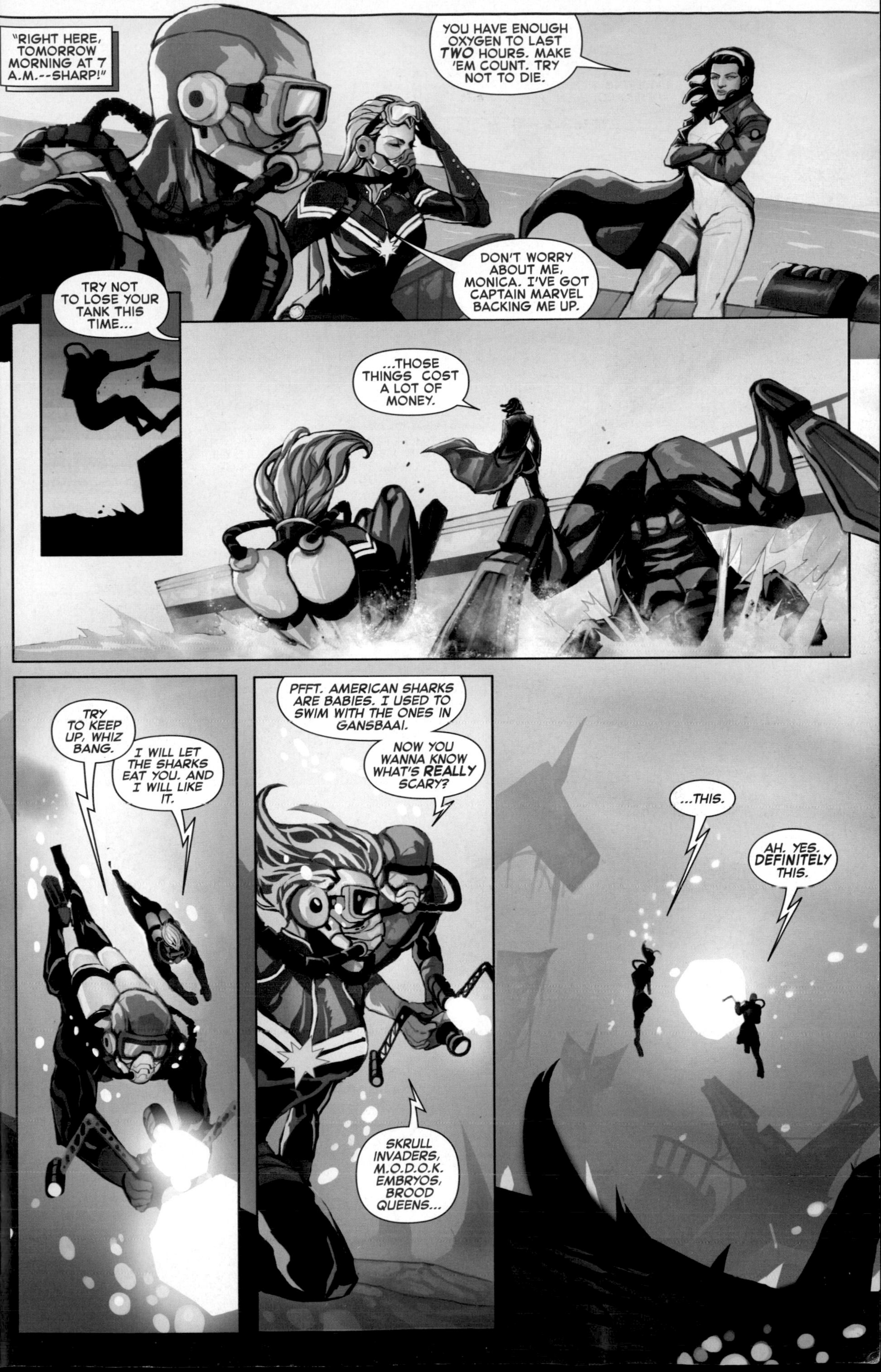
"RIGHT HERE, TOMORROW MORNING AT 7 A.M.--SHARP!"
YOU HAVE ENOUGH OXYGEN TO LAST TWO HOURS. MAKE 'EM COUNT. TRY NOT TO DIE.
DON'T WORRY ABOUT ME, MONICA. I'VE GOT CAPTAIN MARVEL BACKING ME UP.
TRY NOT TO LOSE YOUR TANK THIS TIME...
...THOSE THINGS COST A LOT OF MONEY.
TRY TO KEEP UP, WHIZ BANG.
I WILL LET THE SHARKS EAT YOU. AND I WILL LIKE IT.
PFFT. AMERICAN SHARKS ARE BABIES. I USED TO SWIM WITH THE ONES IN GANSBAAI.
NOW YOU WANNA KNOW WHAT'S REALLY SCARY?
SKRULL INVADERS, M.O.D.O.K. EMBRYOS, BROOD QUEENS...
...THIS.
AH. YES. DEFINITELY THIS.

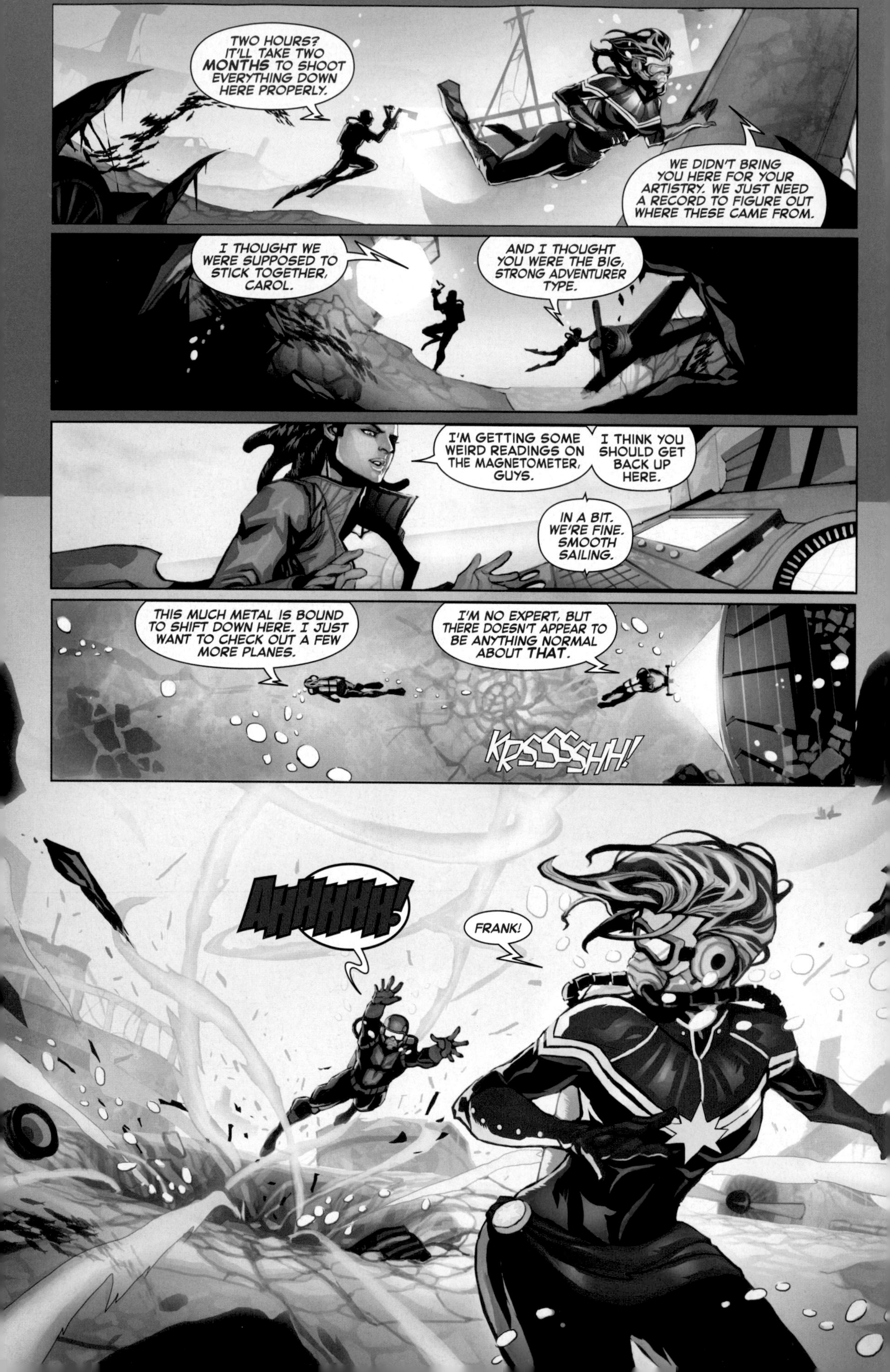
TWO HOURS? IT'LL TAKE TWO MONTHS TO SHOOT EVERYTHING DOWN HERE PROPERLY.
WE DIDN'T BRING YOU HERE FOR YOUR ARTISTRY. WE JUST NEED A RECORD TO FIGURE OUT WHERE THESE CAME FROM.
I THOUGHT WE WERE SUPPOSED TO STICK TOGETHER, CAROL.
AND I THOUGHT YOU WERE THE BIG, STRONG ADVENTURER TYPE.
I'M GETTING SOME WEIRD READINGS ON THE MAGNETOMETER, GUYS.
I THINK YOU SHOULD GET BACK UP HERE.
IN A BIT. WE'RE FINE. SMOOTH SAILING.
THIS MUCH METAL IS BOUND TO SHIFT DOWN HERE. I JUST WANT TO CHECK OUT A FEW MORE PLANES.
I'M NO EXPERT, BUT THERE DOESN'T APPEAR TO BE ANYTHING NORMAL ABOUT THAT.
KRSSSSHH!
AHHHHH!
FRANK!

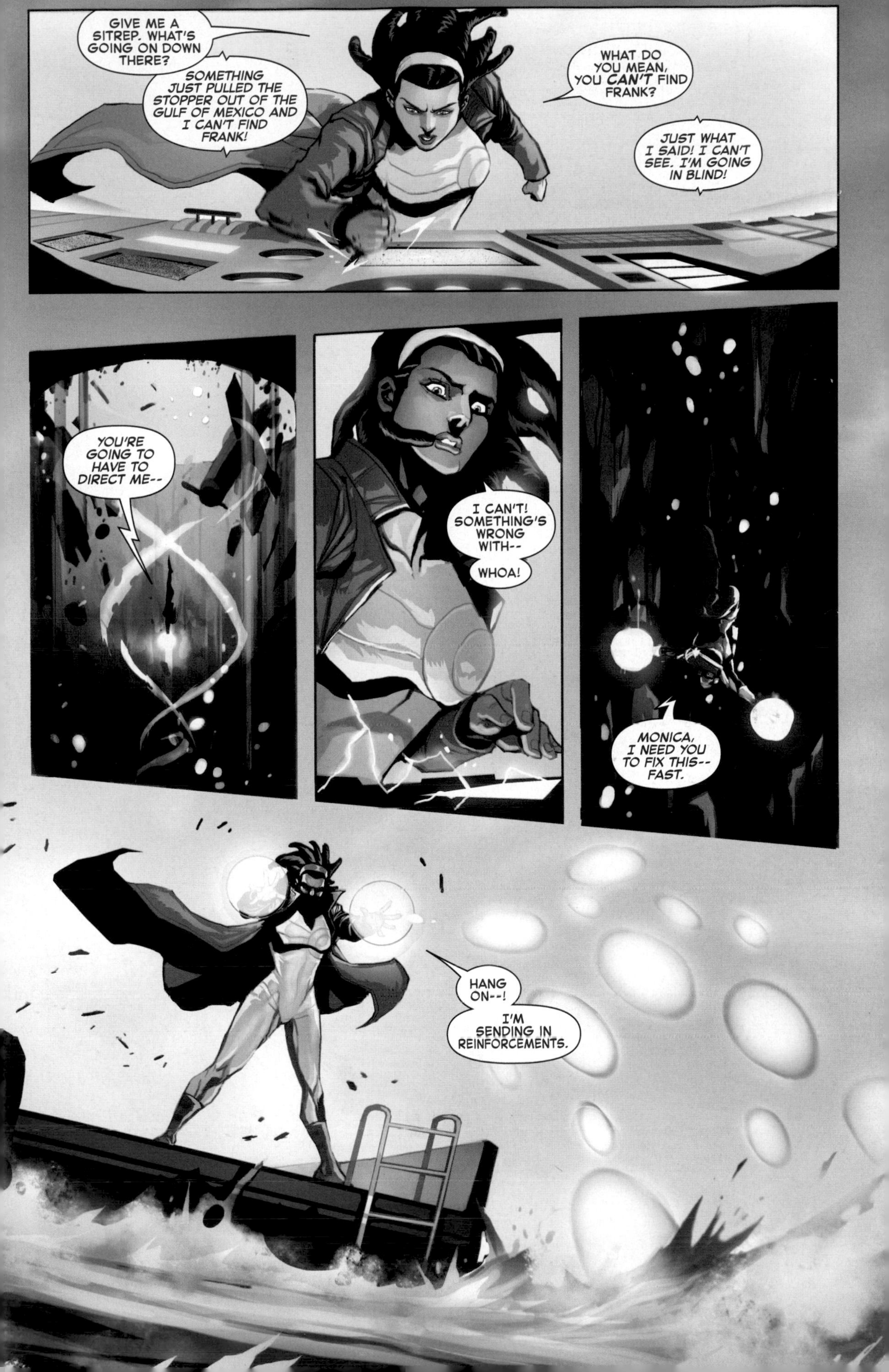
GIVE ME A SITREP. WHAT'S GOING ON DOWN THERE?
SOMETHING JUST PULLED THE STOPPER OUT OF THE GULF OF MEXICO AND I CAN'T FIND FRANK!
WHAT DO YOU MEAN, YOU **CAN'T** FIND FRANK?
JUST WHAT I SAID! I CAN'T SEE. I'M GOING IN BLIND!
YOU'RE GOING TO HAVE TO DIRECT ME--
I CAN'T! SOMETHING'S WRONG WITH--
WHOA!
MONICA, I NEED YOU TO FIX THIS-- FAST.
HANG ON--!
I'M SENDING IN REINFORCEMENTS.

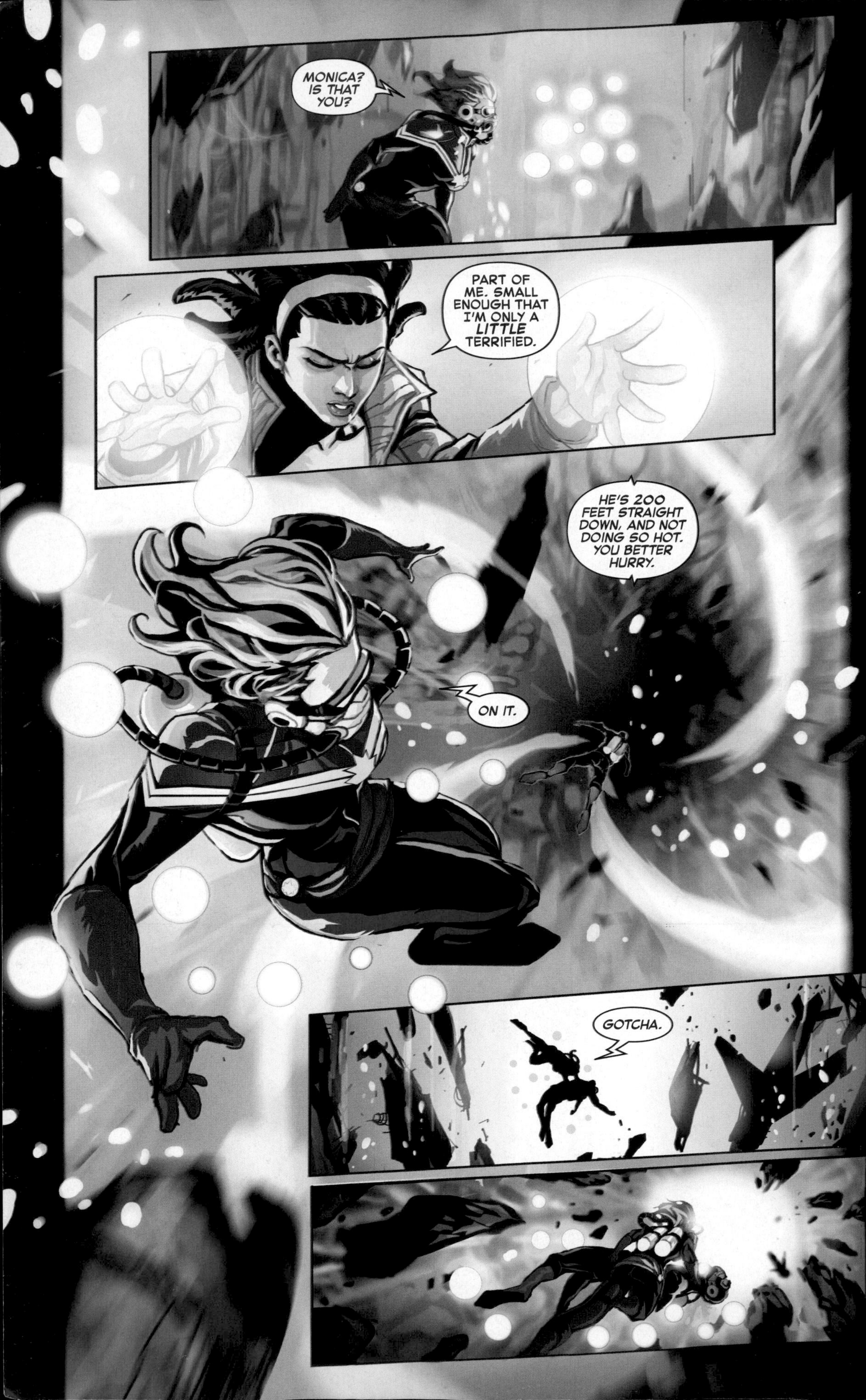
MONICA? IS THAT YOU?
PART OF ME. SMALL ENOUGH THAT I'M ONLY A *LITTLE* TERRIFIED.
HE'S 200 FEET STRAIGHT DOWN, AND NOT DOING SO HOT. YOU BETTER HURRY.
ON IT.
GOTCHA.

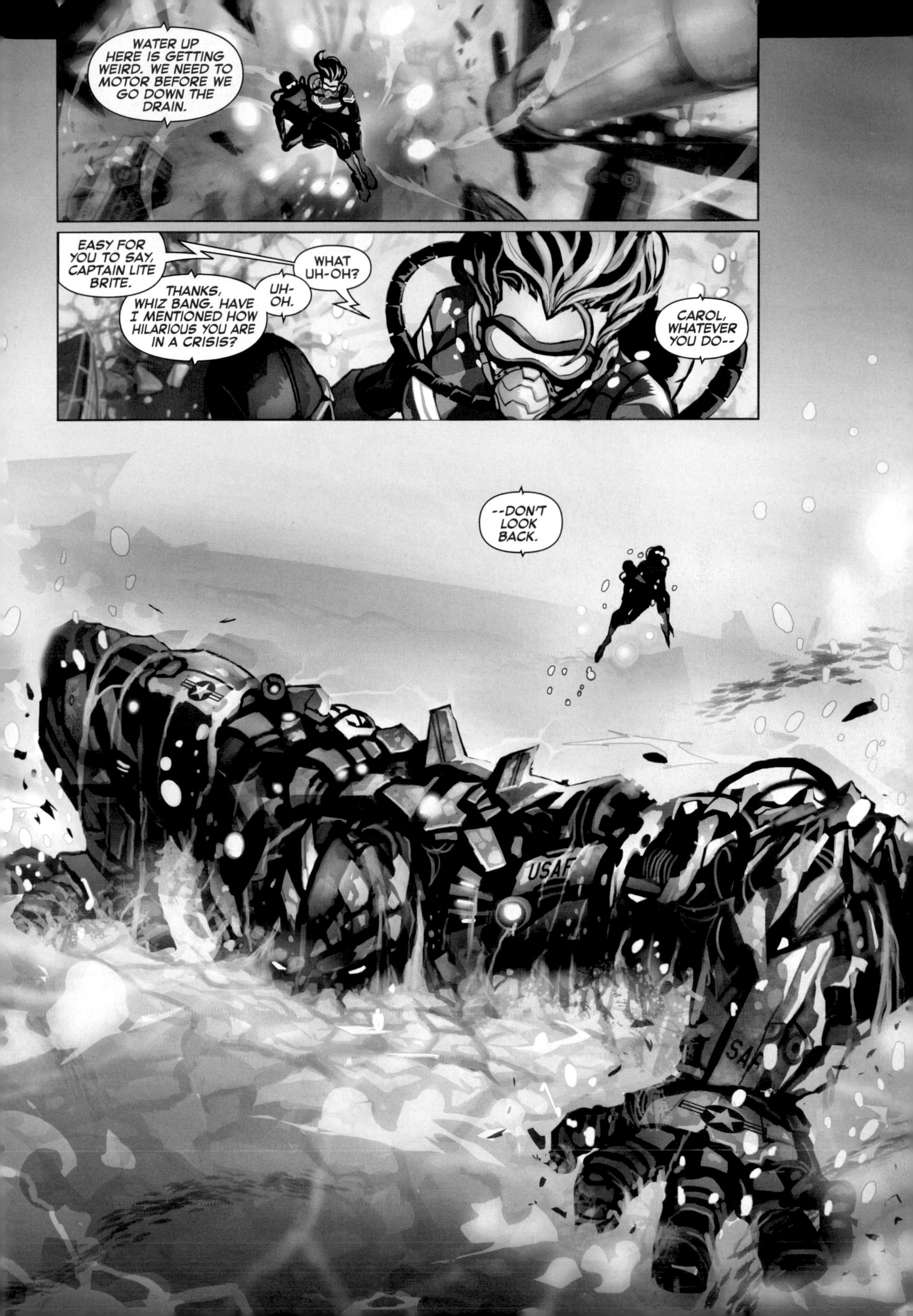
WATER UP HERE IS GETTING WEIRD. WE NEED TO MOTOR BEFORE WE GO DOWN THE DRAIN.
EASY FOR YOU TO SAY, CAPTAIN LITE BRITE.
THANKS, WHIZ BANG. HAVE I MENTIONED HOW HILARIOUS YOU ARE IN A CRISIS?
WHAT UH-OH?
UH-OH.
CAROL, WHATEVER YOU DO--
--DON'T LOOK BACK.
USAF
SAF

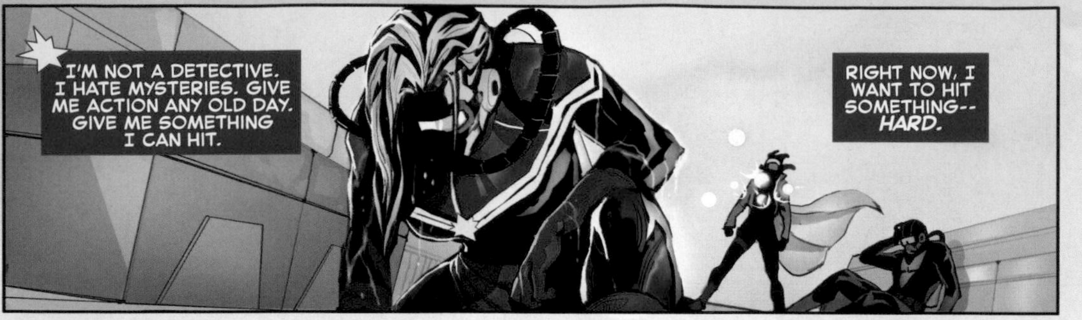
I'M NOT A DETECTIVE. I HATE MYSTERIES. GIVE ME ACTION ANY OLD DAY. GIVE ME SOMETHING I CAN HIT.
RIGHT NOW, I WANT TO HIT SOMETHING-- *HARD.*

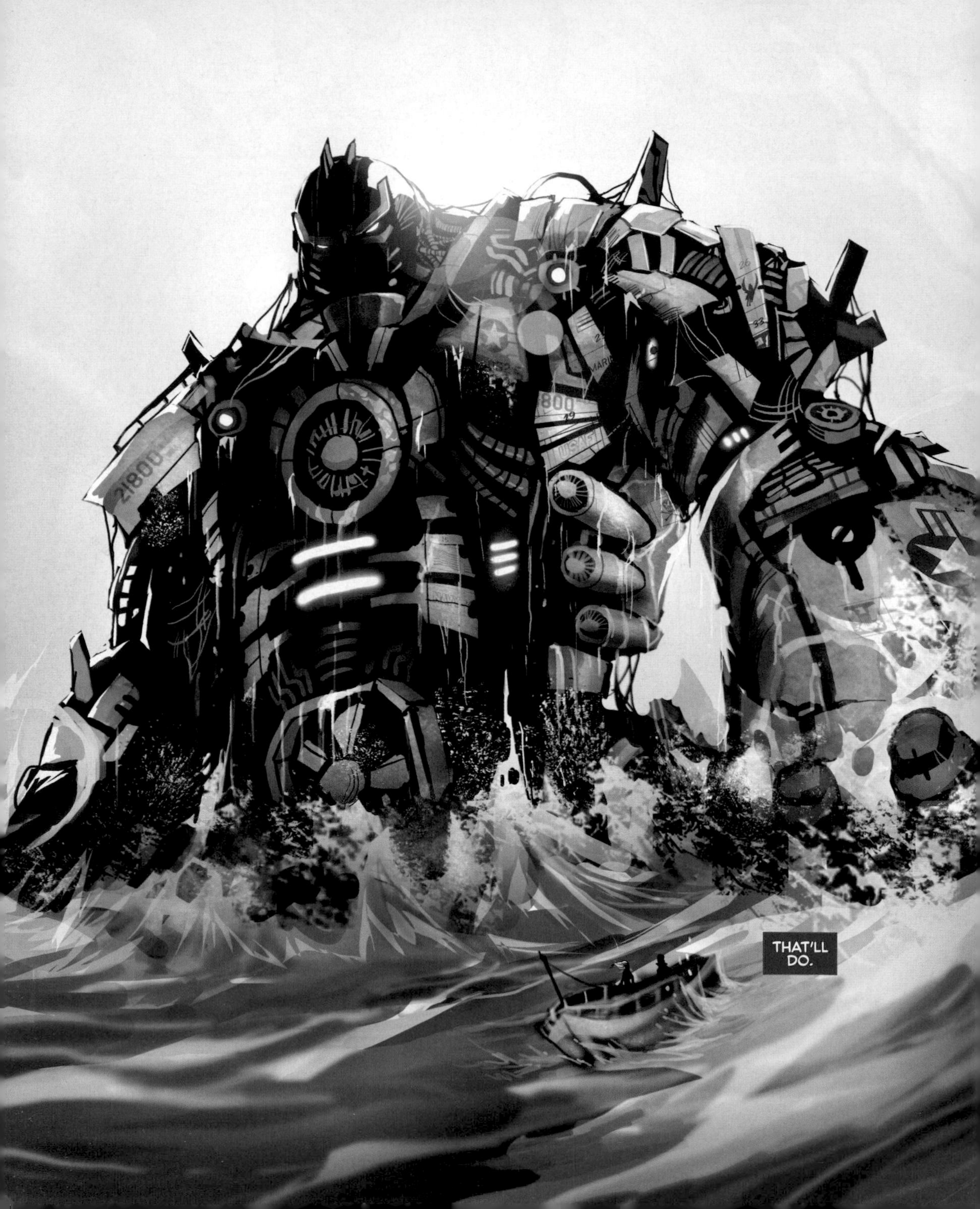
THAT'LL DO.

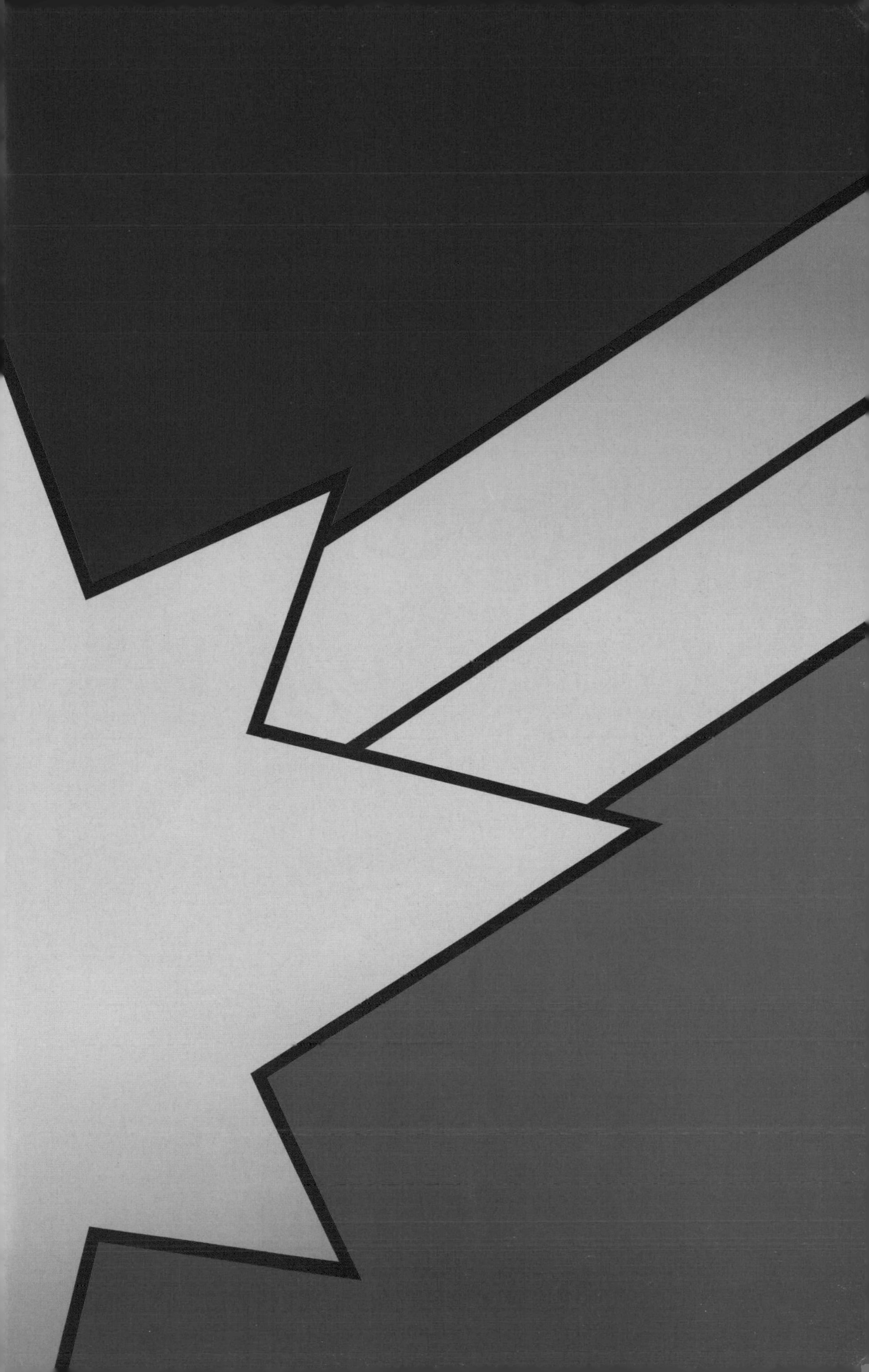

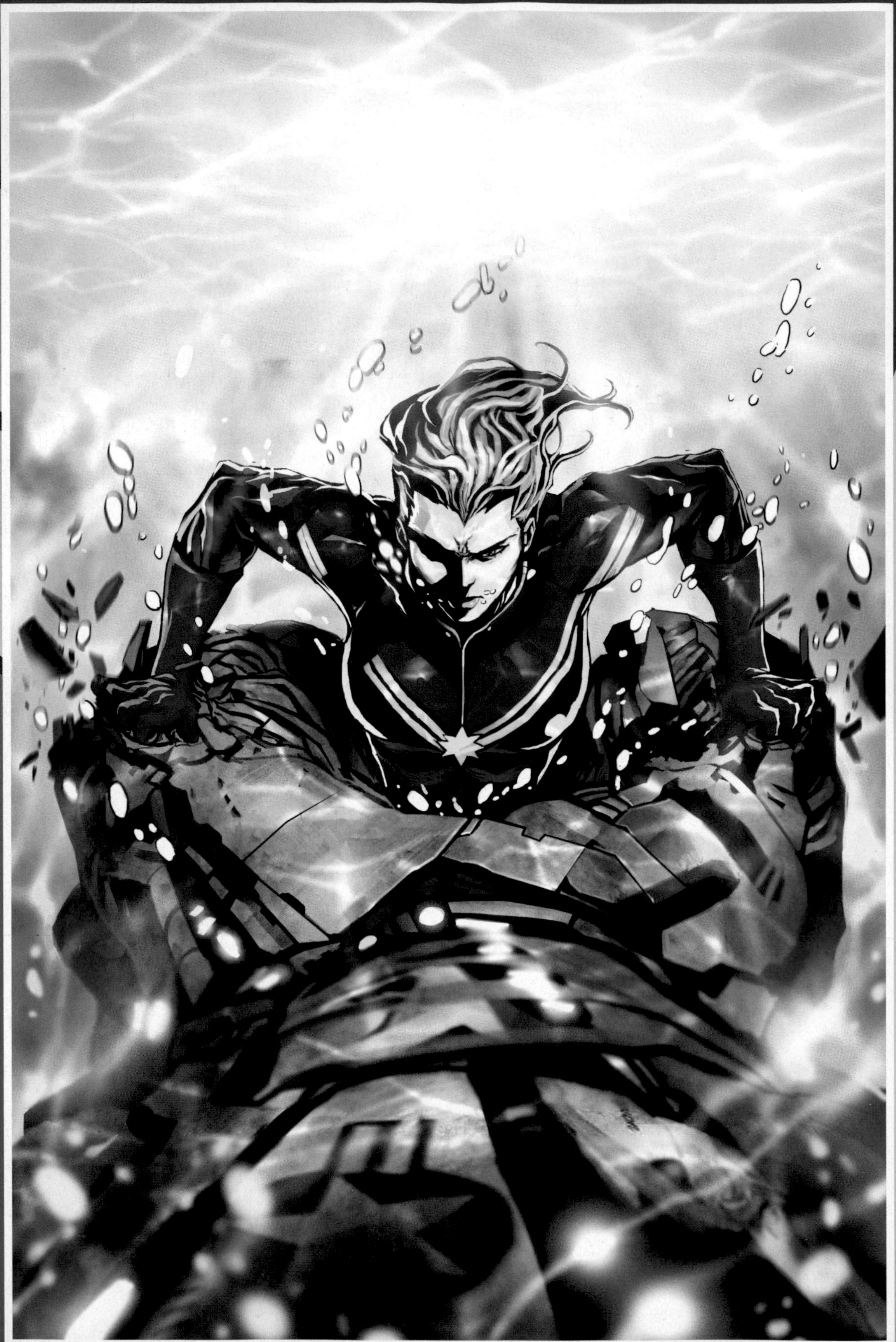

EIGHT

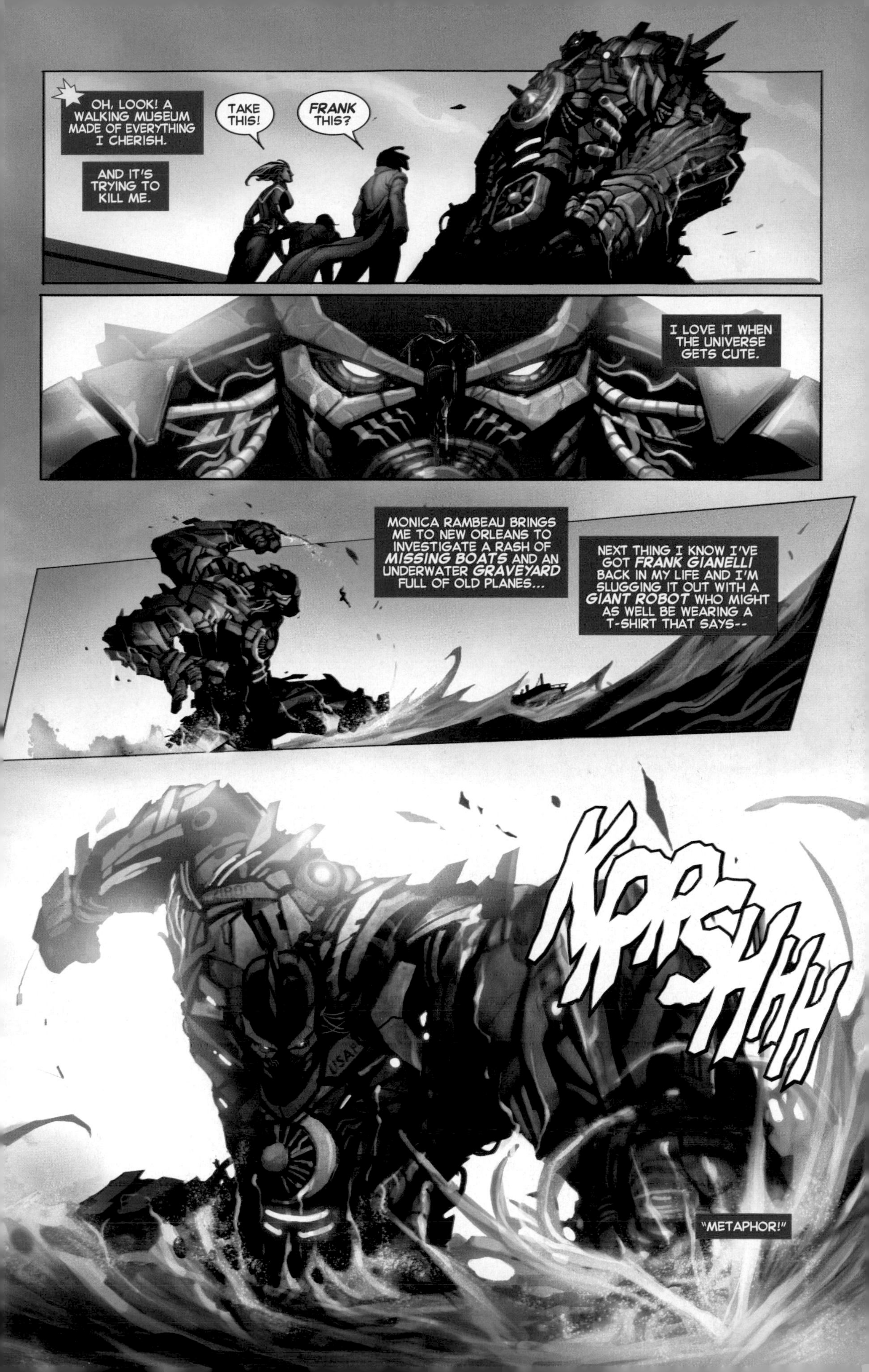
OH, LOOK! A WALKING MUSEUM MADE OF EVERYTHING I CHERISH.
AND IT'S TRYING TO KILL ME.
TAKE THIS!
FRANK THIS?
I LOVE IT WHEN THE UNIVERSE GETS CUTE.
MONICA RAMBEAU BRINGS ME TO NEW ORLEANS TO INVESTIGATE A RASH OF MISSING BOATS AND AN UNDERWATER GRAVEYARD FULL OF OLD PLANES...
NEXT THING I KNOW I'VE GOT FRANK GIANELLI BACK IN MY LIFE AND I'M SLUGGING IT OUT WITH A GIANT ROBOT WHO MIGHT AS WELL BE WEARING A T-SHIRT THAT SAYS--
KROSHHH
"METAPHOR!"

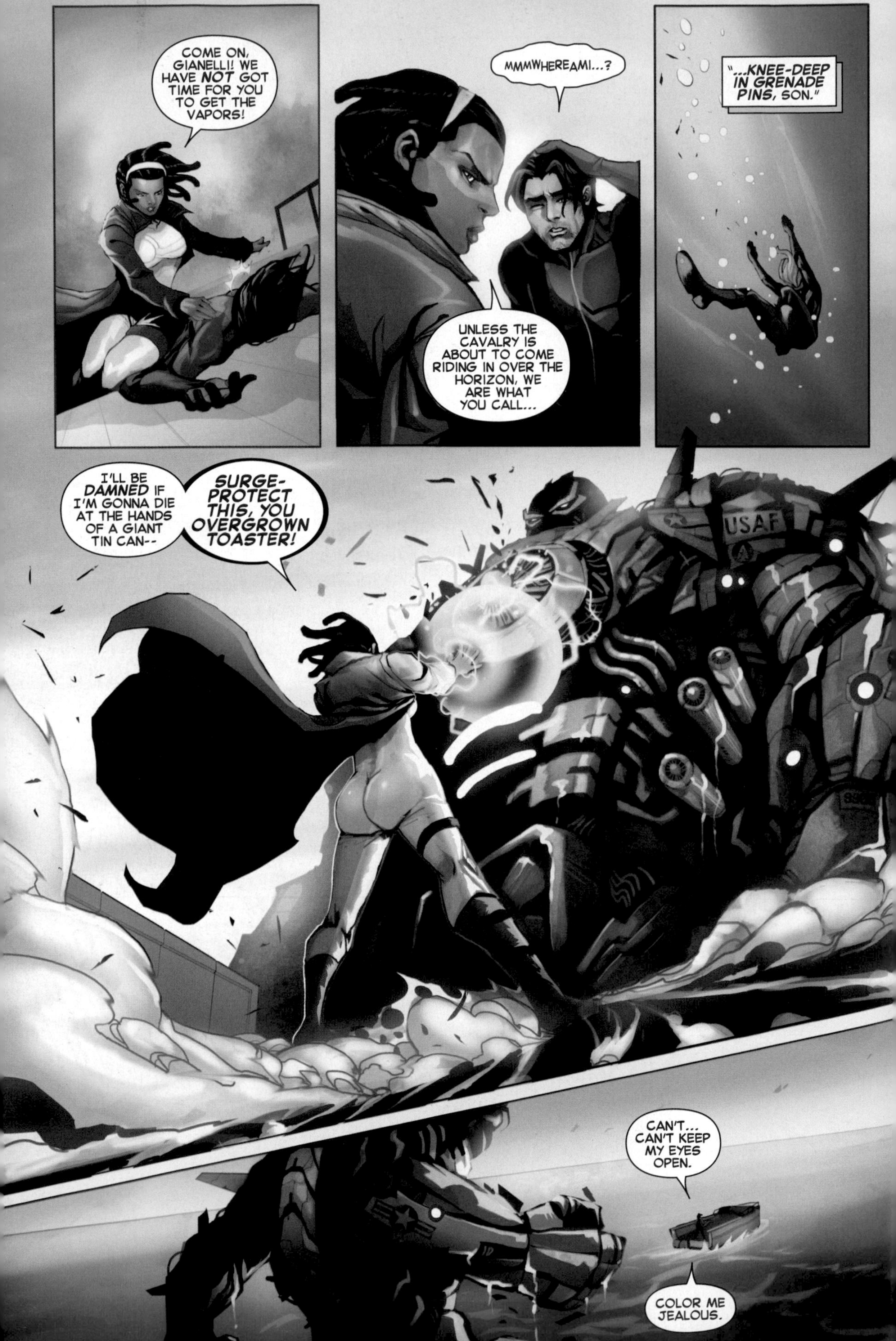
COME ON, GIANELLI! WE HAVE NOT GOT TIME FOR YOU TO GET THE VAPORS!
MMMWHEREAMI...?
UNLESS THE CAVALRY IS ABOUT TO COME RIDING IN OVER THE HORIZON, WE ARE WHAT YOU CALL...
"...KNEE-DEEP IN GRENADE PINS, SON."
I'LL BE DAMNED IF I'M GONNA DIE AT THE HANDS OF A GIANT TIN CAN--
SURGE-PROTECT THIS, YOU OVERGROWN TOASTER!
USAF
CAN'T... CAN'T KEEP MY EYES OPEN.
COLOR ME JEALOUS.

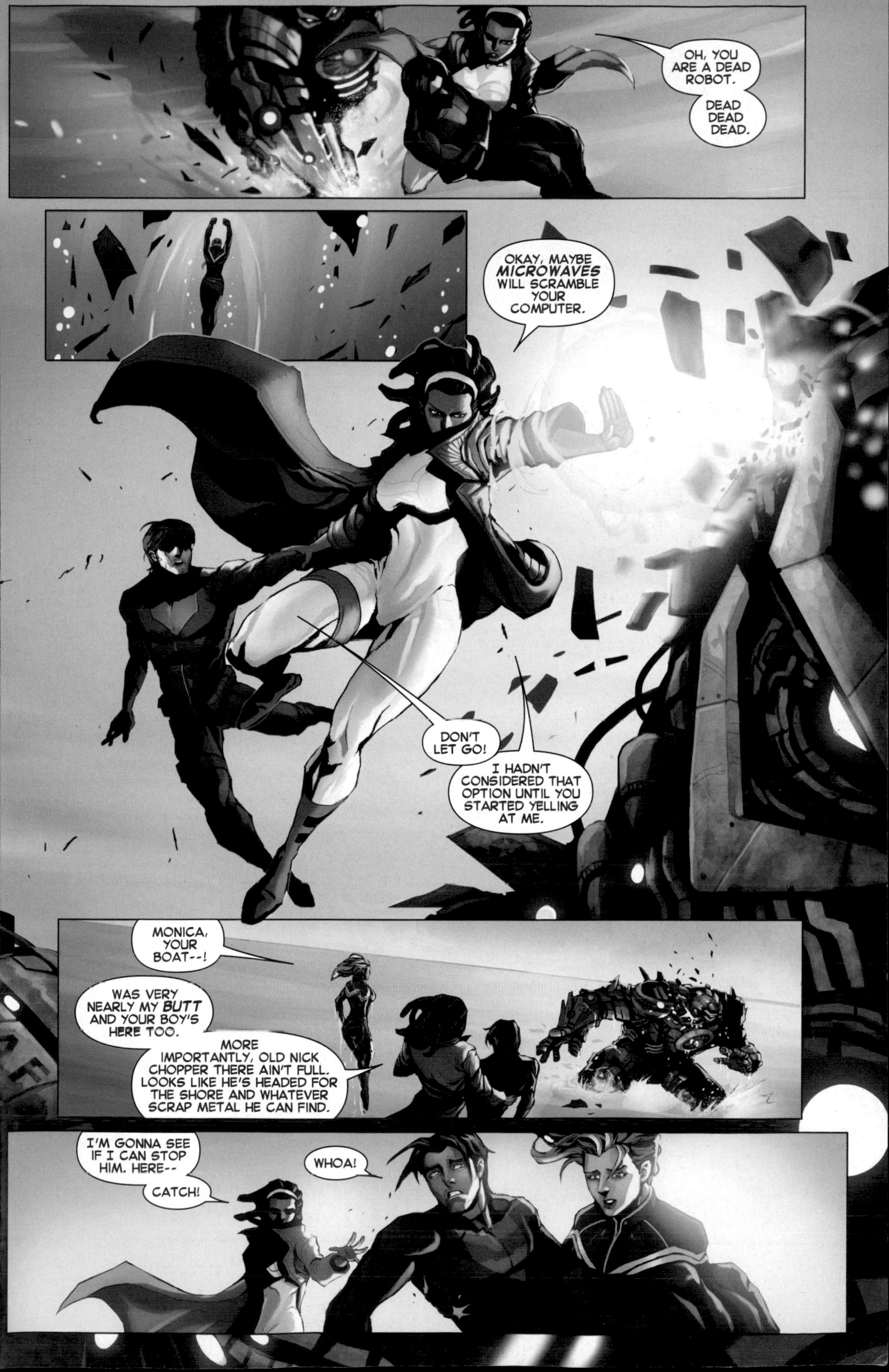
OH, YOU ARE A DEAD ROBOT.
DEAD DEAD DEAD.
OKAY, MAYBE MICROWAVES WILL SCRAMBLE YOUR COMPUTER.
DON'T LET GO!
I HADN'T CONSIDERED THAT OPTION UNTIL YOU STARTED YELLING AT ME.
MONICA, YOUR BOAT--!
WAS VERY NEARLY MY BUTT AND YOUR BOY'S HERE TOO.
MORE IMPORTANTLY, OLD NICK CHOPPER THERE AIN'T FULL. LOOKS LIKE HE'S HEADED FOR THE SHORE AND WHATEVER SCRAP METAL HE CAN FIND.
I'M GONNA SEE IF I CAN STOP HIM. HERE--
CATCH!
WHOA!

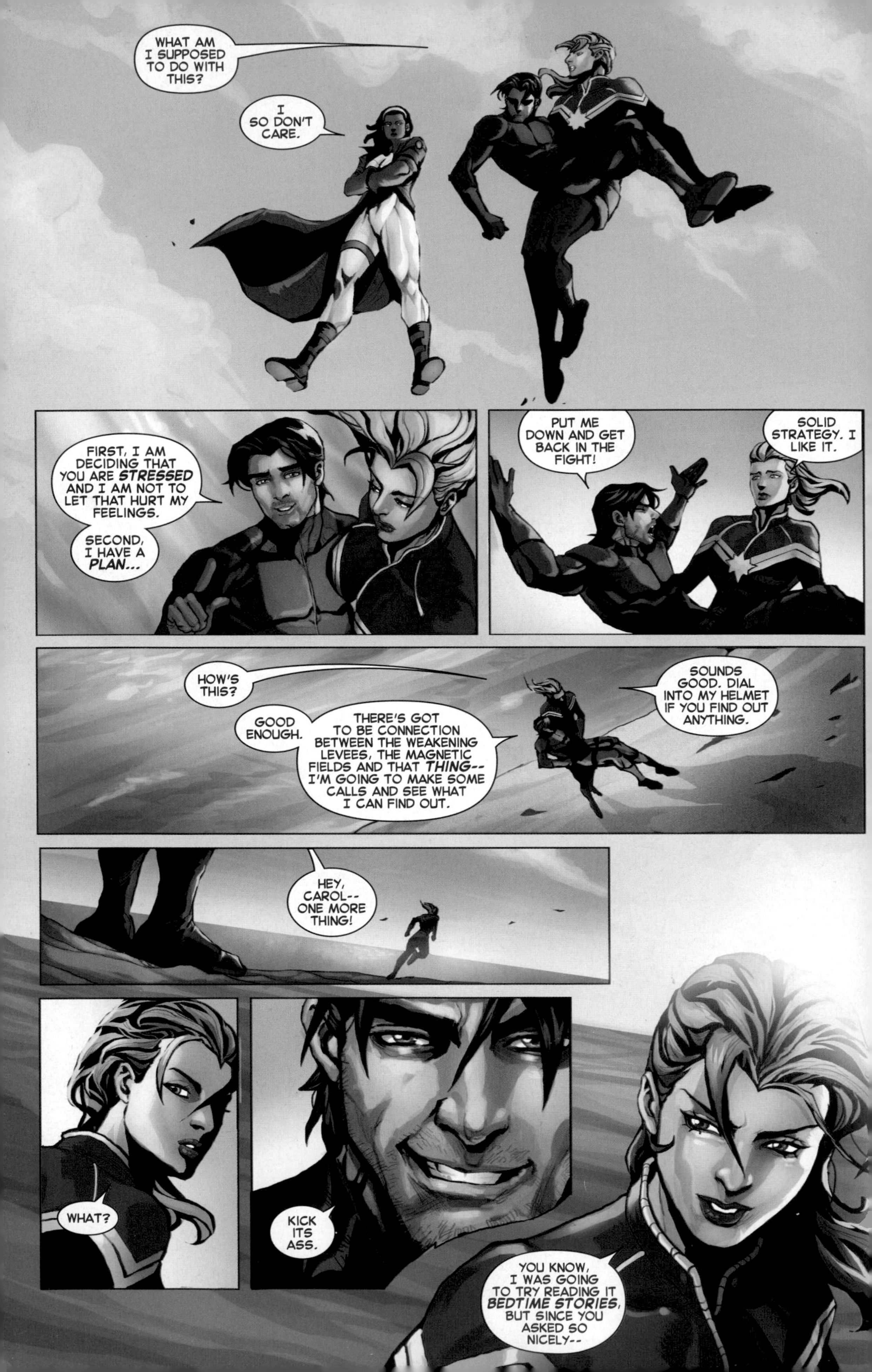
WHAT AM I SUPPOSED TO DO WITH THIS?
I SO DON'T CARE.
FIRST, I AM DECIDING THAT YOU ARE STRESSED AND I AM NOT TO LET THAT HURT MY FEELINGS.
SECOND, I HAVE A PLAN...
PUT ME DOWN AND GET BACK IN THE FIGHT!
SOLID STRATEGY. I LIKE IT.
HOW'S THIS?
GOOD ENOUGH.
THERE'S GOT TO BE CONNECTION BETWEEN THE WEAKENING LEVEES, THE MAGNETIC FIELDS AND THAT THING-- I'M GOING TO MAKE SOME CALLS AND SEE WHAT I CAN FIND OUT.
SOUNDS GOOD. DIAL INTO MY HELMET IF YOU FIND OUT ANYTHING.
HEY, CAROL-- ONE MORE THING!
WHAT?
KICK ITS ASS.
YOU KNOW, I WAS GOING TO TRY READING IT BEDTIME STORIES, BUT SINCE YOU ASKED SO NICELY--

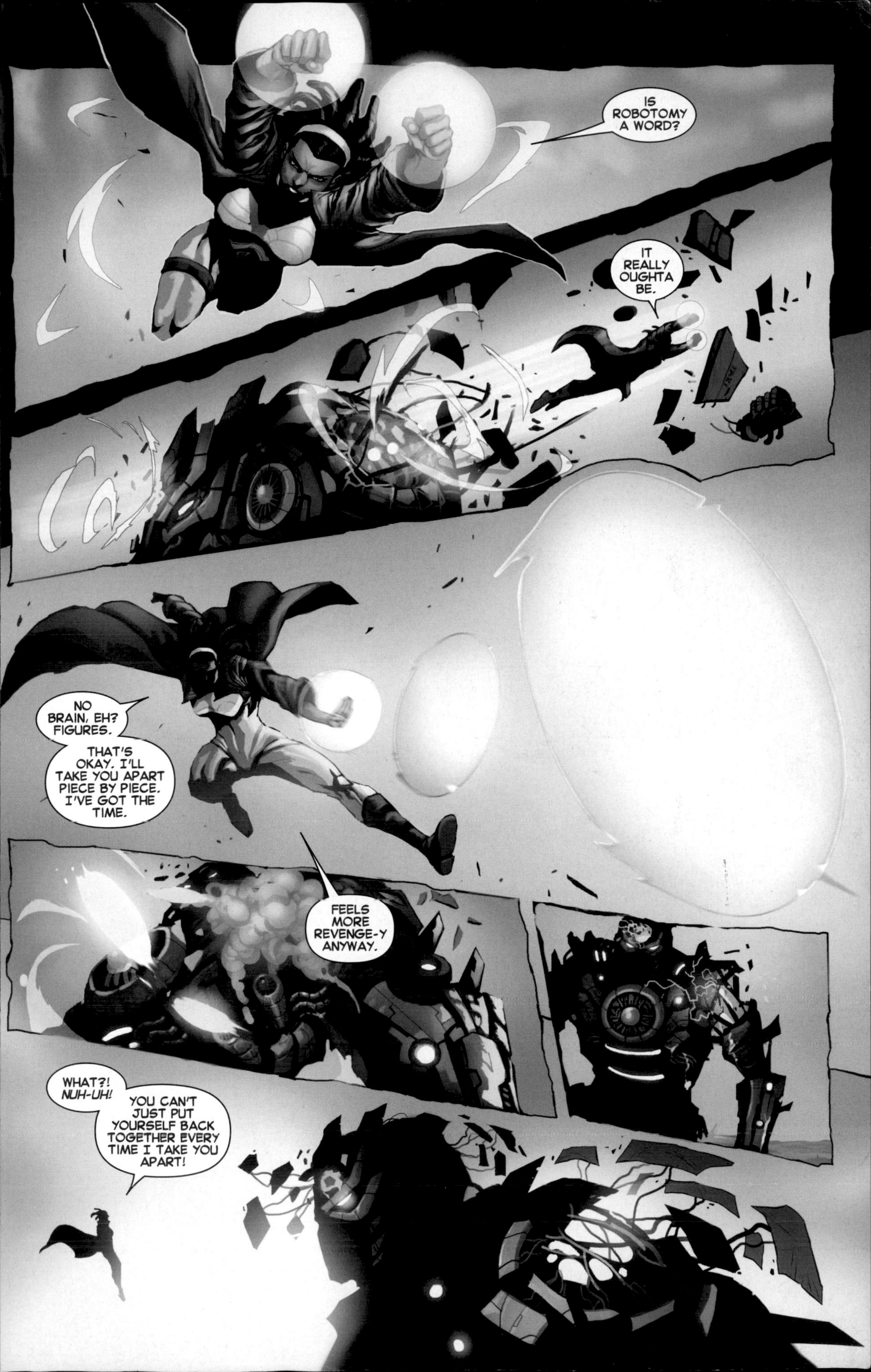
IS ROBOTOMY A WORD?
IT REALLY OUGHTA BE.
NO BRAIN, EH? FIGURES.
THAT'S OKAY. I'LL TAKE YOU APART PIECE BY PIECE. I'VE GOT THE TIME.
FEELS MORE REVENGE-Y ANYWAY.
WHAT?! NUH-UH!
YOU CAN'T JUST PUT YOURSELF BACK TOGETHER EVERY TIME I TAKE YOU APART!

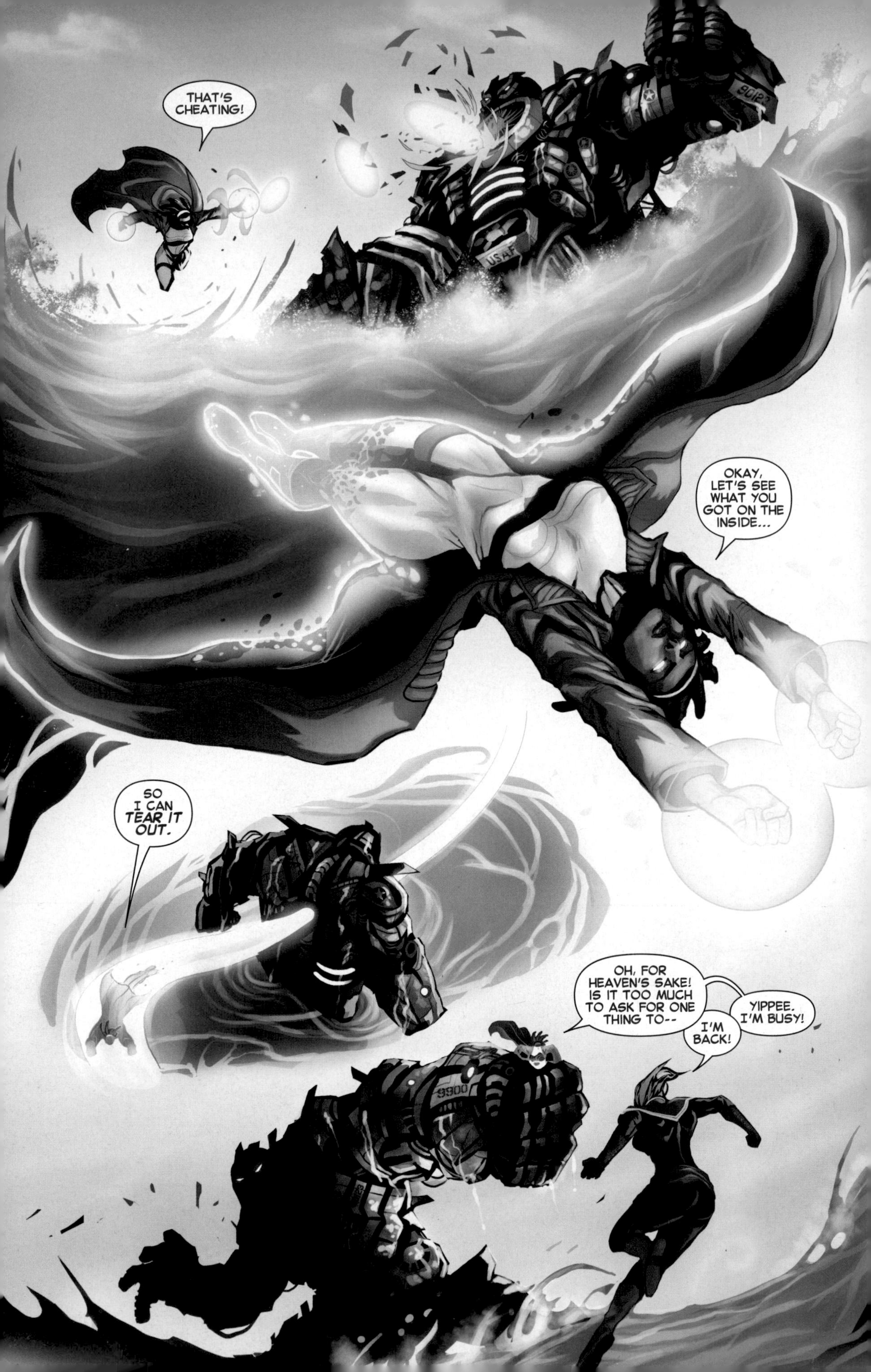
THAT'S CHEATING!
OKAY, LET'S SEE WHAT YOU GOT ON THE INSIDE...
SO I CAN TEAR IT OUT.
OH, FOR HEAVEN'S SAKE! IS IT TOO MUCH TO ASK FOR ONE THING TO--
I'M BACK!
YIPPEE. I'M BUSY!

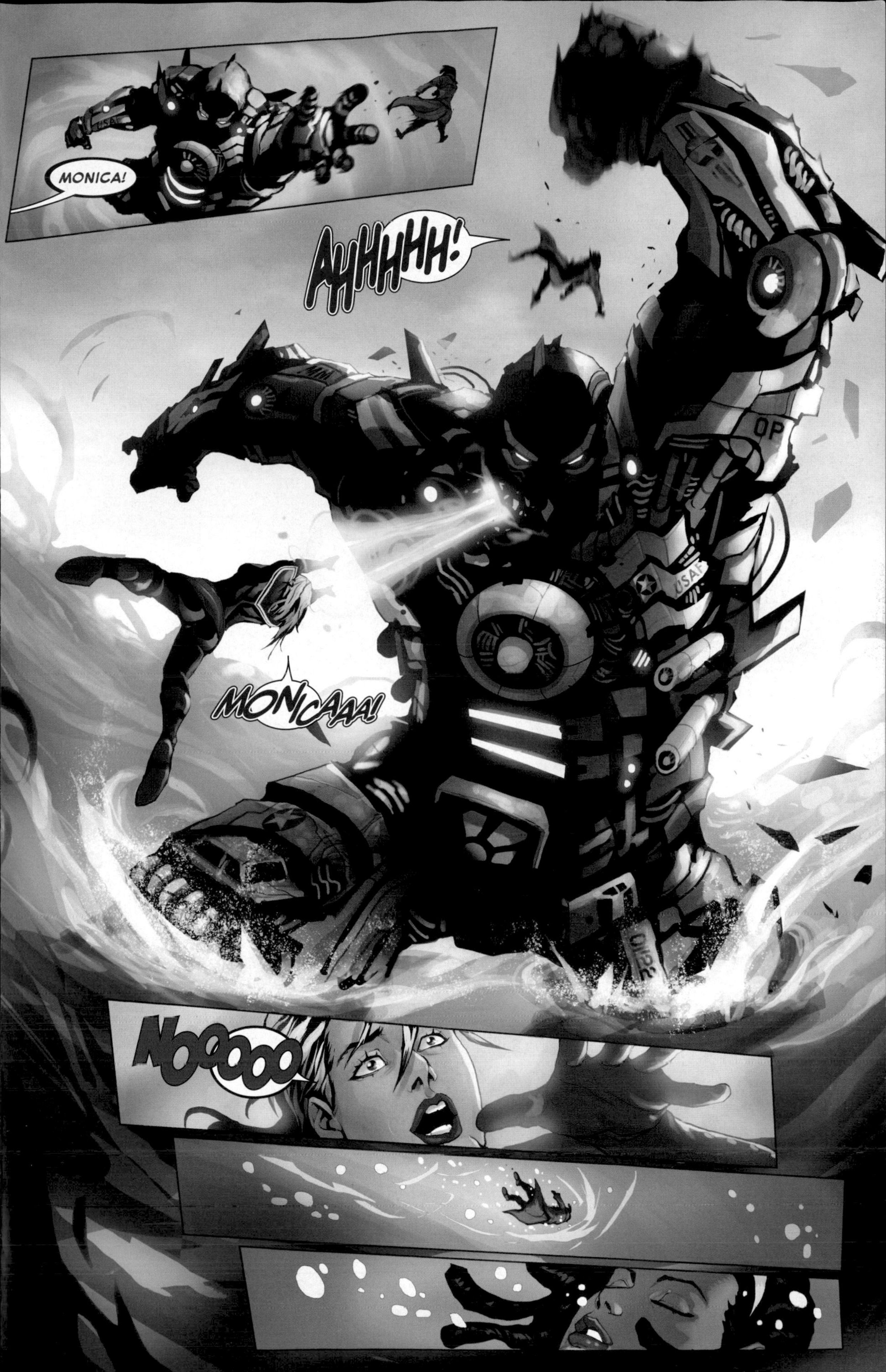
MONICA!
AHHHHH!
MONICAAA!
NOOOOO

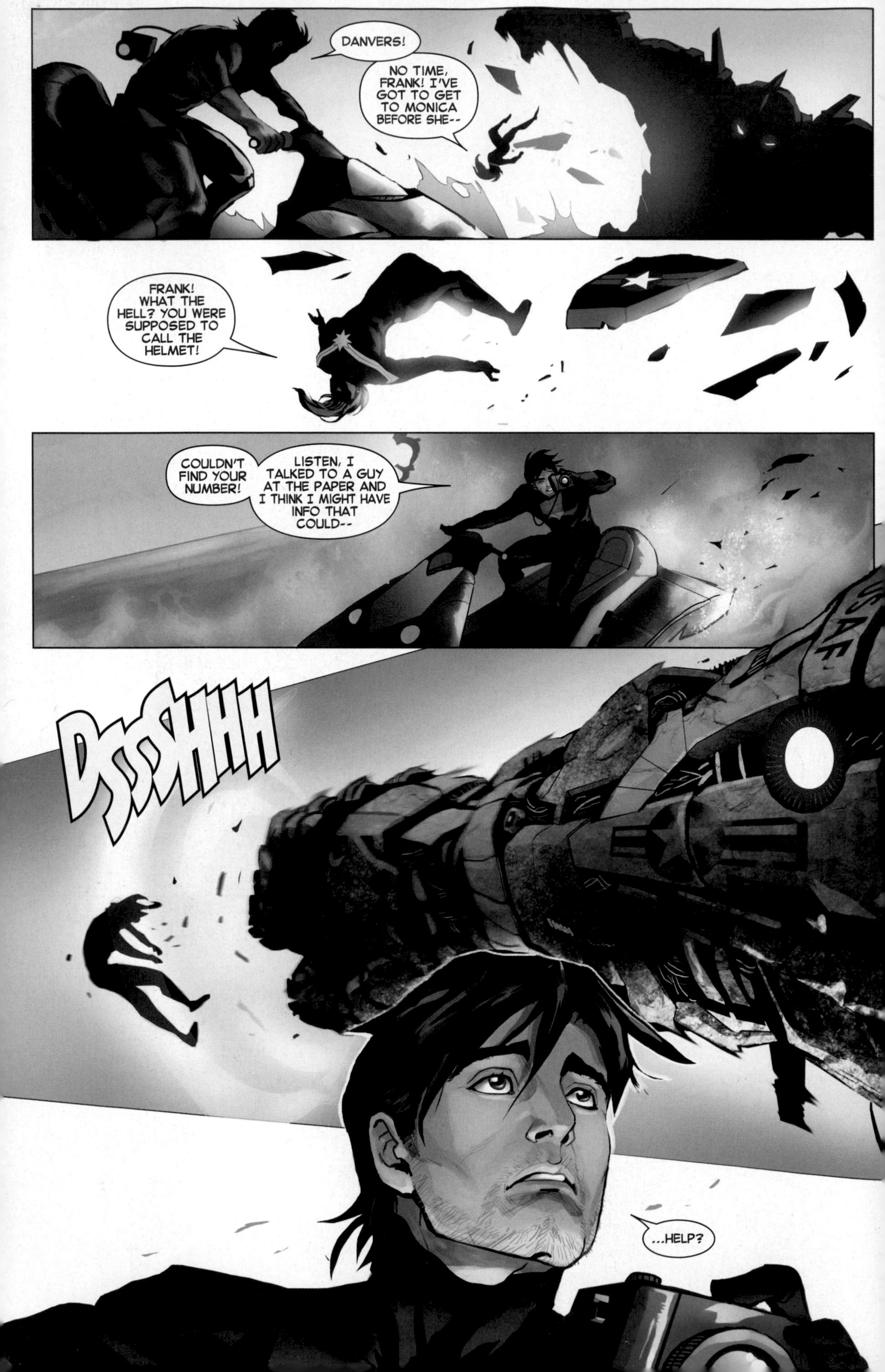
DANVERS!
NO TIME, FRANK! I'VE GOT TO GET TO MONICA BEFORE SHE--
FRANK! WHAT THE HELL? YOU WERE SUPPOSED TO CALL THE HELMET!
COULDN'T FIND YOUR NUMBER!
LISTEN, I TALKED TO A GUY AT THE PAPER AND I THINK I MIGHT HAVE INFO THAT COULD--
USAF
DSSSHHH
...HELP?

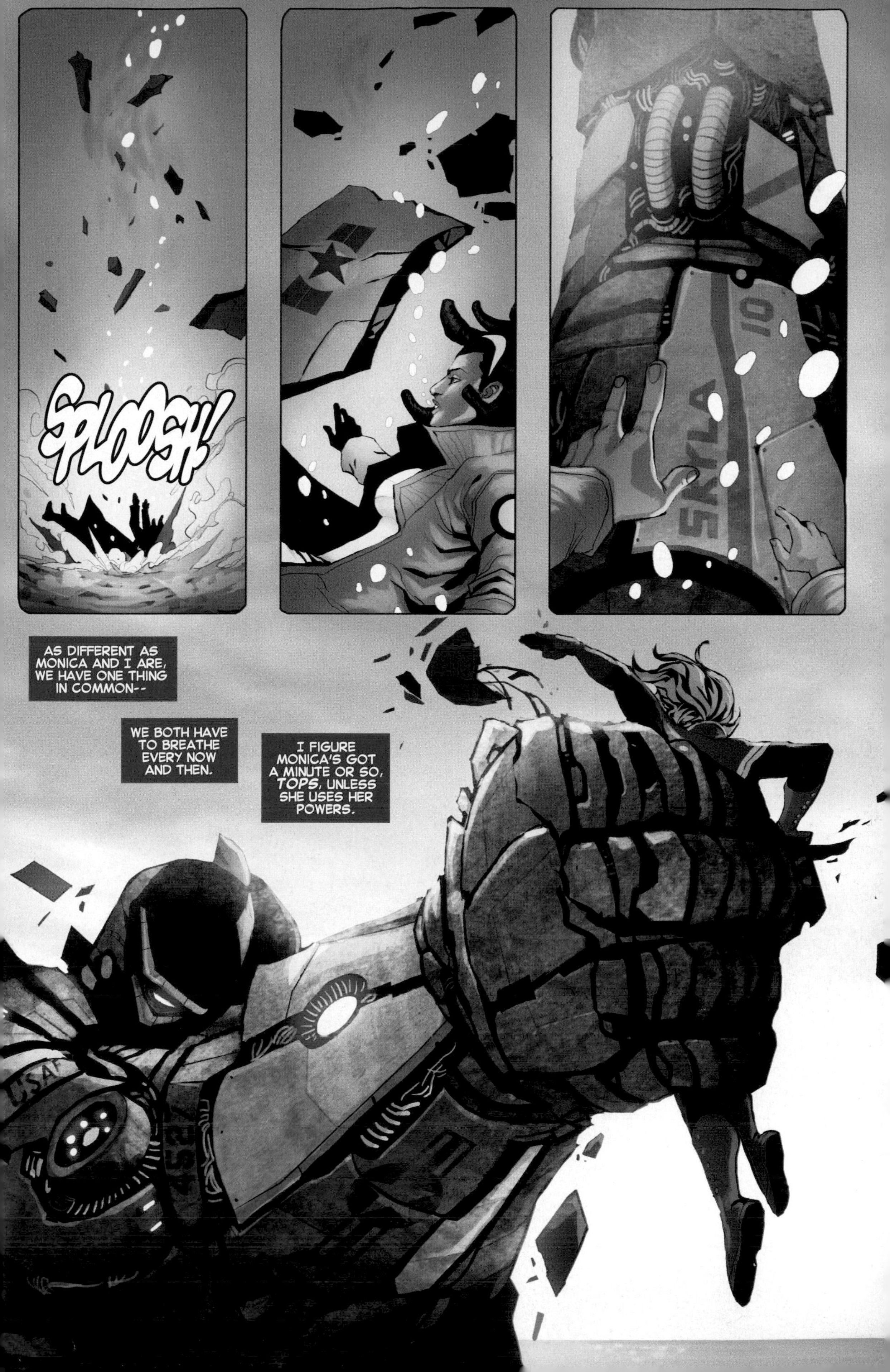

SPLOOSH!
AS DIFFERENT AS MONICA AND I ARE, WE HAVE ONE THING IN COMMON--
WE BOTH HAVE TO BREATHE EVERY NOW AND THEN.
I FIGURE MONICA'S GOT A MINUTE OR SO, TOPS, UNLESS SHE USES HER POWERS.

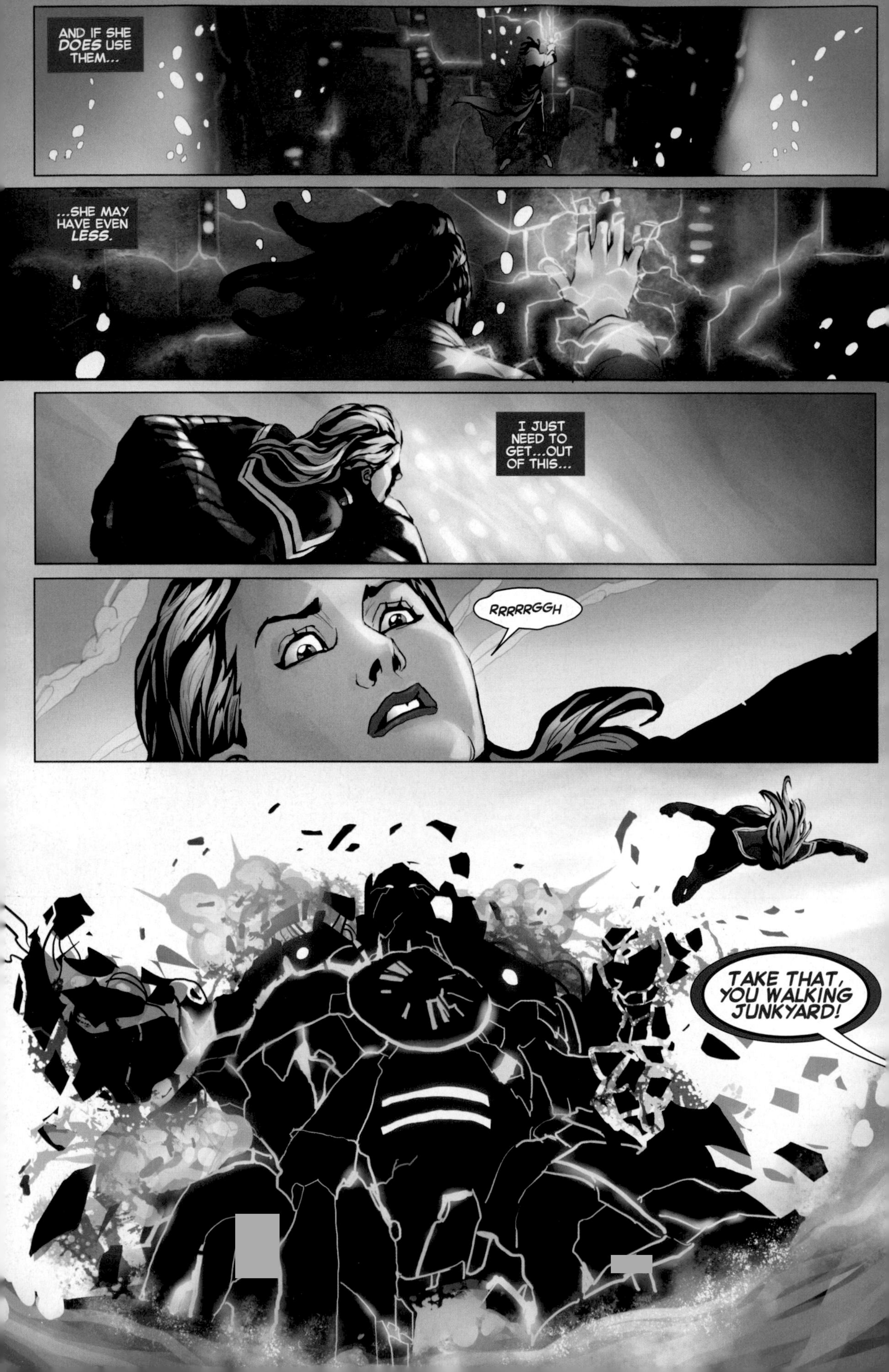
AND IF SHE DOES USE THEM...
...SHE MAY HAVE EVEN LESS.
I JUST NEED TO GET...OUT OF THIS...
RRRRRGGH
TAKE THAT, YOU WALKING JUNKYARD!

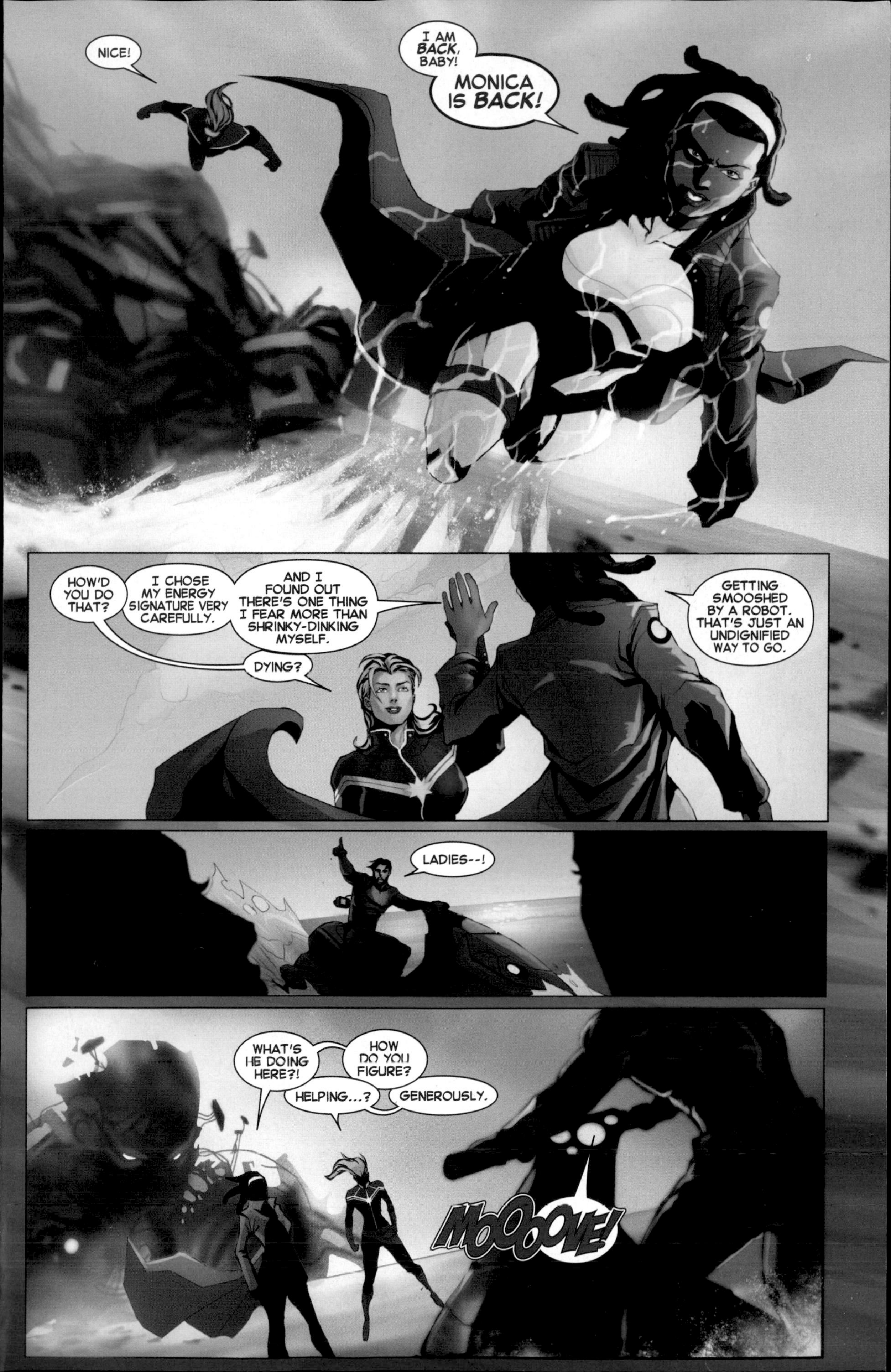
NICE!
I AM BACK, BABY!
MONICA IS BACK!
HOW'D YOU DO THAT?
I CHOSE MY ENERGY SIGNATURE VERY CAREFULLY.
AND I FOUND OUT THERE'S ONE THING I FEAR MORE THAN SHRINKY-DINKING MYSELF.
DYING?
GETTING SMOOSHED BY A ROBOT. THAT'S JUST AN UNDIGNIFIED WAY TO GO.
LADIES--!
WHAT'S HE DOING HERE?!
HOW DO YOU FIGURE?
HELPING...?
GENEROUSLY.
MOOOOOVE!

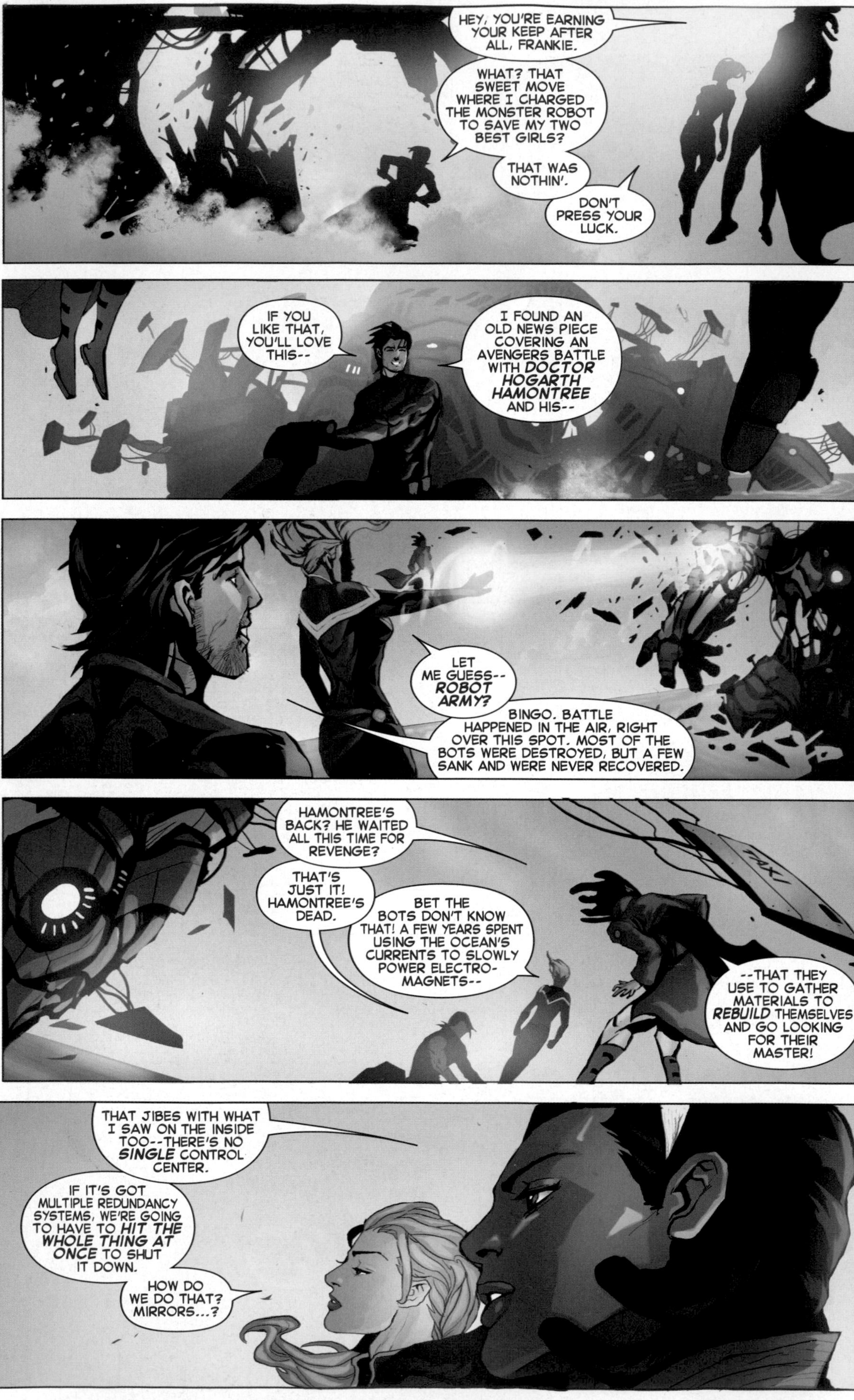
HEY, YOU'RE EARNING YOUR KEEP AFTER ALL, FRANKIE.
WHAT? THAT SWEET MOVE WHERE I CHARGED THE MONSTER ROBOT TO SAVE MY TWO BEST GIRLS?
THAT WAS NOTHIN'.
DON'T PRESS YOUR LUCK.
IF YOU LIKE THAT, YOU'LL LOVE THIS--
I FOUND AN OLD NEWS PIECE COVERING AN AVENGERS BATTLE WITH DOCTOR HOGARTH HAMONTREE AND HIS--
LET ME GUESS-- ROBOT ARMY?
BINGO. BATTLE HAPPENED IN THE AIR, RIGHT OVER THIS SPOT. MOST OF THE BOTS WERE DESTROYED, BUT A FEW SANK AND WERE NEVER RECOVERED.
HAMONTREE'S BACK? HE WAITED ALL THIS TIME FOR REVENGE?
THAT'S JUST IT! HAMONTREE'S DEAD.
BET THE BOTS DON'T KNOW THAT! A FEW YEARS SPENT USING THE OCEAN'S CURRENTS TO SLOWLY POWER ELECTRO-MAGNETS--
--THAT THEY USE TO GATHER MATERIALS TO REBUILD THEMSELVES AND GO LOOKING FOR THEIR MASTER!
TAXI
THAT JIBES WITH WHAT I SAW ON THE INSIDE TOO--THERE'S NO SINGLE CONTROL CENTER.
IF IT'S GOT MULTIPLE REDUNDANCY SYSTEMS, WE'RE GOING TO HAVE TO HIT THE WHOLE THING AT ONCE TO SHUT IT DOWN.
HOW DO WE DO THAT? MIRRORS...?

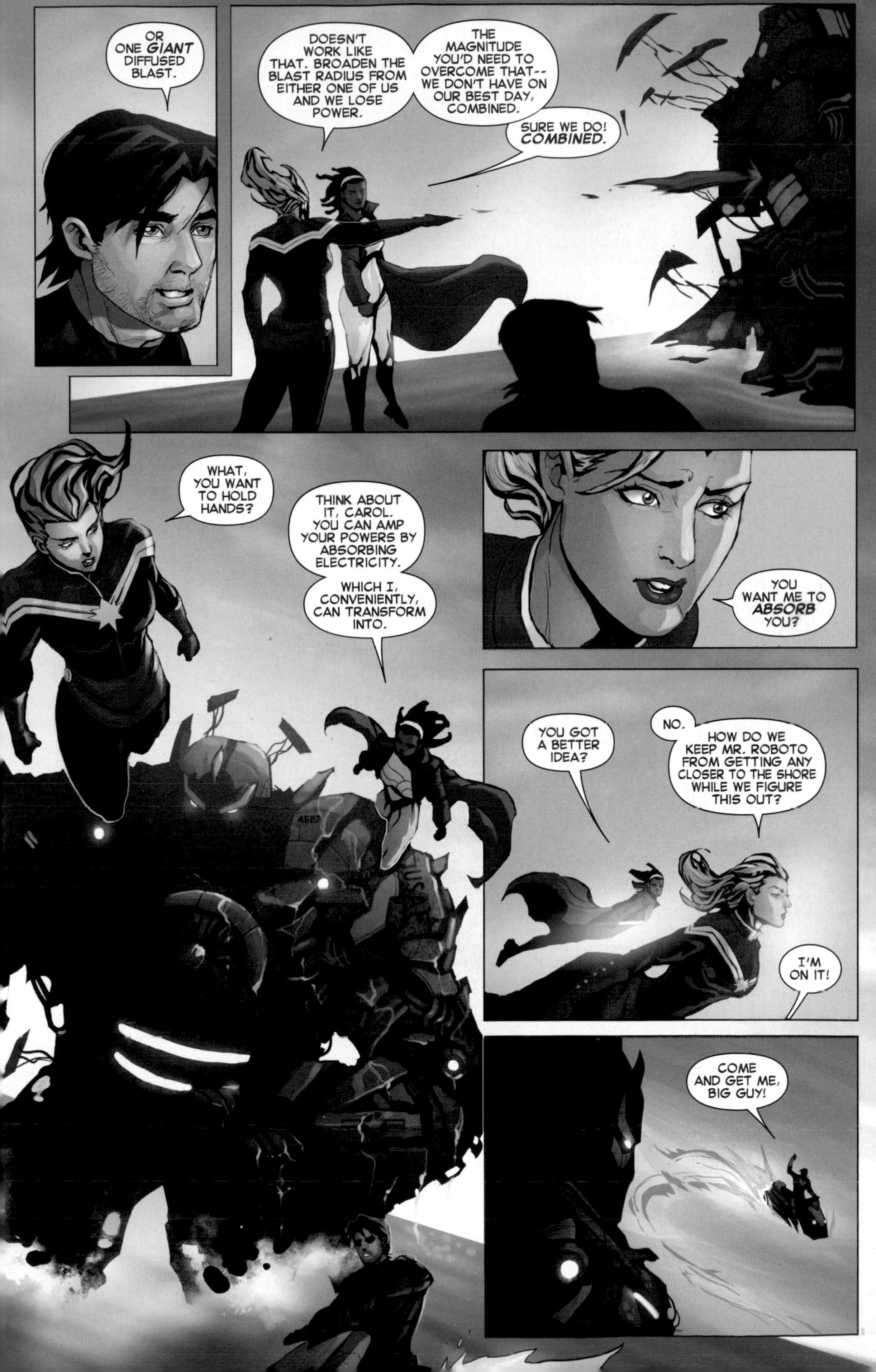

OR ONE GIANT DIFFUSED BLAST.
DOESN'T WORK LIKE THAT. BROADEN THE BLAST RADIUS FROM EITHER ONE OF US AND WE LOSE POWER.
THE MAGNITUDE YOU'D NEED TO OVERCOME THAT-- WE DON'T HAVE ON OUR BEST DAY, COMBINED.
SURE WE DO! COMBINED.
WHAT, YOU WANT TO HOLD HANDS?
THINK ABOUT IT, CAROL. YOU CAN AMP YOUR POWERS BY ABSORBING ELECTRICITY.
WHICH I, CONVENIENTLY, CAN TRANSFORM INTO.
4527
YOU WANT ME TO ABSORB YOU?
NO.
YOU GOT A BETTER IDEA?
HOW DO WE KEEP MR. ROBOTO FROM GETTING ANY CLOSER TO THE SHORE WHILE WE FIGURE THIS OUT?
I'M ON IT!
COME AND GET ME, BIG GUY!

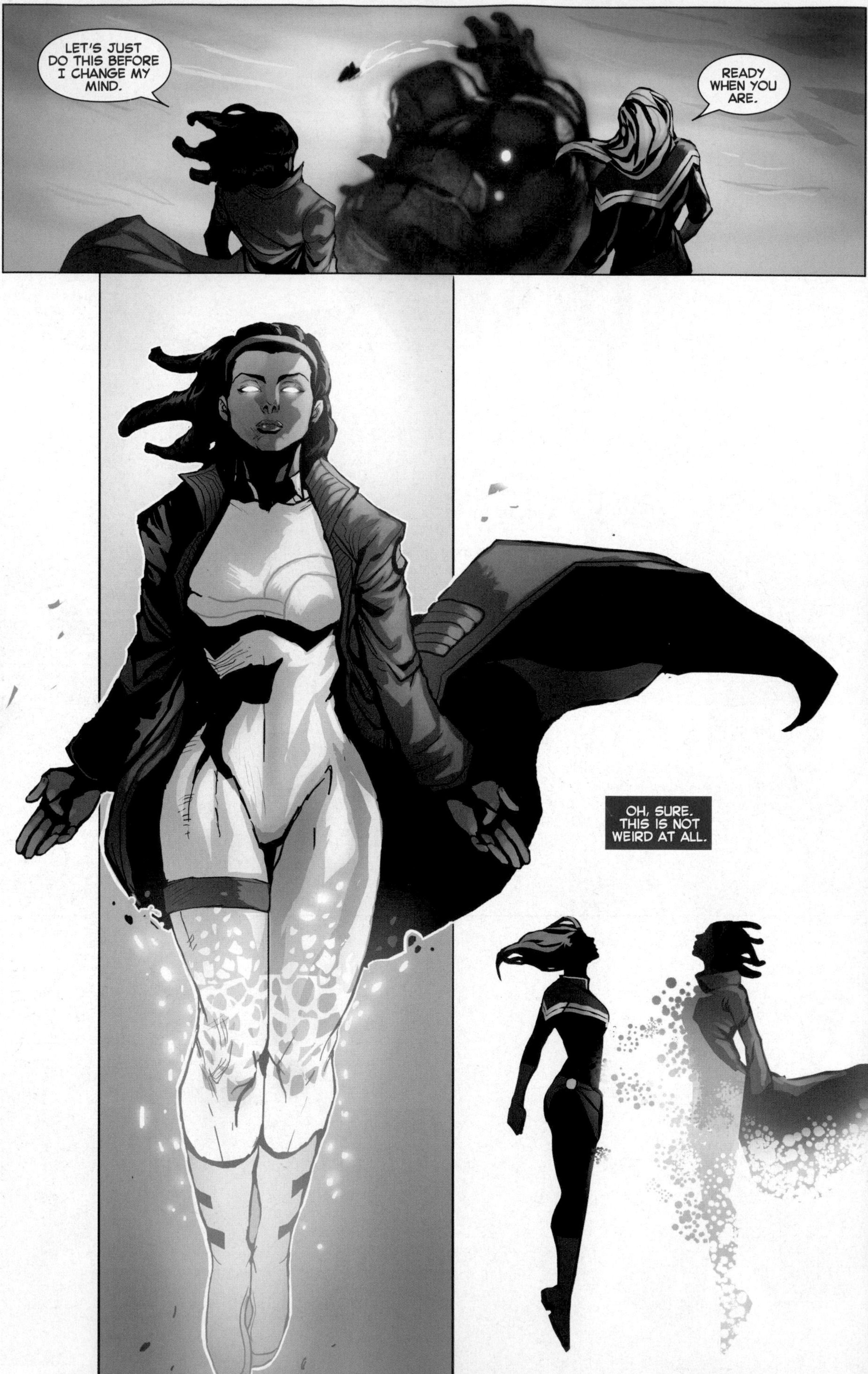
LET'S JUST DO THIS BEFORE I CHANGE MY MIND.
READY WHEN YOU ARE.
OH, SURE. THIS IS NOT WEIRD AT ALL.

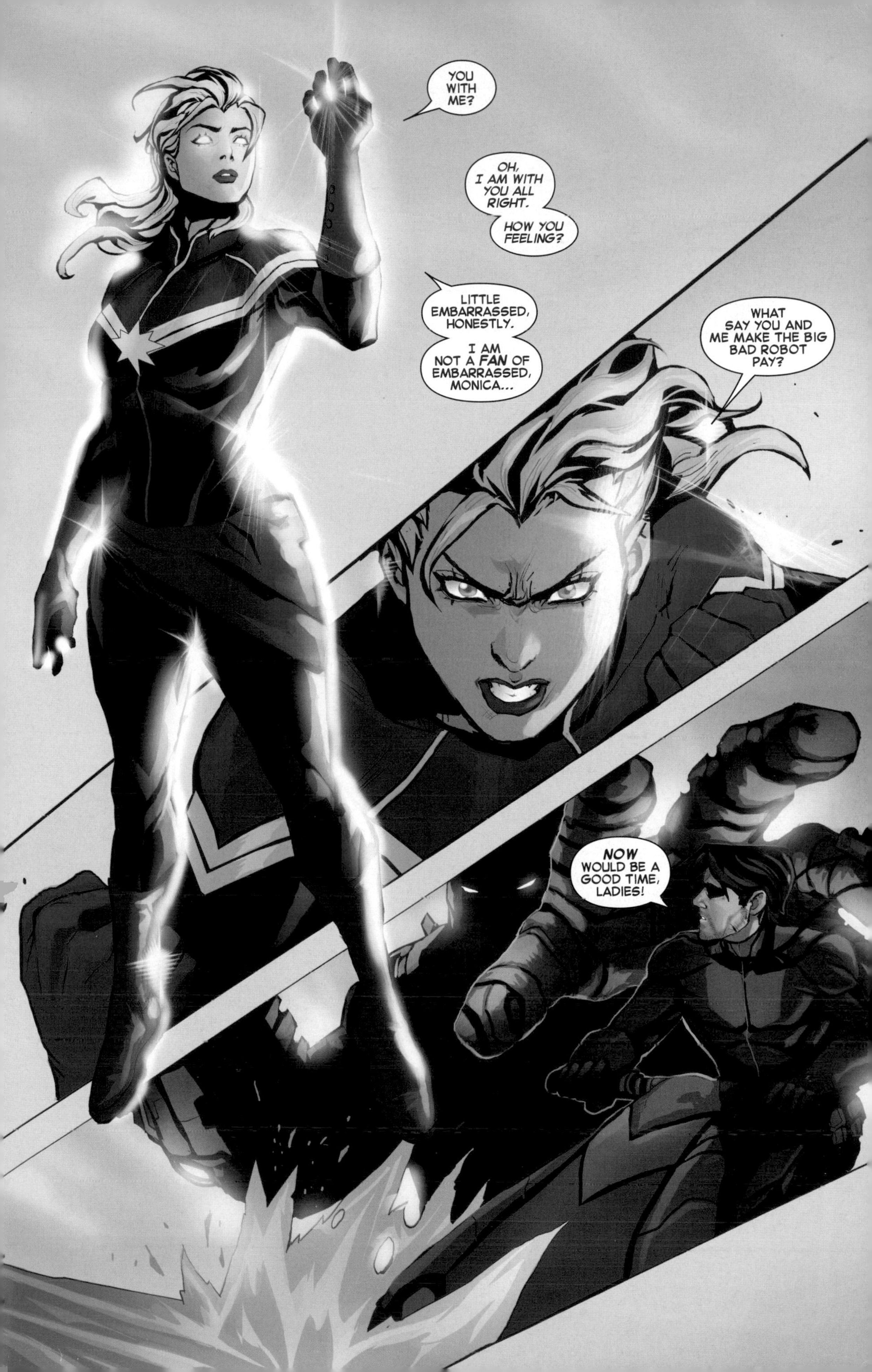
YOU WITH ME?
OH, I AM WITH YOU ALL RIGHT.
HOW YOU FEELING?
LITTLE EMBARRASSED, HONESTLY.
I AM NOT A *FAN* OF EMBARRASSED, MONICA...
WHAT SAY YOU AND ME MAKE THE BIG BAD ROBOT PAY?
NOW WOULD BE A GOOD TIME, LADIES!

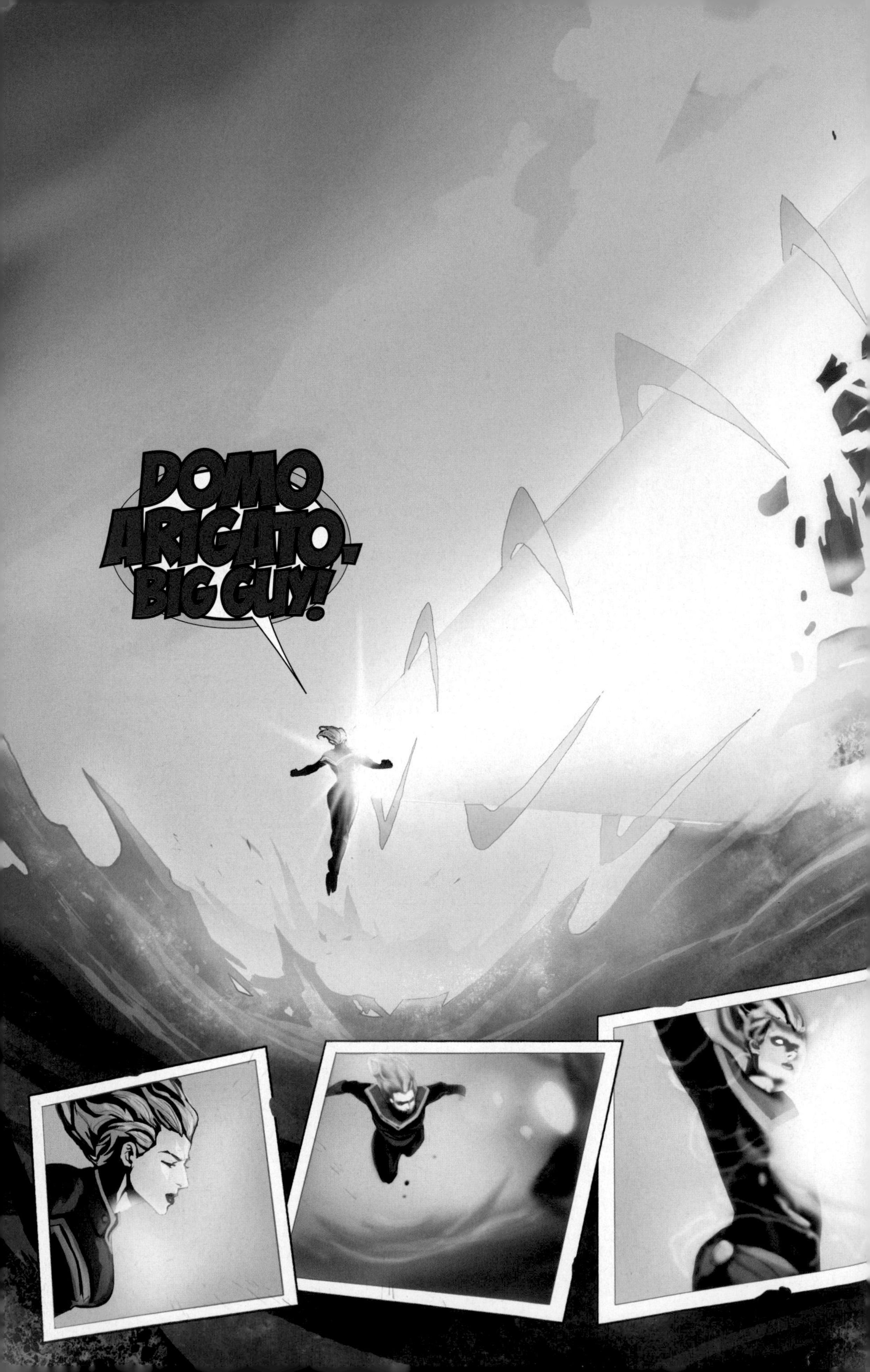
DOMO ARIGATO, BIG GUY!

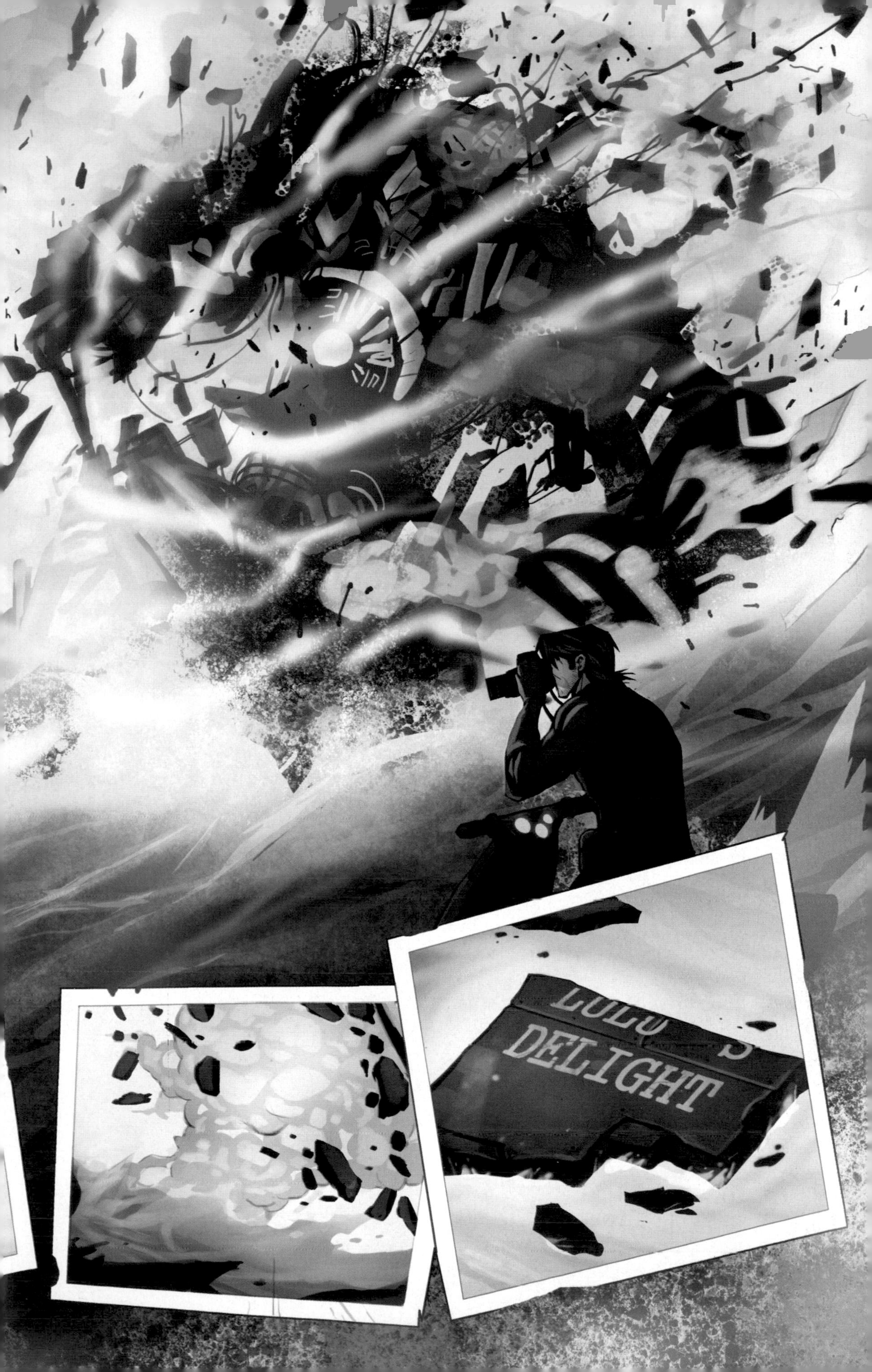
DELIGHT

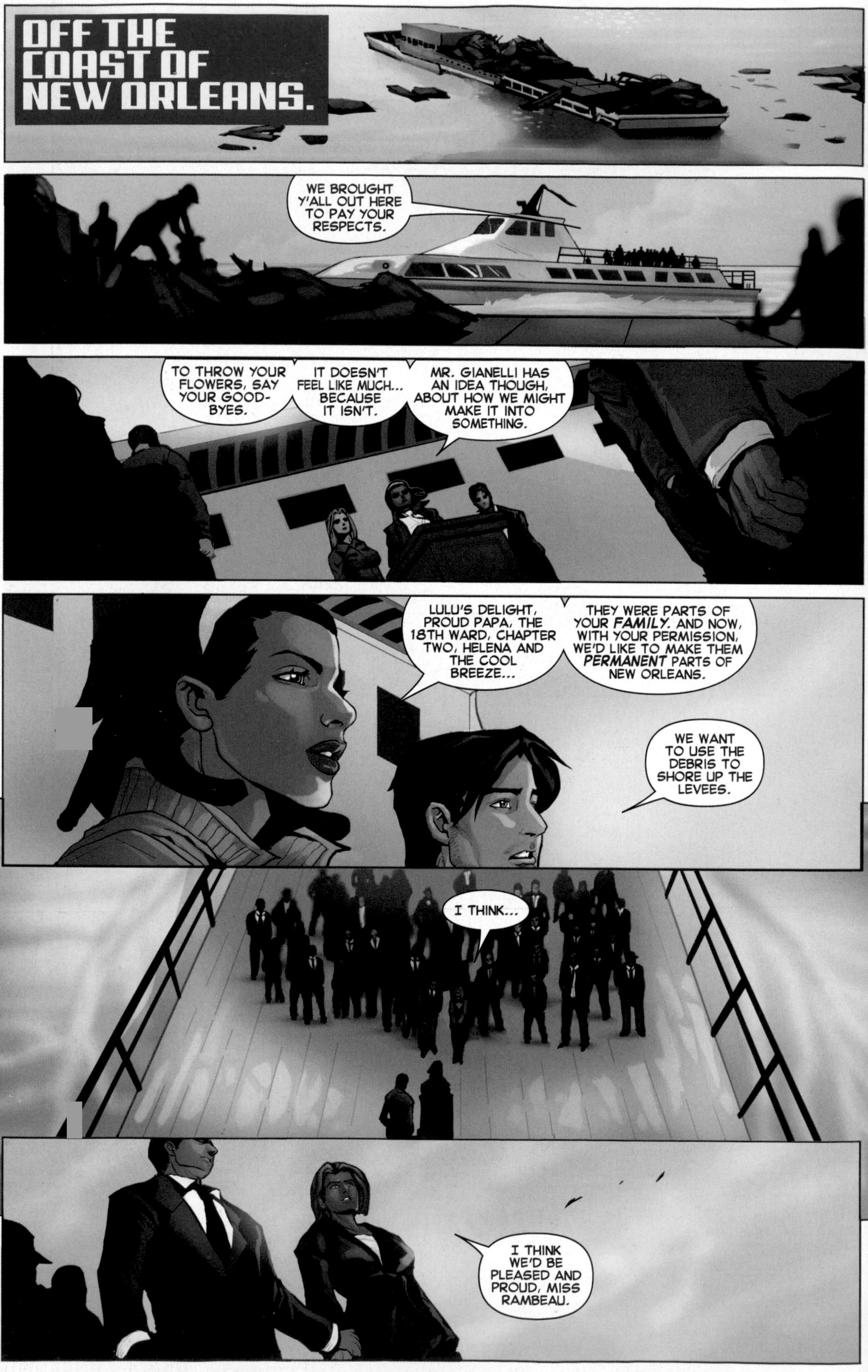
OFF THE COAST OF NEW ORLEANS.
WE BROUGHT Y'ALL OUT HERE TO PAY YOUR RESPECTS.
TO THROW YOUR FLOWERS, SAY YOUR GOOD-BYES.
IT DOESN'T FEEL LIKE MUCH... BECAUSE IT ISN'T.
MR. GIANELLI HAS AN IDEA THOUGH, ABOUT HOW WE MIGHT MAKE IT INTO SOMETHING.
LULU'S DELIGHT, PROUD PAPA, THE 18TH WARD, CHAPTER TWO, HELENA AND THE COOL BREEZE...
THEY WERE PARTS OF YOUR *FAMILY.* AND NOW, WITH YOUR PERMISSION, WE'D LIKE TO MAKE THEM *PERMANENT* PARTS OF NEW ORLEANS.
WE WANT TO USE THE DEBRIS TO SHORE UP THE LEVEES.
I THINK...
I THINK WE'D BE PLEASED AND PROUD, MISS RAMBEAU.

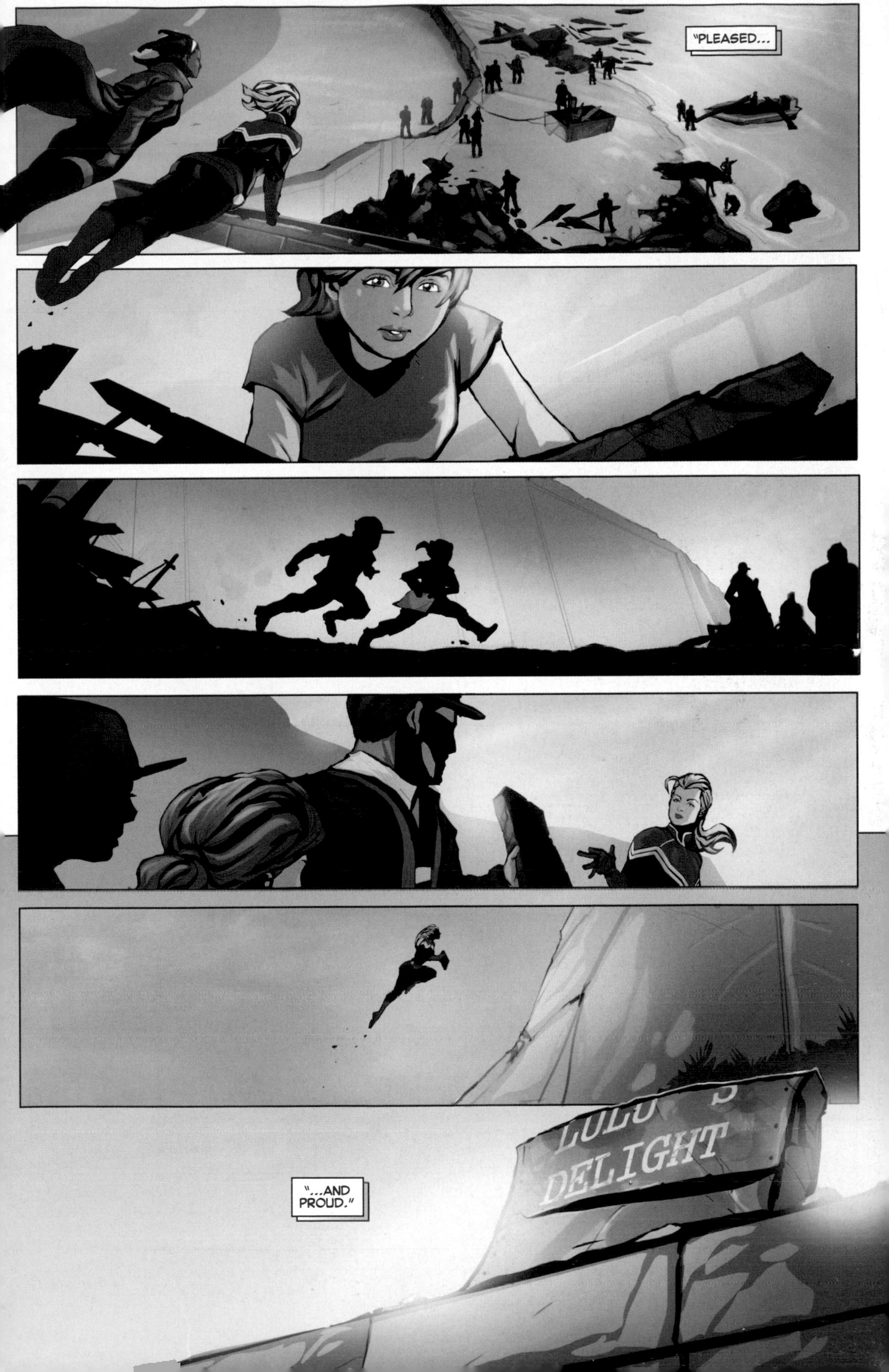
"PLEASED...
LULU S
DELIGHT
"...AND PROUD."

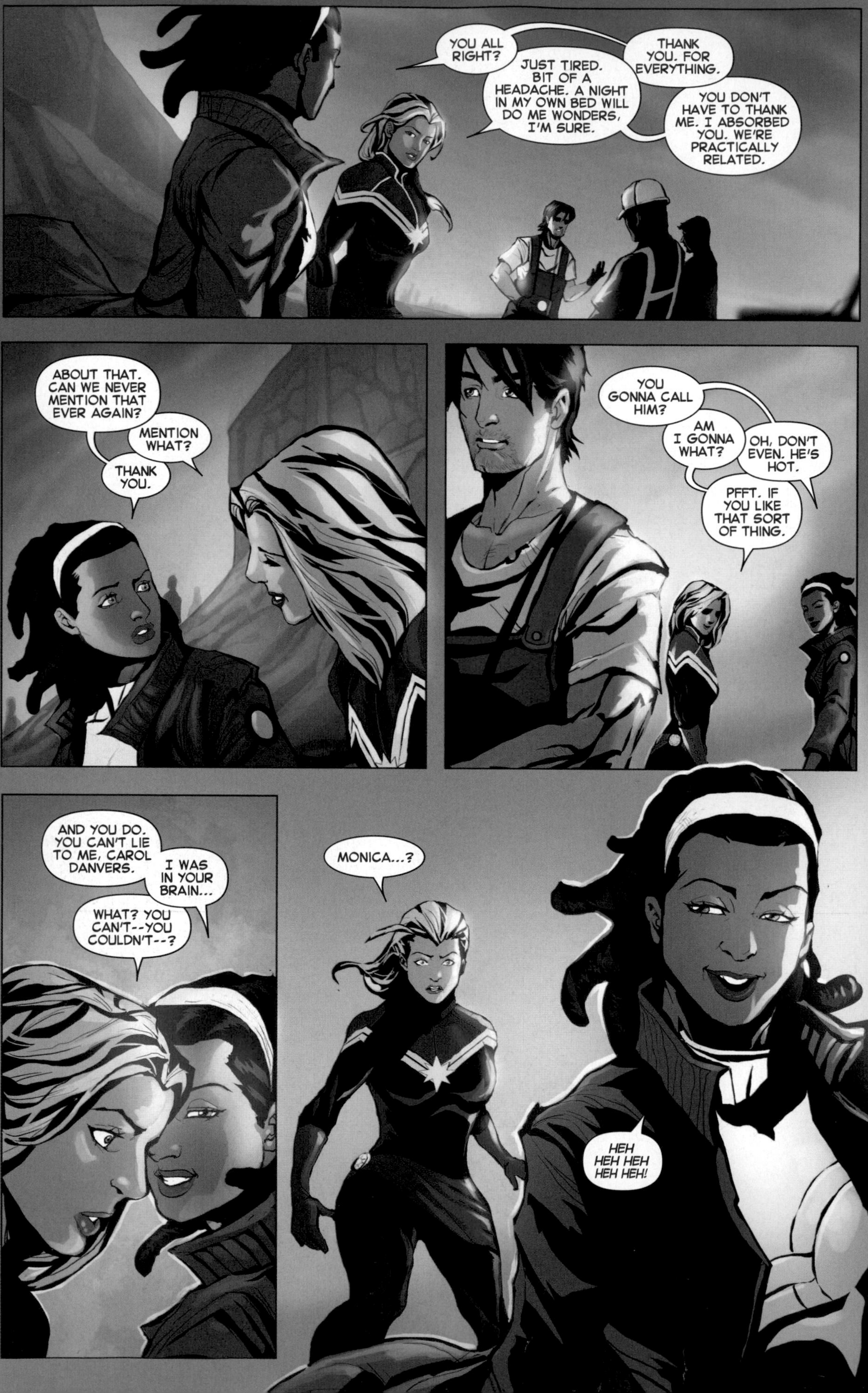
YOU ALL RIGHT?
JUST TIRED. BIT OF A HEADACHE. A NIGHT IN MY OWN BED WILL DO ME WONDERS, I'M SURE.
THANK YOU. FOR EVERYTHING.
YOU DON'T HAVE TO THANK ME. I ABSORBED YOU. WE'RE PRACTICALLY RELATED.
ABOUT THAT. CAN WE NEVER MENTION THAT EVER AGAIN?
MENTION WHAT?
THANK YOU.
YOU GONNA CALL HIM?
AM I GONNA WHAT?
OH, DON'T EVEN. HE'S HOT.
PFFT. IF YOU LIKE THAT SORT OF THING.
AND YOU DO. YOU CAN'T LIE TO ME, CAROL DANVERS.
I WAS IN YOUR BRAIN...
WHAT? YOU CAN'T--YOU COULDN'T--?
MONICA...?
HEH HEH HEH HEH HEH!

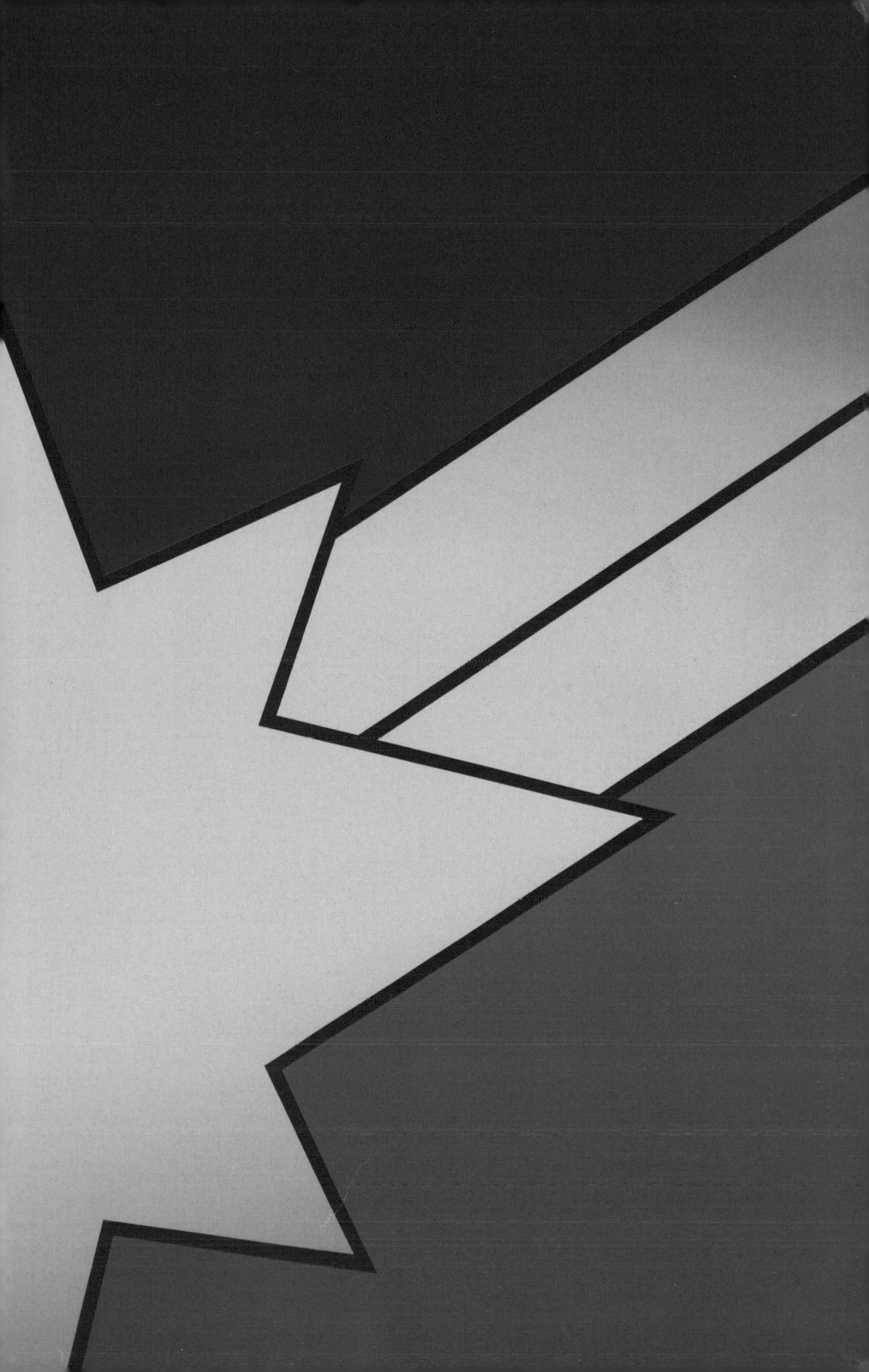

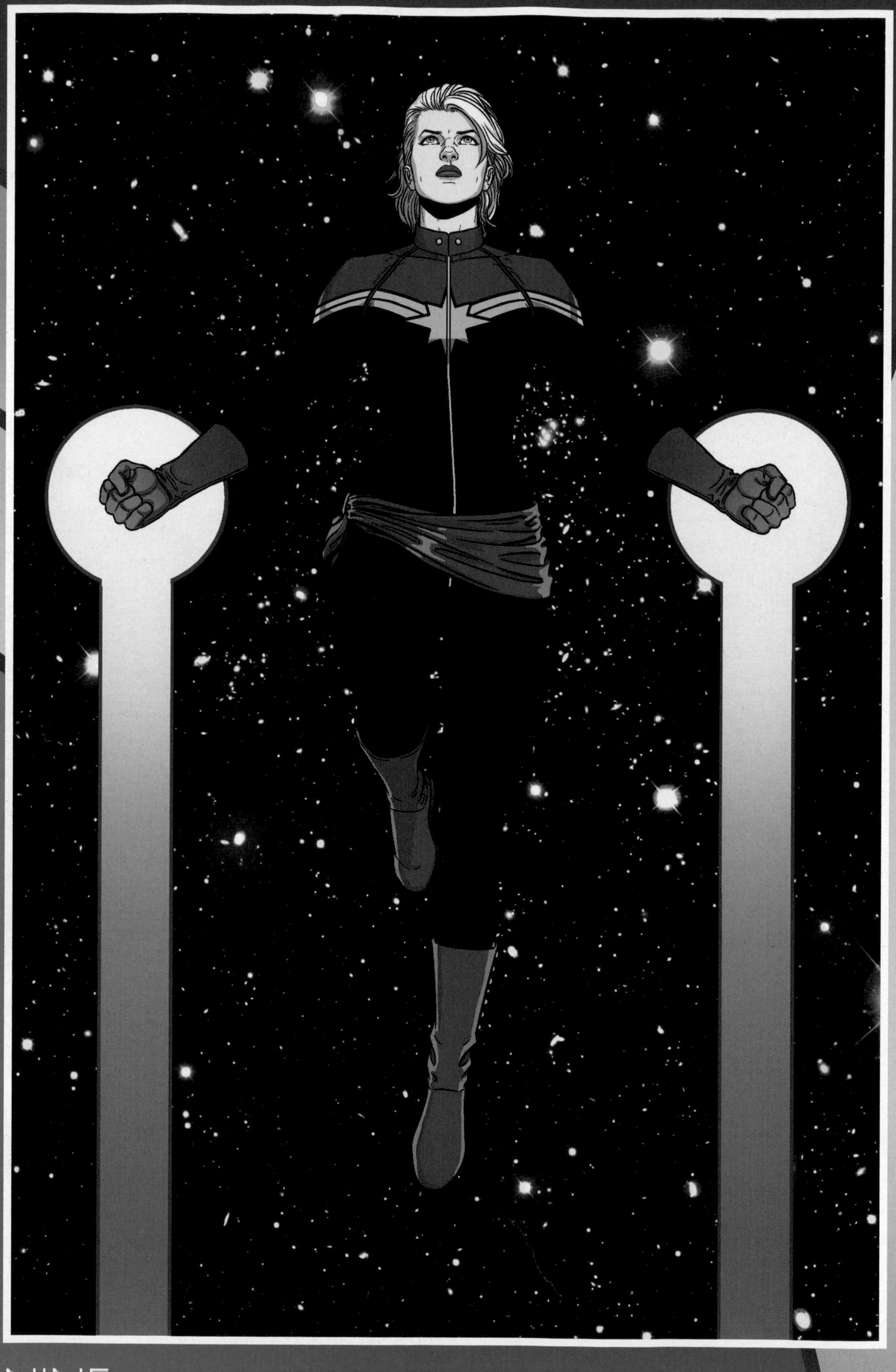

NINE

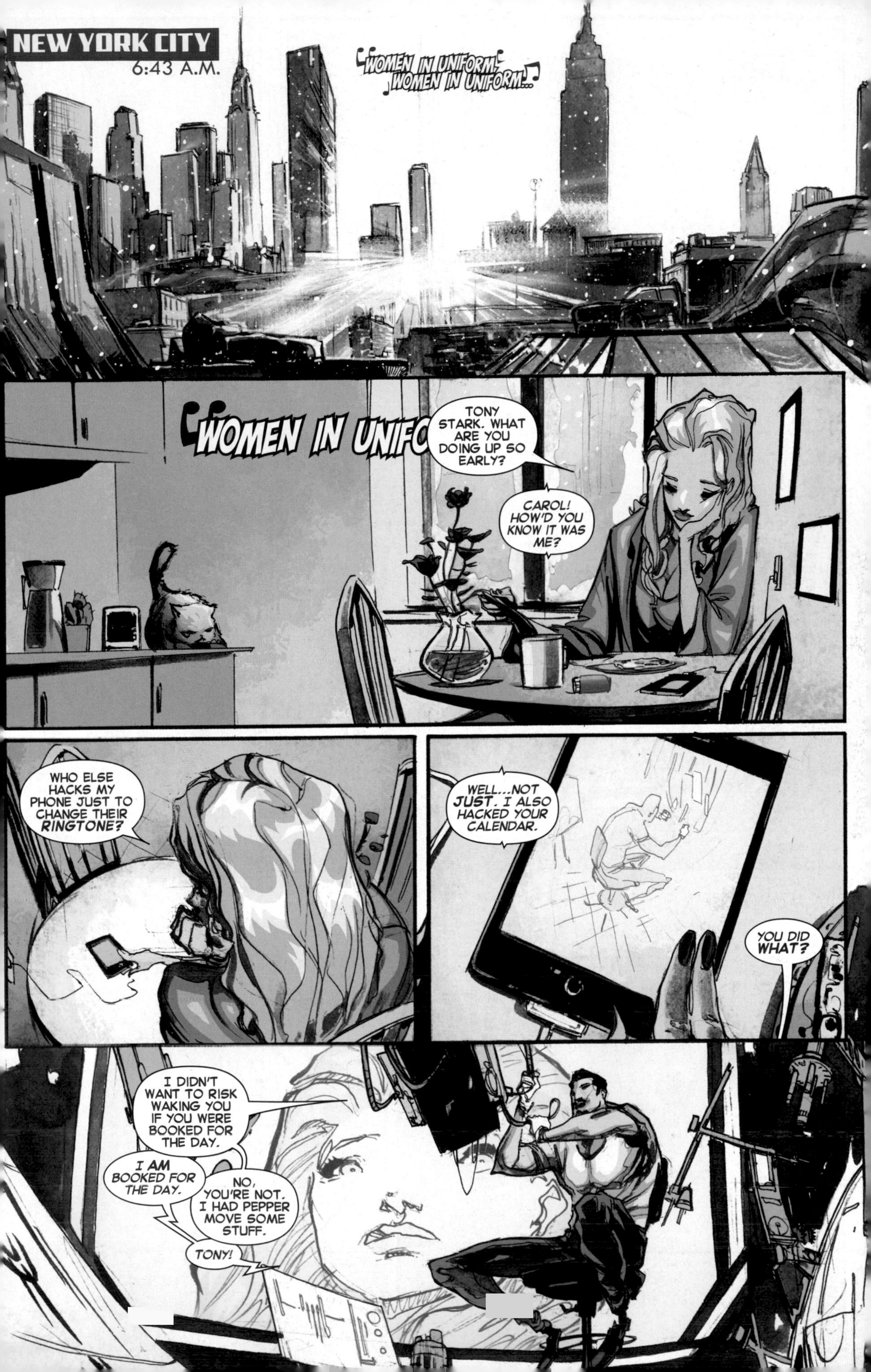

NEW YORK CITY
6:43 A.M.
"WOMEN IN UNIFORM, WOMEN IN UNIFORM..."
"WOMEN IN UNIFO
TONY STARK. WHAT ARE YOU DOING UP SO EARLY?
CAROL! HOW'D YOU KNOW IT WAS ME?
WHO ELSE HACKS MY PHONE JUST TO CHANGE THEIR RINGTONE?
WELL...NOT JUST. I ALSO HACKED YOUR CALENDAR.
YOU DID WHAT?
I DIDN'T WANT TO RISK WAKING YOU IF YOU WERE BOOKED FOR THE DAY.
I AM BOOKED FOR THE DAY.
NO, YOU'RE NOT. I HAD PEPPER MOVE SOME STUFF.
TONY!

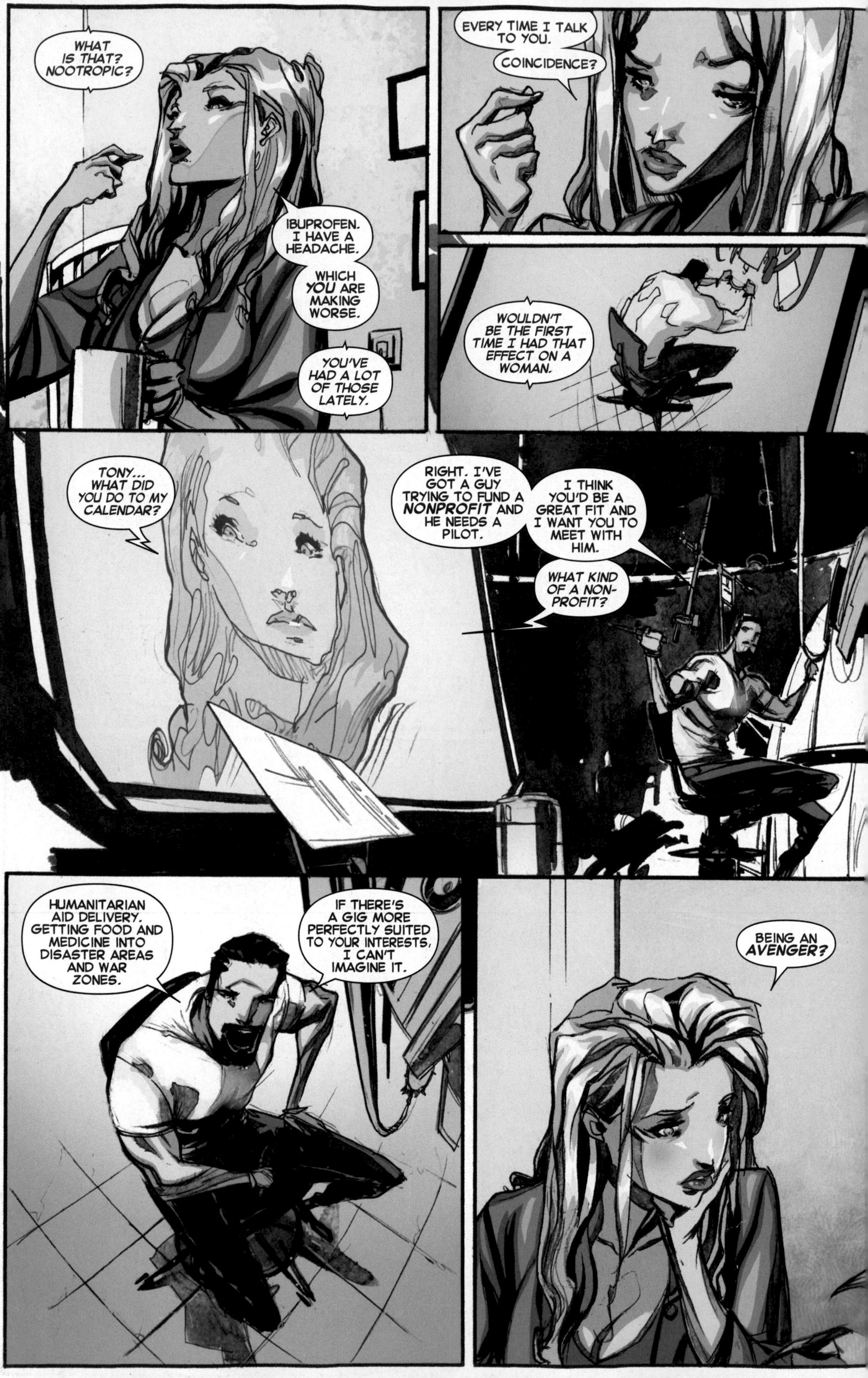
WHAT IS THAT? NOOTROPIC?
IBUPROFEN. I HAVE A HEADACHE.
WHICH YOU ARE MAKING WORSE.
YOU'VE HAD A LOT OF THOSE LATELY.
EVERY TIME I TALK TO YOU.
COINCIDENCE?
WOULDN'T BE THE FIRST TIME I HAD THAT EFFECT ON A WOMAN.
TONY... WHAT DID YOU DO TO MY CALENDAR?
RIGHT. I'VE GOT A GUY TRYING TO FUND A NONPROFIT AND HE NEEDS A PILOT.
I THINK YOU'D BE A GREAT FIT AND I WANT YOU TO MEET WITH HIM.
WHAT KIND OF A NON-PROFIT?
HUMANITARIAN AID DELIVERY. GETTING FOOD AND MEDICINE INTO DISASTER AREAS AND WAR ZONES.
IF THERE'S A GIG MORE PERFECTLY SUITED TO YOUR INTERESTS, I CAN'T IMAGINE IT.
BEING AN AVENGER?

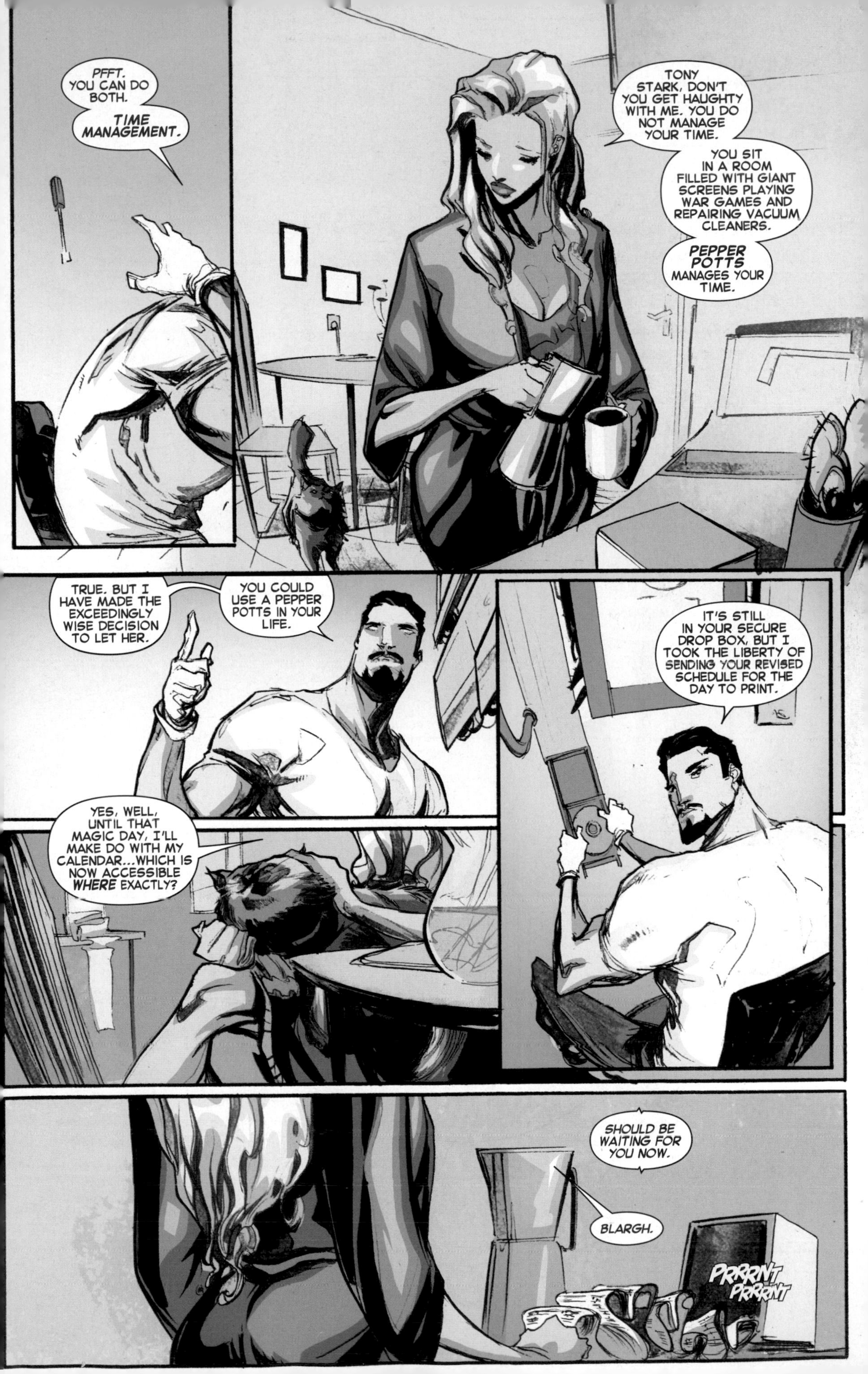
PFFT. YOU CAN DO BOTH.
TIME MANAGEMENT.
TONY STARK, DON'T YOU GET HAUGHTY WITH ME. YOU DO NOT MANAGE YOUR TIME.
YOU SIT IN A ROOM FILLED WITH GIANT SCREENS PLAYING WAR GAMES AND REPAIRING VACUUM CLEANERS.
PEPPER POTTS MANAGES YOUR TIME.
YOU COULD USE A PEPPER POTTS IN YOUR LIFE.
TRUE. BUT I HAVE MADE THE EXCEEDINGLY WISE DECISION TO LET HER.
YES, WELL, UNTIL THAT MAGIC DAY, I'LL MAKE DO WITH MY CALENDAR...WHICH IS NOW ACCESSIBLE WHERE EXACTLY?
IT'S STILL IN YOUR SECURE DROP BOX, BUT I TOOK THE LIBERTY OF SENDING YOUR REVISED SCHEDULE FOR THE DAY TO PRINT.
SHOULD BE WAITING FOR YOU NOW.
BLARGH.
PRRRNT PRRRNT

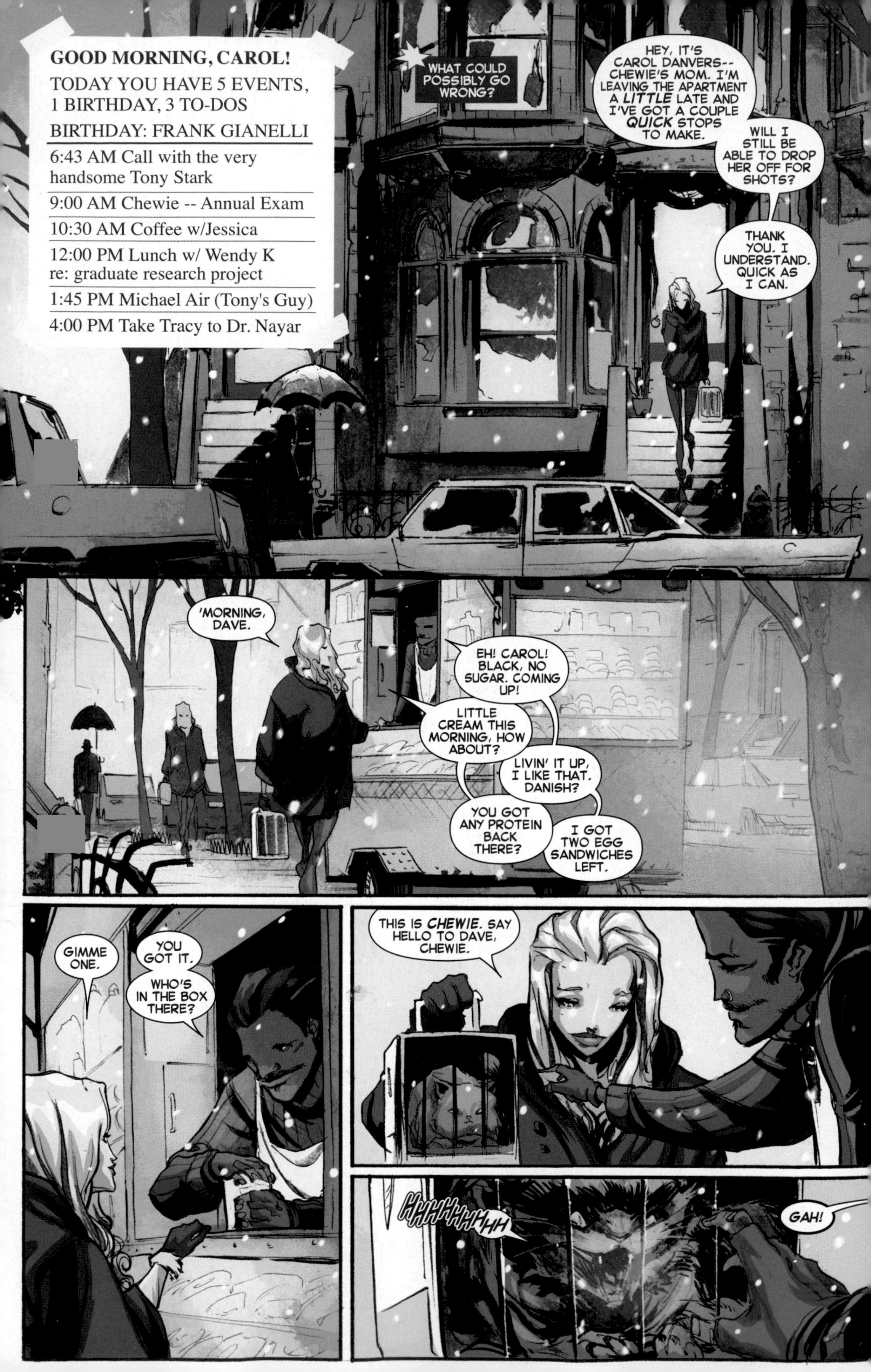
GOOD MORNING, CAROL!
TODAY YOU HAVE 5 EVENTS, 1 BIRTHDAY, 3 TO-DOS
BIRTHDAY: FRANK GIANELLI
6:43 AM Call with the very handsome Tony Stark
9:00 AM Chewie -- Annual Exam
10:30 AM Coffee w/Jessica
12:00 PM Lunch w/ Wendy K re: graduate research project
1:45 PM Michael Air (Tony's Guy)
4:00 PM Take Tracy to Dr. Nayar
WHAT COULD POSSIBLY GO WRONG?
HEY, IT'S CAROL DANVERS-- CHEWIE'S MOM. I'M LEAVING THE APARTMENT A LITTLE LATE AND I'VE GOT A COUPLE QUICK STOPS TO MAKE.
WILL I STILL BE ABLE TO DROP HER OFF FOR SHOTS?
THANK YOU. I UNDERSTAND. QUICK AS I CAN.
'MORNING, DAVE.
EH! CAROL! BLACK, NO SUGAR. COMING UP!
LITTLE CREAM THIS MORNING, HOW ABOUT?
LIVIN' IT UP, I LIKE THAT. DANISH?
YOU GOT ANY PROTEIN BACK THERE?
I GOT TWO EGG SANDWICHES LEFT.
GIMME ONE.
YOU GOT IT.
WHO'S IN THE BOX THERE?
THIS IS CHEWIE. SAY HELLO TO DAVE, CHEWIE.
HHHHHHHHH
GAH!

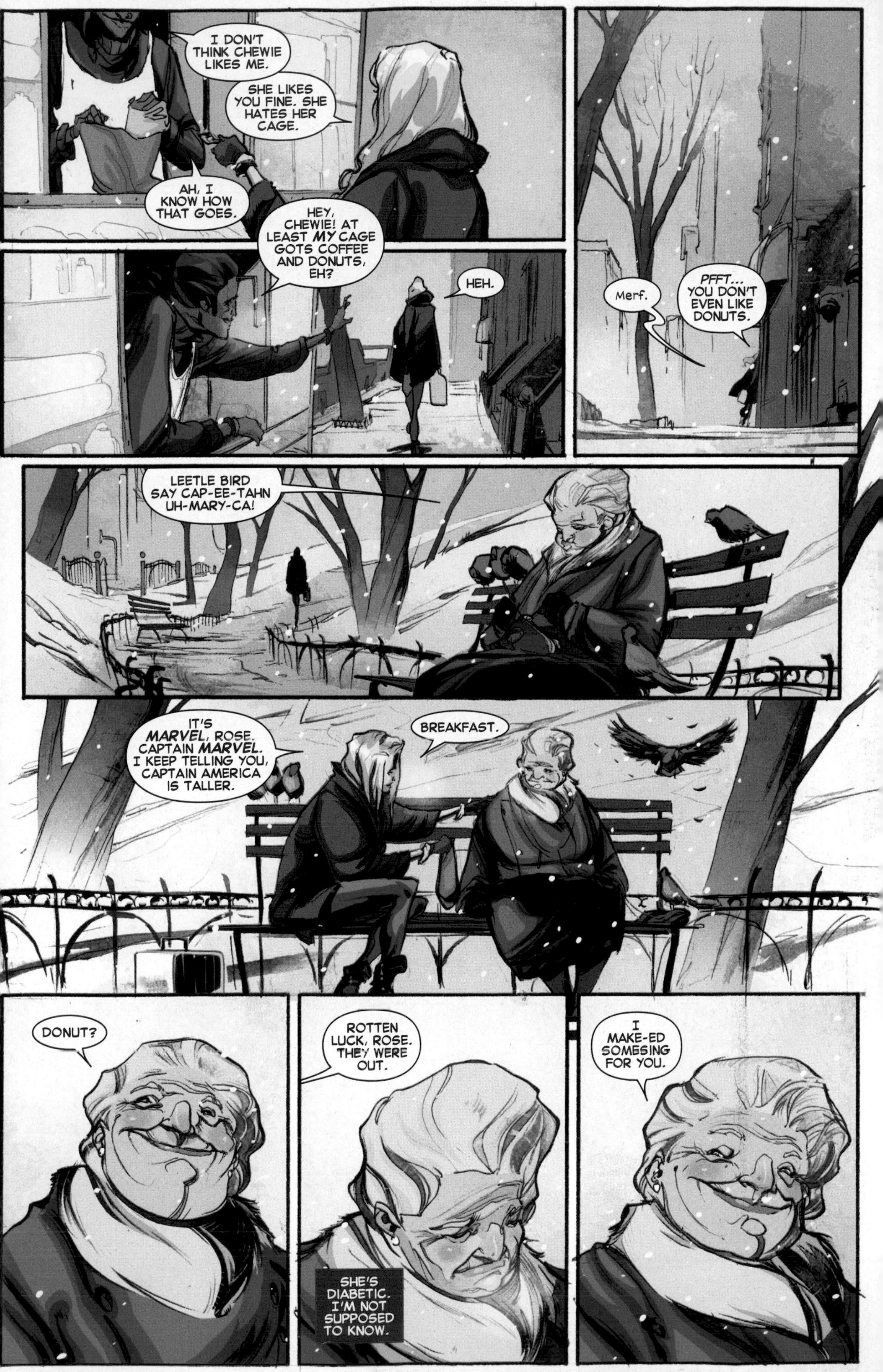
I DON'T THINK CHEWIE LIKES ME.
SHE LIKES YOU FINE. SHE HATES HER CAGE.
AH, I KNOW HOW THAT GOES.
HEY, CHEWIE! AT LEAST MY CAGE GOTS COFFEE AND DONUTS, EH?
HEH.
Merf.
PFFT... YOU DON'T EVEN LIKE DONUTS.
LEETLE BIRD SAY CAP-EE-TAHN UH-MARY-CA!
IT'S MARVEL, ROSE. CAPTAIN MARVEL. I KEEP TELLING YOU, CAPTAIN AMERICA IS TALLER.
BREAKFAST.
DONUT?
ROTTEN LUCK, ROSE. THEY WERE OUT.
SHE'S DIABETIC. I'M NOT SUPPOSED TO KNOW.
I MAKE-ED SOMESING FOR YOU.

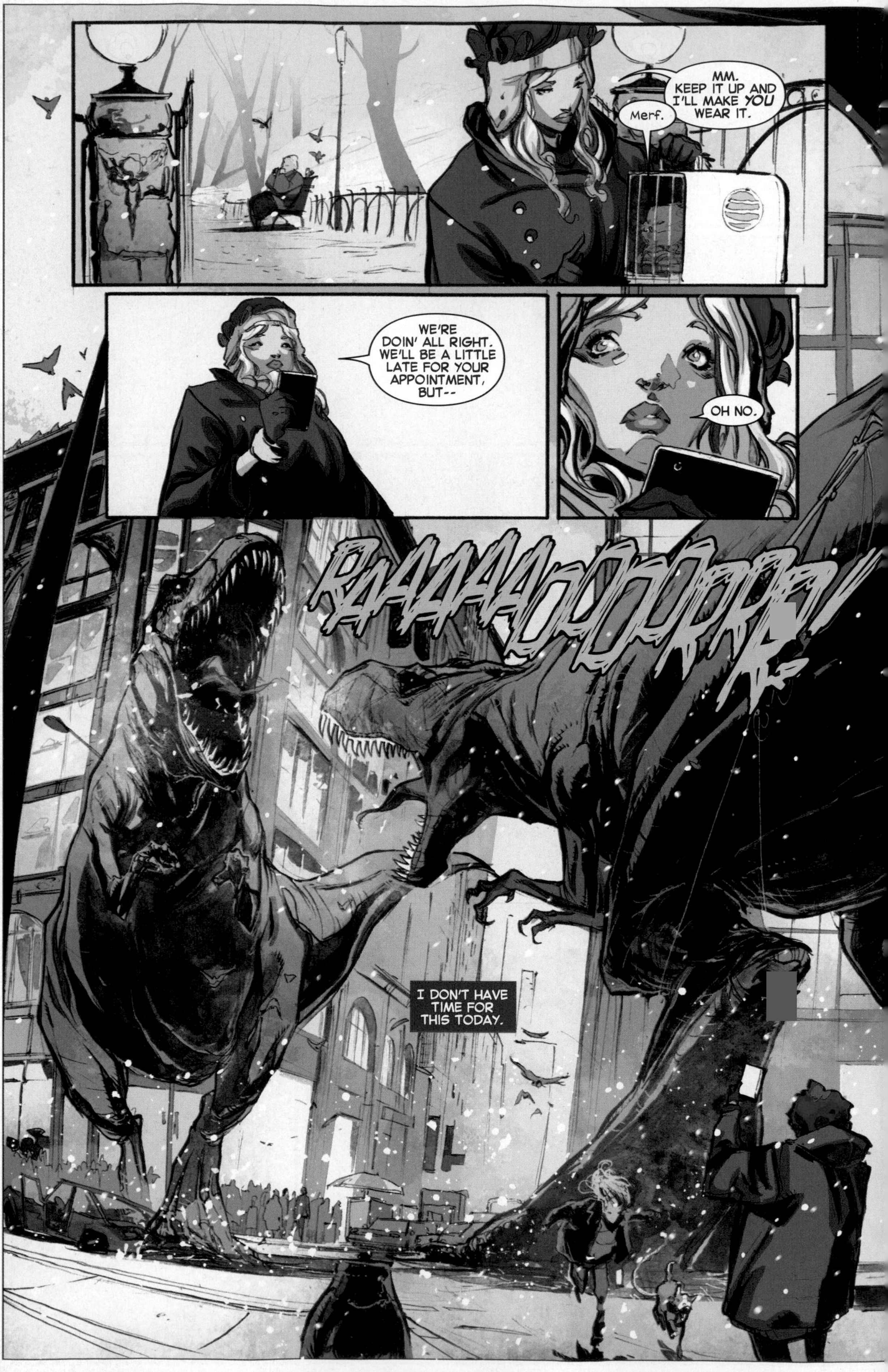
Merf.
MM. KEEP IT UP AND I'LL MAKE *YOU* WEAR IT.
WE'RE DOIN' ALL RIGHT. WE'LL BE A LITTLE LATE FOR YOUR APPOINTMENT, BUT--
OH NO.
I DON'T HAVE TIME FOR THIS TODAY.

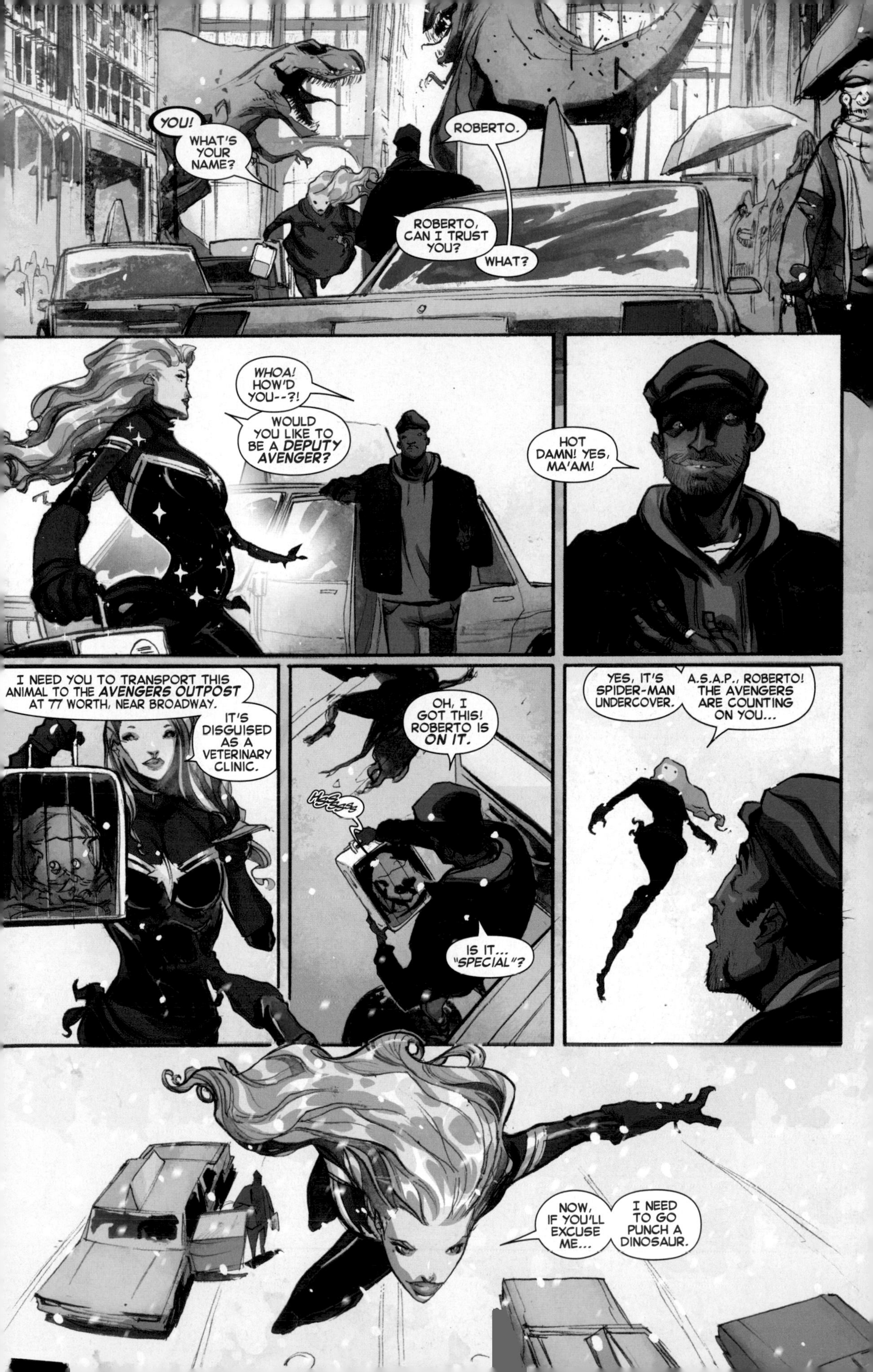
YOU! WHAT'S YOUR NAME?
ROBERTO.
ROBERTO, CAN I TRUST YOU?
WHAT?
WHOA! HOW'D YOU--?!
WOULD YOU LIKE TO BE A DEPUTY AVENGER?
HOT DAMN! YES, MA'AM!
I NEED YOU TO TRANSPORT THIS ANIMAL TO THE AVENGERS OUTPOST AT 77 WORTH, NEAR BROADWAY.
IT'S DISGUISED AS A VETERINARY CLINIC.
OH, I GOT THIS! ROBERTO IS ON IT.
IS IT... "SPECIAL"?
YES, IT'S SPIDER-MAN UNDERCOVER.
A.S.A.P., ROBERTO! THE AVENGERS ARE COUNTING ON YOU...
NOW, IF YOU'LL EXCUSE ME...
I NEED TO GO PUNCH A DINOSAUR.

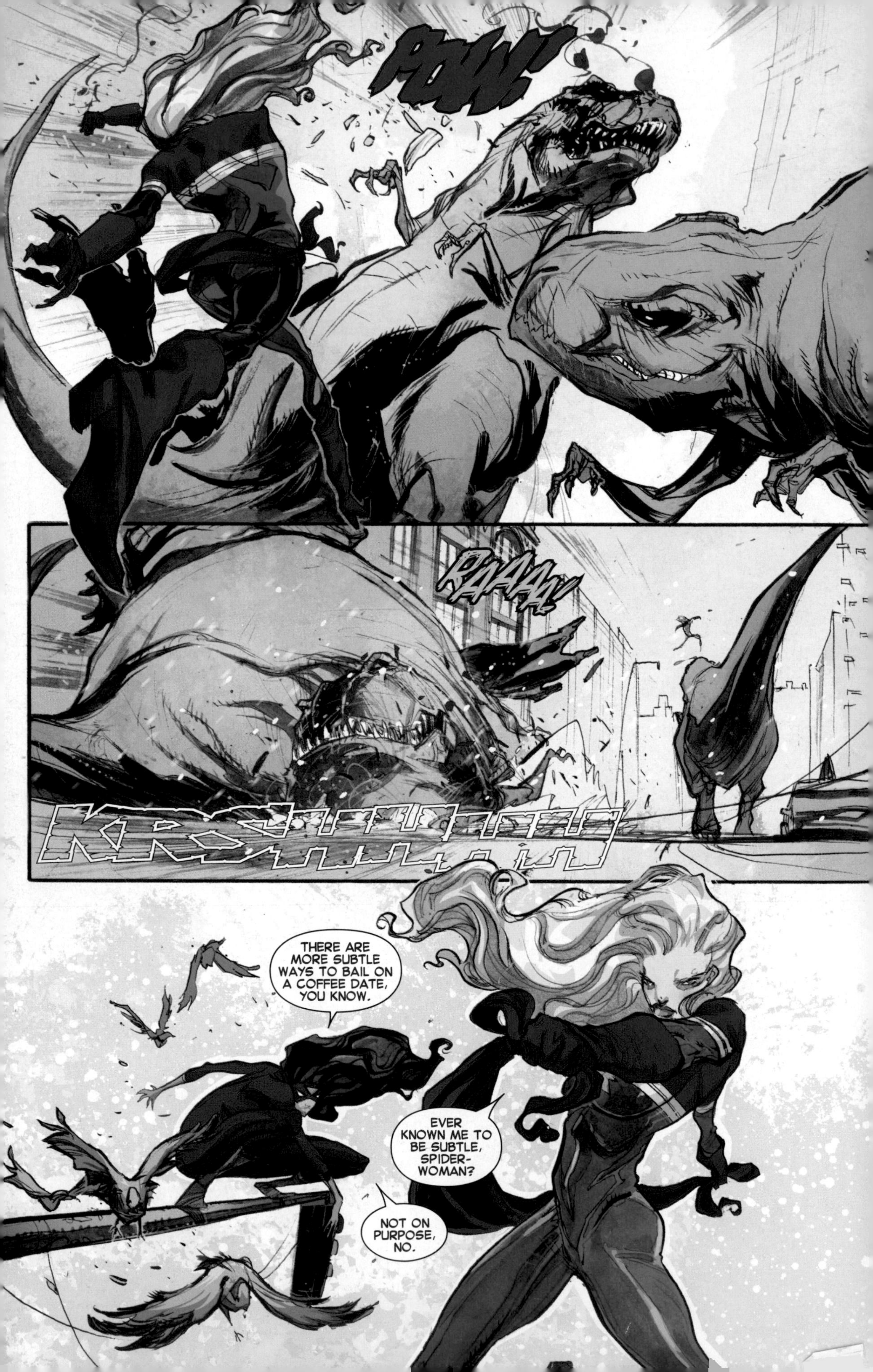
POW!!
RAAAA!
KRSHHHHHHHH
THERE ARE MORE SUBTLE WAYS TO BAIL ON A COFFEE DATE, YOU KNOW.
EVER KNOWN ME TO BE SUBTLE, SPIDER-WOMAN?
NOT ON PURPOSE, NO.

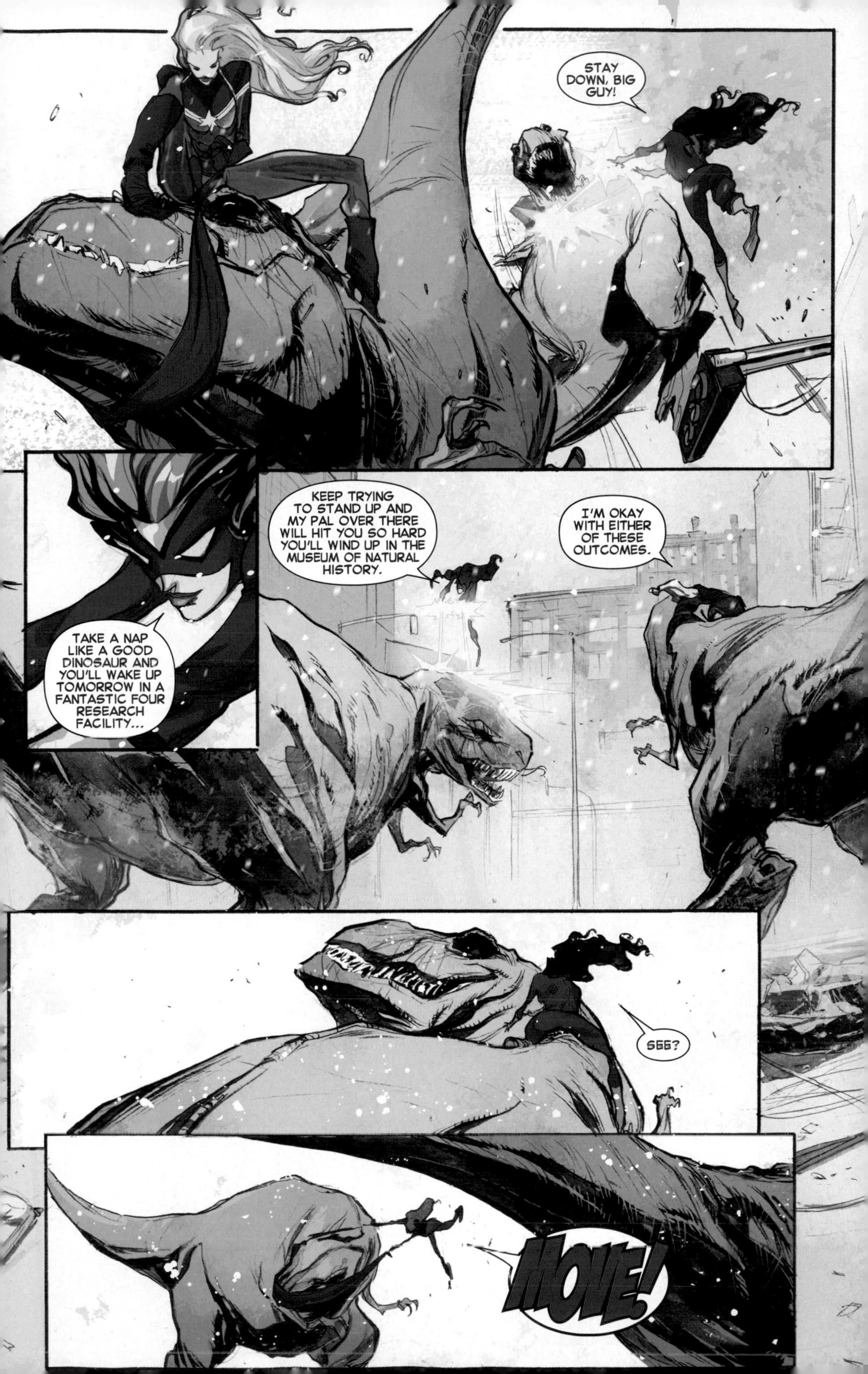
STAY DOWN, BIG GUY!
TAKE A NAP LIKE A GOOD DINOSAUR AND YOU'LL WAKE UP TOMORROW IN A FANTASTIC FOUR RESEARCH FACILITY...
KEEP TRYING TO STAND UP AND MY PAL OVER THERE WILL HIT YOU SO HARD YOU'LL WIND UP IN THE MUSEUM OF NATURAL HISTORY.
I'M OKAY WITH EITHER OF THESE OUTCOMES.
SEE?
MOVE!

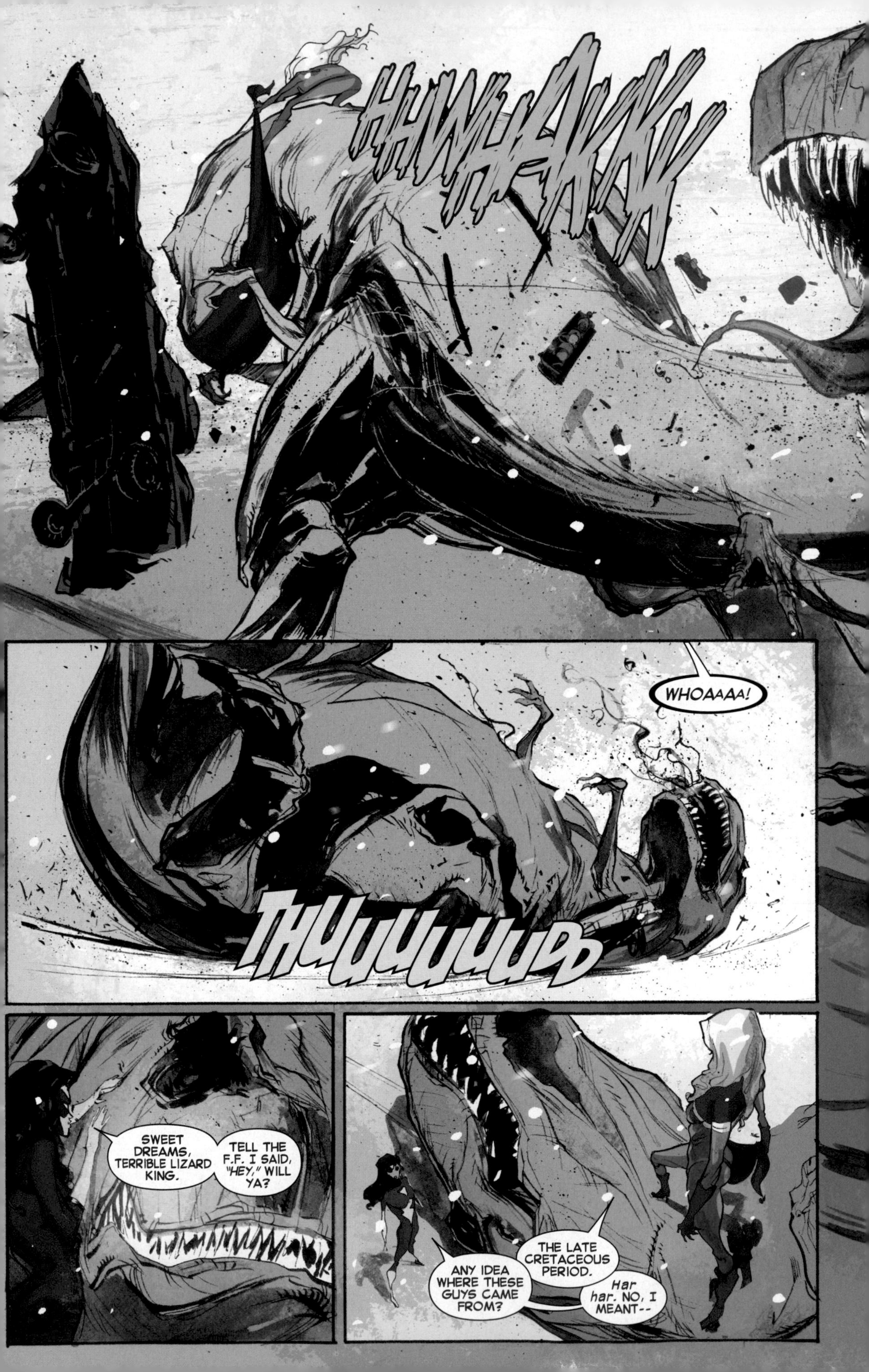

THWHAKK
WHOAAAA!
THUUUUUUD
SWEET DREAMS, TERRIBLE LIZARD KING.
TELL THE F.F. I SAID, "HEY," WILL YA?
ANY IDEA WHERE THESE GUYS CAME FROM?
THE LATE CRETACEOUS PERIOD.
Har har. NO, I MEANT--

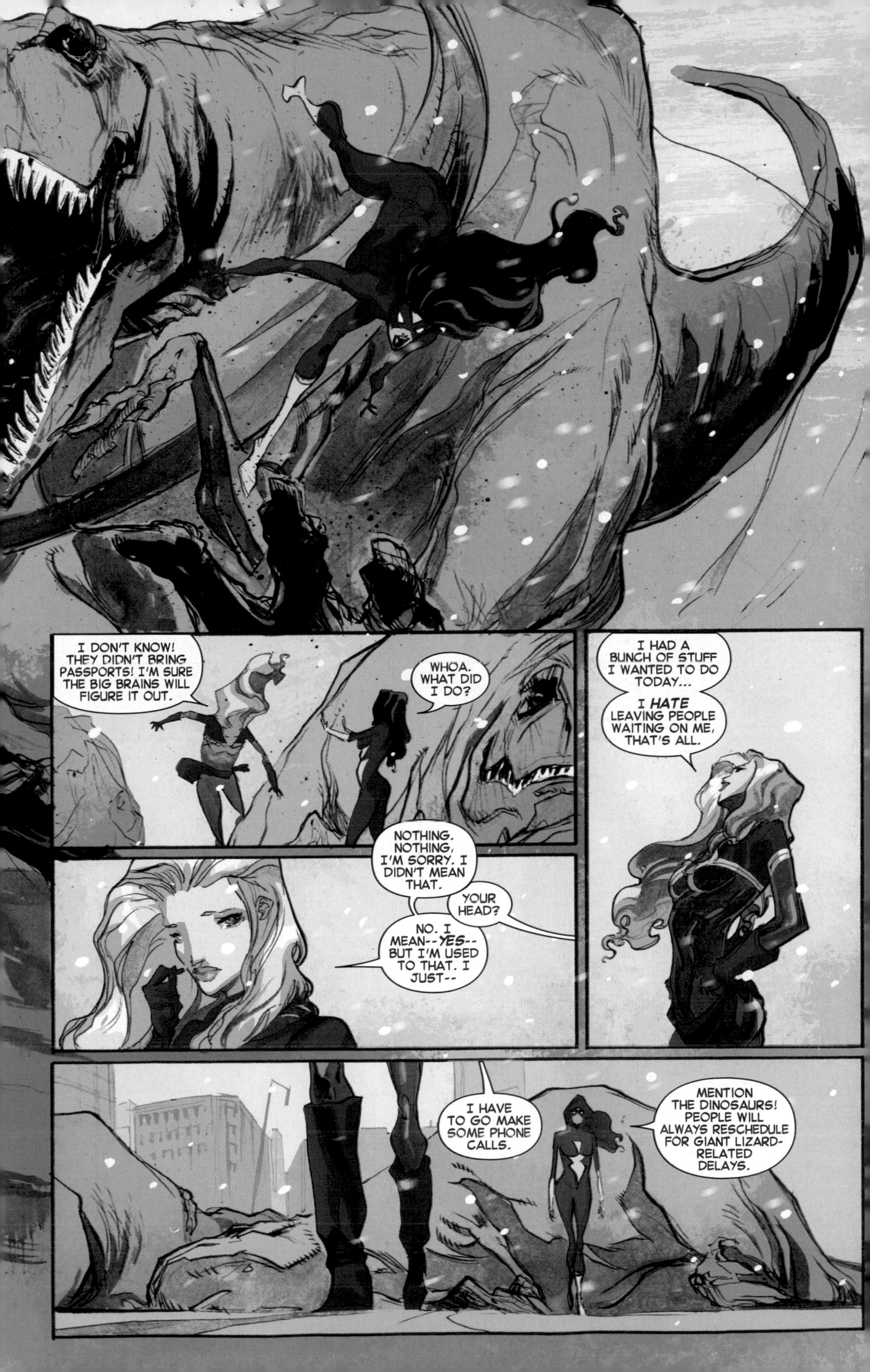
I DON'T KNOW! THEY DIDN'T BRING PASSPORTS! I'M SURE THE BIG BRAINS WILL FIGURE IT OUT.
WHOA. WHAT DID I DO?
I HAD A BUNCH OF STUFF I WANTED TO DO TODAY...
I HATE LEAVING PEOPLE WAITING ON ME, THAT'S ALL.
NOTHING. NOTHING, I'M SORRY. I DIDN'T MEAN THAT.
YOUR HEAD?
NO. I MEAN--YES--BUT I'M USED TO THAT. I JUST--
I HAVE TO GO MAKE SOME PHONE CALLS.
MENTION THE DINOSAURS! PEOPLE WILL ALWAYS RESCHEDULE FOR GIANT LIZARD-RELATED DELAYS.

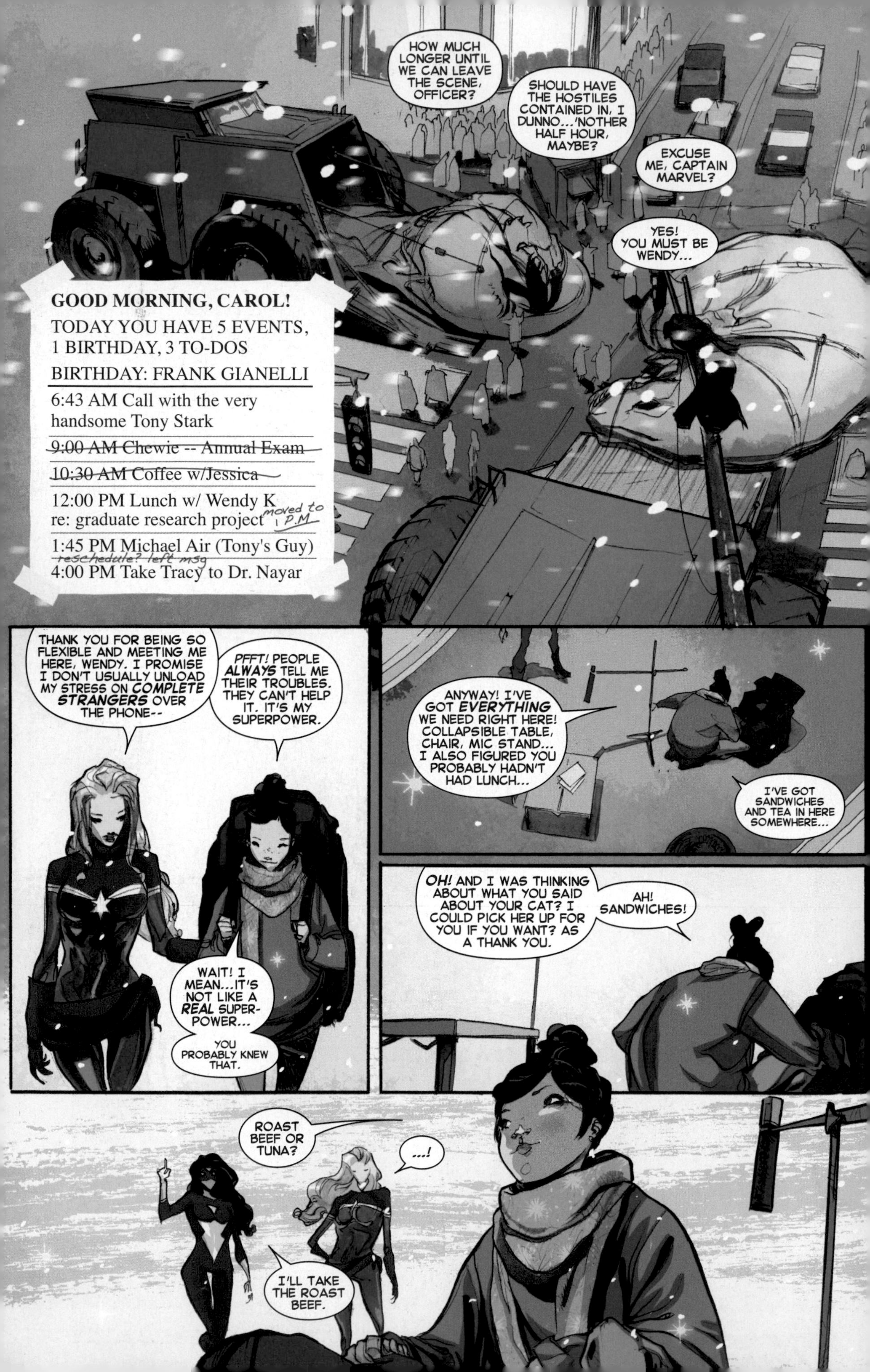
HOW MUCH LONGER UNTIL WE CAN LEAVE THE SCENE, OFFICER?
SHOULD HAVE THE HOSTILES CONTAINED IN, I DUNNO...'NOTHER HALF HOUR, MAYBE?
EXCUSE ME, CAPTAIN MARVEL?
YES! YOU MUST BE WENDY...
GOOD MORNING, CAROL!
TODAY YOU HAVE 5 EVENTS, 1 BIRTHDAY, 3 TO-DOS
BIRTHDAY: FRANK GIANELLI
6:43 AM Call with the very handsome Tony Stark
~~9:00 AM Chewie -- Annual Exam~~
~~10:30 AM Coffee w/Jessica~~
12:00 PM Lunch w/ Wendy K re: graduate research project
moved to 1 P.M
1:45 PM Michael Air (Tony's Guy)
reschedule? left msg
4:00 PM Take Tracy to Dr. Nayar
THANK YOU FOR BEING SO FLEXIBLE AND MEETING ME HERE, WENDY. I PROMISE I DON'T USUALLY UNLOAD MY STRESS ON COMPLETE STRANGERS OVER THE PHONE--
PFFT! PEOPLE ALWAYS TELL ME THEIR TROUBLES. THEY CAN'T HELP IT. IT'S MY SUPERPOWER.
WAIT! I MEAN...IT'S NOT LIKE A REAL SUPER-POWER...
YOU PROBABLY KNEW THAT.
ANYWAY! I'VE GOT EVERYTHING WE NEED RIGHT HERE! COLLAPSIBLE TABLE, CHAIR, MIC STAND... I ALSO FIGURED YOU PROBABLY HADN'T HAD LUNCH...
I'VE GOT SANDWICHES AND TEA IN HERE SOMEWHERE...
OH! AND I WAS THINKING ABOUT WHAT YOU SAID ABOUT YOUR CAT? I COULD PICK HER UP FOR YOU IF YOU WANT? AS A THANK YOU.
AH! SANDWICHES!
ROAST BEEF OR TUNA?
...!
I'LL TAKE THE ROAST BEEF.

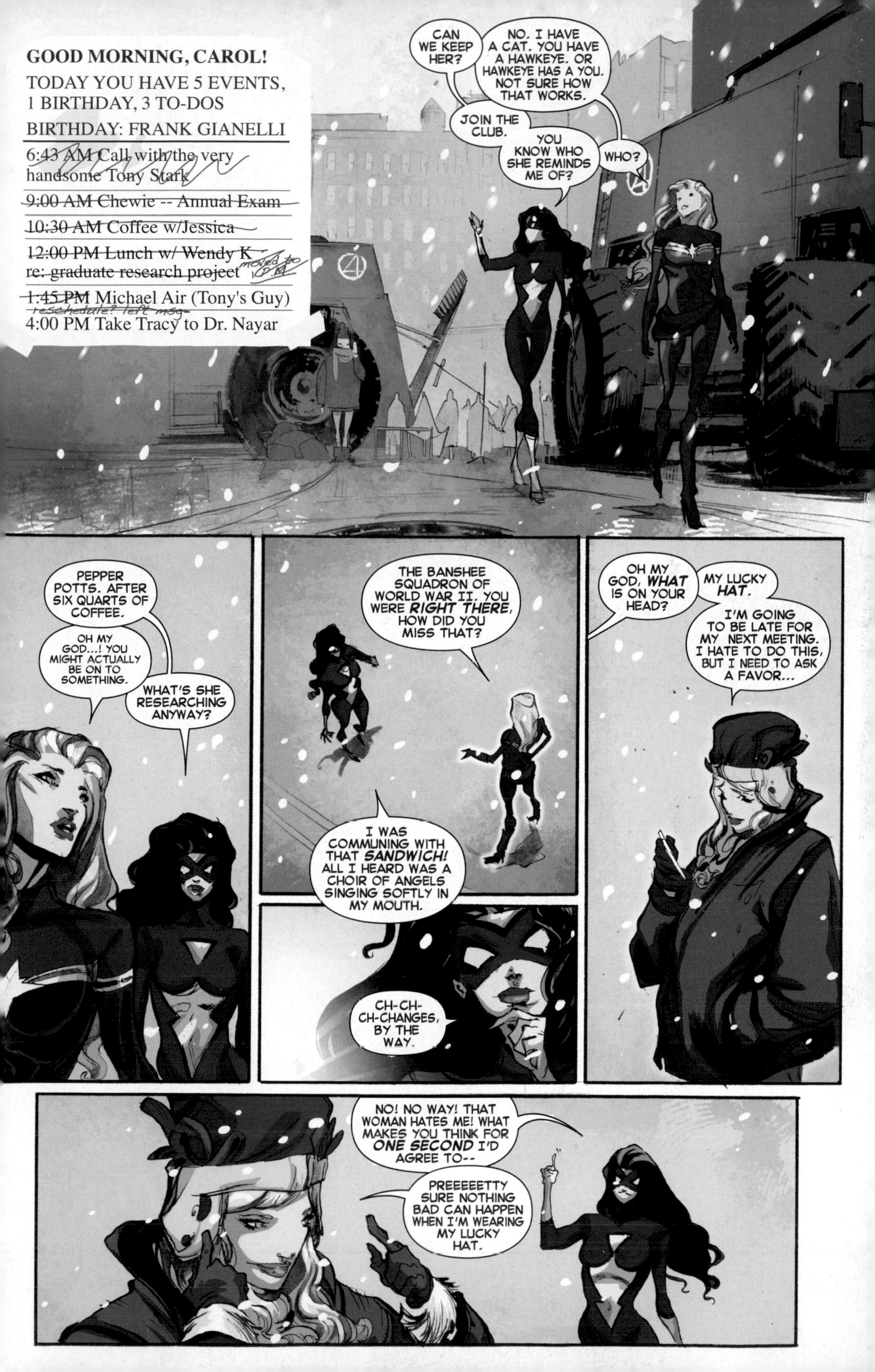
GOOD MORNING, CAROL!
TODAY YOU HAVE 5 EVENTS, 1 BIRTHDAY, 3 TO-DOS
BIRTHDAY: FRANK GIANELLI
6:43 AM Call with the very handsome Tony Stark
9:00 AM Chewie -- Annual Exam
10:30 AM Coffee w/Jessica
12:00 PM Lunch w/ Wendy K re: graduate research project
moved to 1 P.M.
1:45 PM Michael Air (Tony's Guy)
reschedule? left msg
4:00 PM Take Tracy to Dr. Nayar
CAN WE KEEP HER?
NO. I HAVE A CAT. YOU HAVE A HAWKEYE. OR HAWKEYE HAS A YOU. NOT SURE HOW THAT WORKS.
JOIN THE CLUB.
YOU KNOW WHO SHE REMINDS ME OF?
WHO?
PEPPER POTTS. AFTER SIX QUARTS OF COFFEE.
OH MY GOD...! YOU MIGHT ACTUALLY BE ON TO SOMETHING.
WHAT'S SHE RESEARCHING ANYWAY?
THE BANSHEE SQUADRON OF WORLD WAR II. YOU WERE RIGHT THERE, HOW DID YOU MISS THAT?
I WAS COMMUNING WITH THAT SANDWICH! ALL I HEARD WAS A CHOIR OF ANGELS SINGING SOFTLY IN MY MOUTH.
CH-CH-CH-CHANGES, BY THE WAY.
OH MY GOD, WHAT IS ON YOUR HEAD?
MY LUCKY HAT.
I'M GOING TO BE LATE FOR MY NEXT MEETING. I HATE TO DO THIS, BUT I NEED TO ASK A FAVOR...
NO! NO WAY! THAT WOMAN HATES ME! WHAT MAKES YOU THINK FOR ONE SECOND I'D AGREE TO--
PREEEEETTY SURE NOTHING BAD CAN HAPPEN WHEN I'M WEARING MY LUCKY HAT.

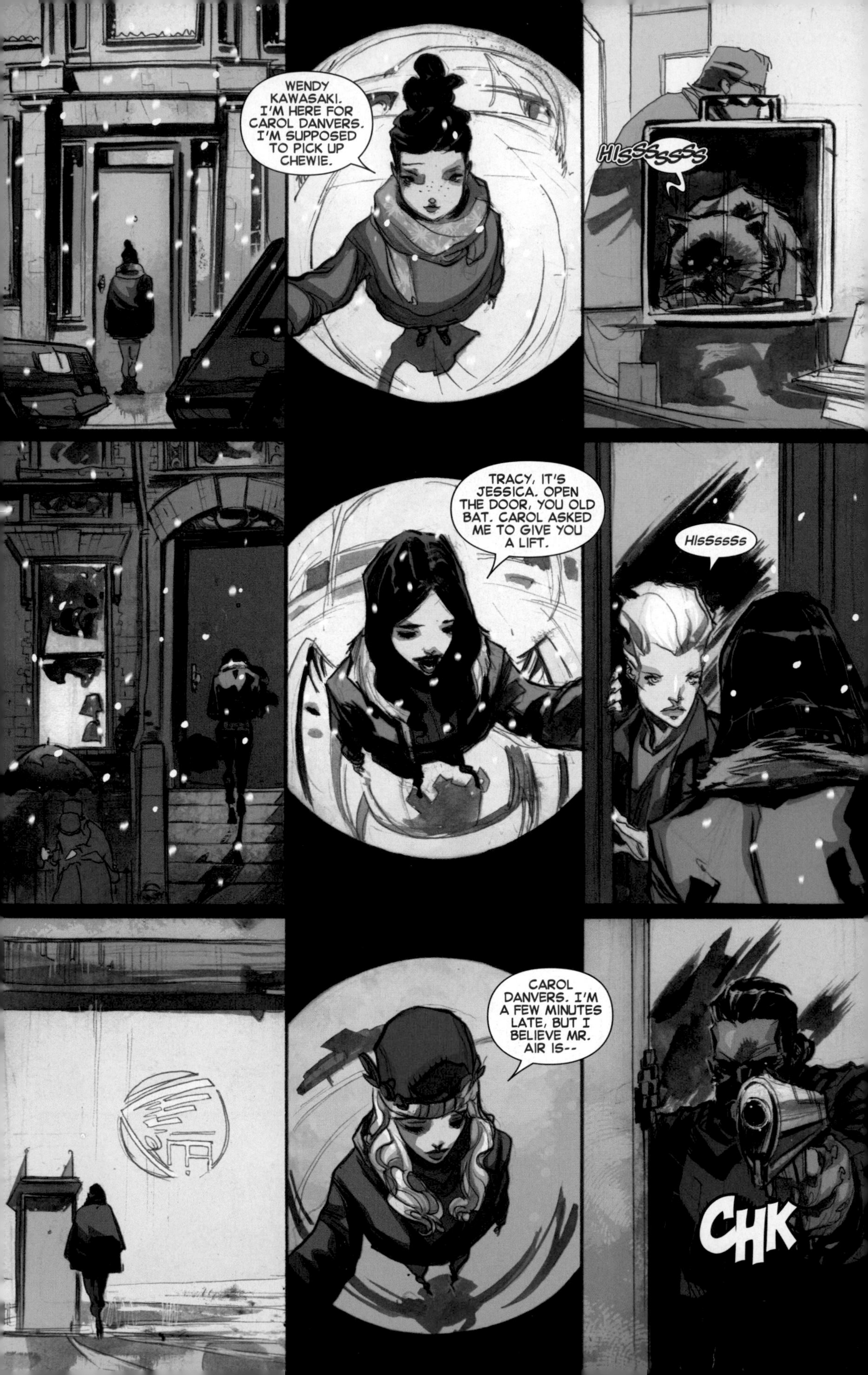
WENDY KAWASAKI. I'M HERE FOR CAROL DANVERS. I'M SUPPOSED TO PICK UP CHEWIE.
HISSSSSSS
TRACY, IT'S JESSICA. OPEN THE DOOR, YOU OLD BAT. CAROL ASKED ME TO GIVE YOU A LIFT.
HISSSSSS
CAROL DANVERS. I'M A FEW MINUTES LATE, BUT I BELIEVE MR. AIR IS--
CHK

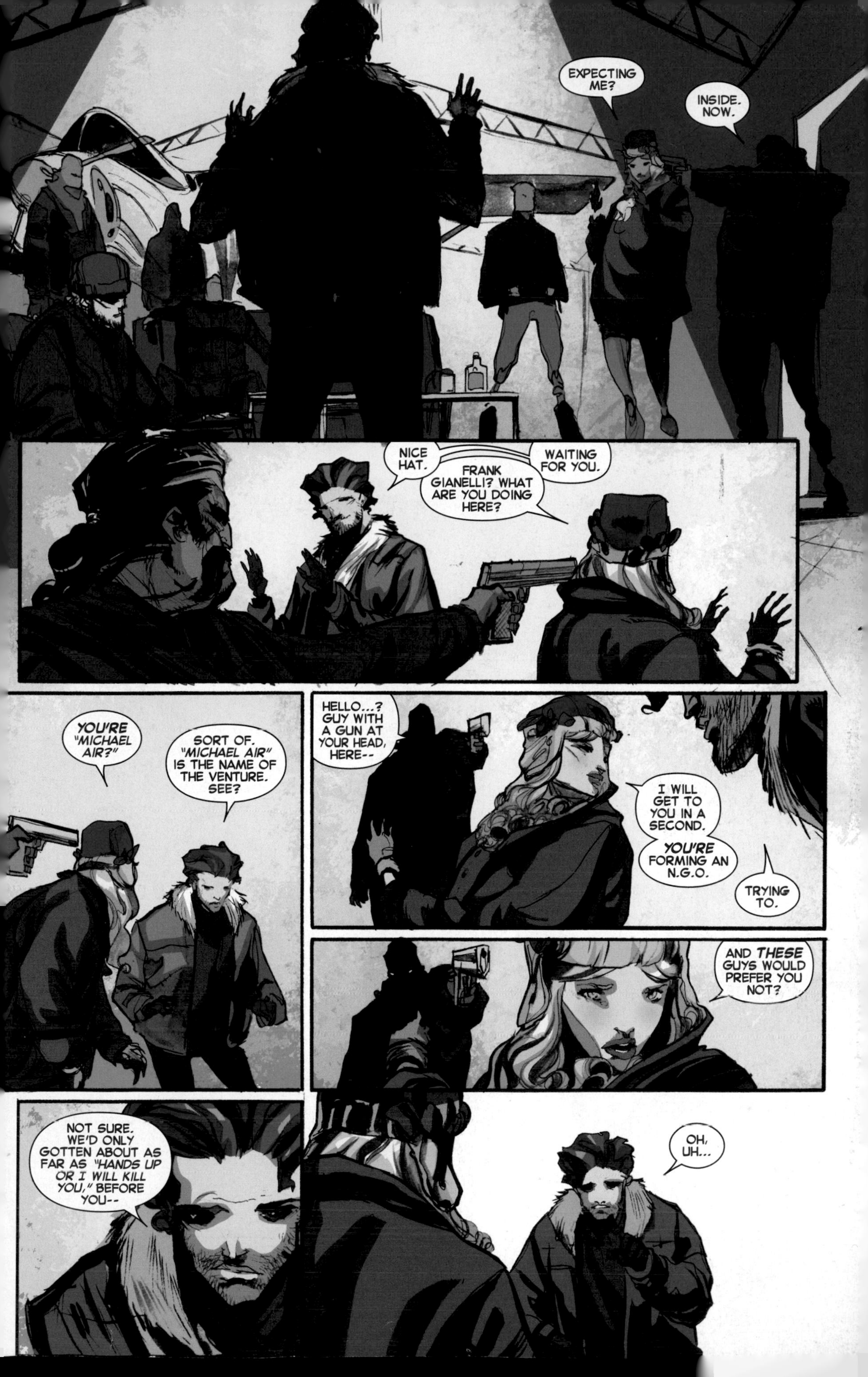
EXPECTING ME?
INSIDE. NOW.
NICE HAT.
WAITING FOR YOU.
FRANK GIANELLI? WHAT ARE YOU DOING HERE?
YOU'RE "MICHAEL AIR?"
SORT OF. "MICHAEL AIR" IS THE NAME OF THE VENTURE. SEE?
HELLO...? GUY WITH A GUN AT YOUR HEAD, HERE--
I WILL GET TO YOU IN A SECOND.
YOU'RE FORMING AN N.G.O.
TRYING TO.
AND THESE GUYS WOULD PREFER YOU NOT?
NOT SURE. WE'D ONLY GOTTEN ABOUT AS FAR AS "HANDS UP OR I WILL KILL YOU," BEFORE YOU--
OH, UH...

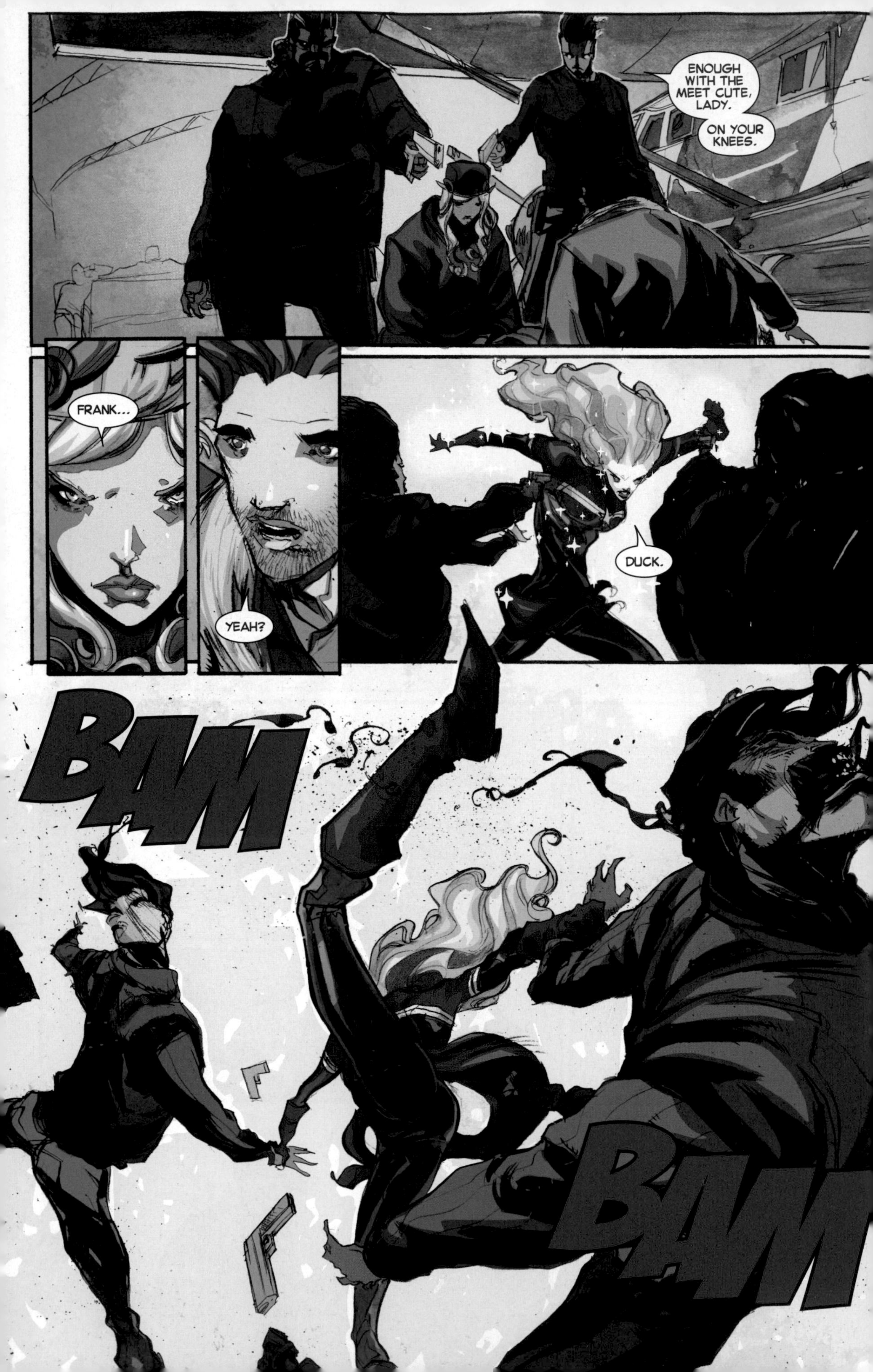
ENOUGH WITH THE MEET CUTE, LADY.
ON YOUR KNEES.
FRANK...
YEAH?
DUCK.
BAM
BAM

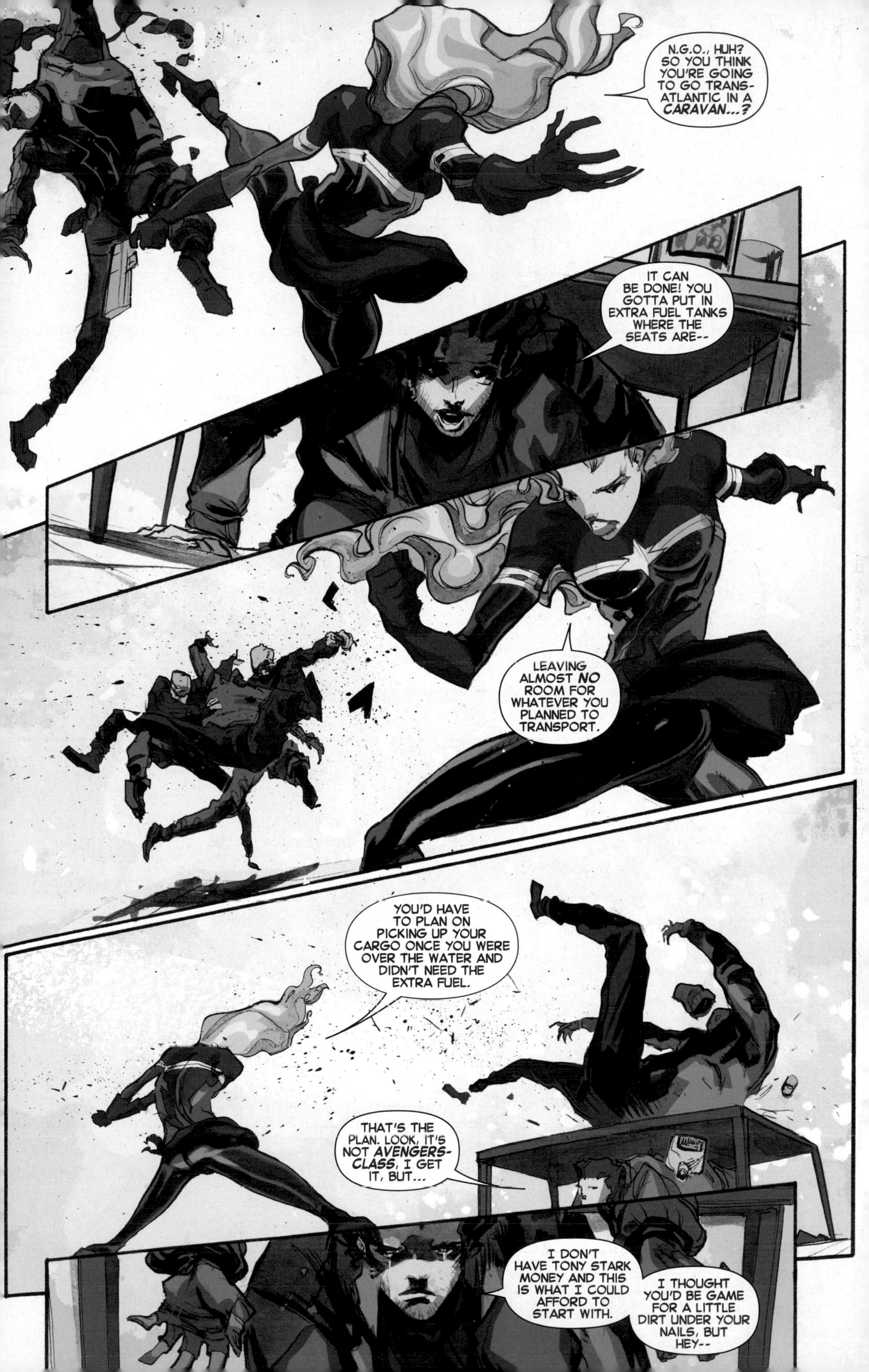
N.G.O., HUH? SO YOU THINK YOU'RE GOING TO GO TRANS-ATLANTIC IN A CARAVAN...?
IT CAN BE DONE! YOU GOTTA PUT IN EXTRA FUEL TANKS WHERE THE SEATS ARE--
LEAVING ALMOST NO ROOM FOR WHATEVER YOU PLANNED TO TRANSPORT.
YOU'D HAVE TO PLAN ON PICKING UP YOUR CARGO ONCE YOU WERE OVER THE WATER AND DIDN'T NEED THE EXTRA FUEL.
THAT'S THE PLAN. LOOK, IT'S NOT AVENGERS-CLASS, I GET IT, BUT...
I DON'T HAVE TONY STARK MONEY AND THIS IS WHAT I COULD AFFORD TO START WITH.
I THOUGHT YOU'D BE GAME FOR A LITTLE DIRT UNDER YOUR NAILS, BUT HEY--

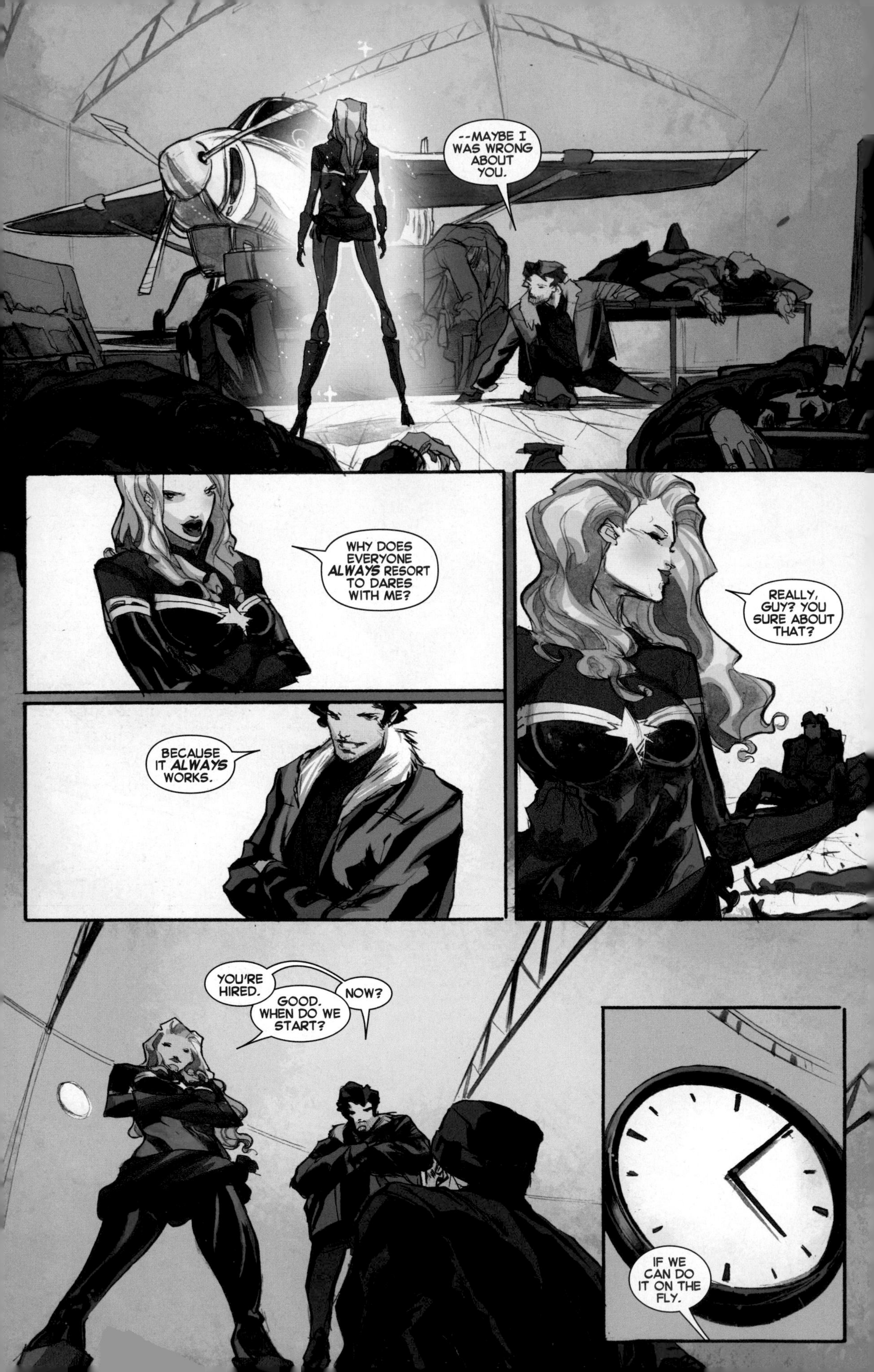
--MAYBE I WAS WRONG ABOUT YOU.
WHY DOES EVERYONE *ALWAYS* RESORT TO DARES WITH ME?
REALLY, GUY? YOU SURE ABOUT THAT?
BECAUSE IT *ALWAYS* WORKS.
YOU'RE HIRED.
GOOD. WHEN DO WE START?
NOW?
IF WE CAN DO IT ON THE FLY.

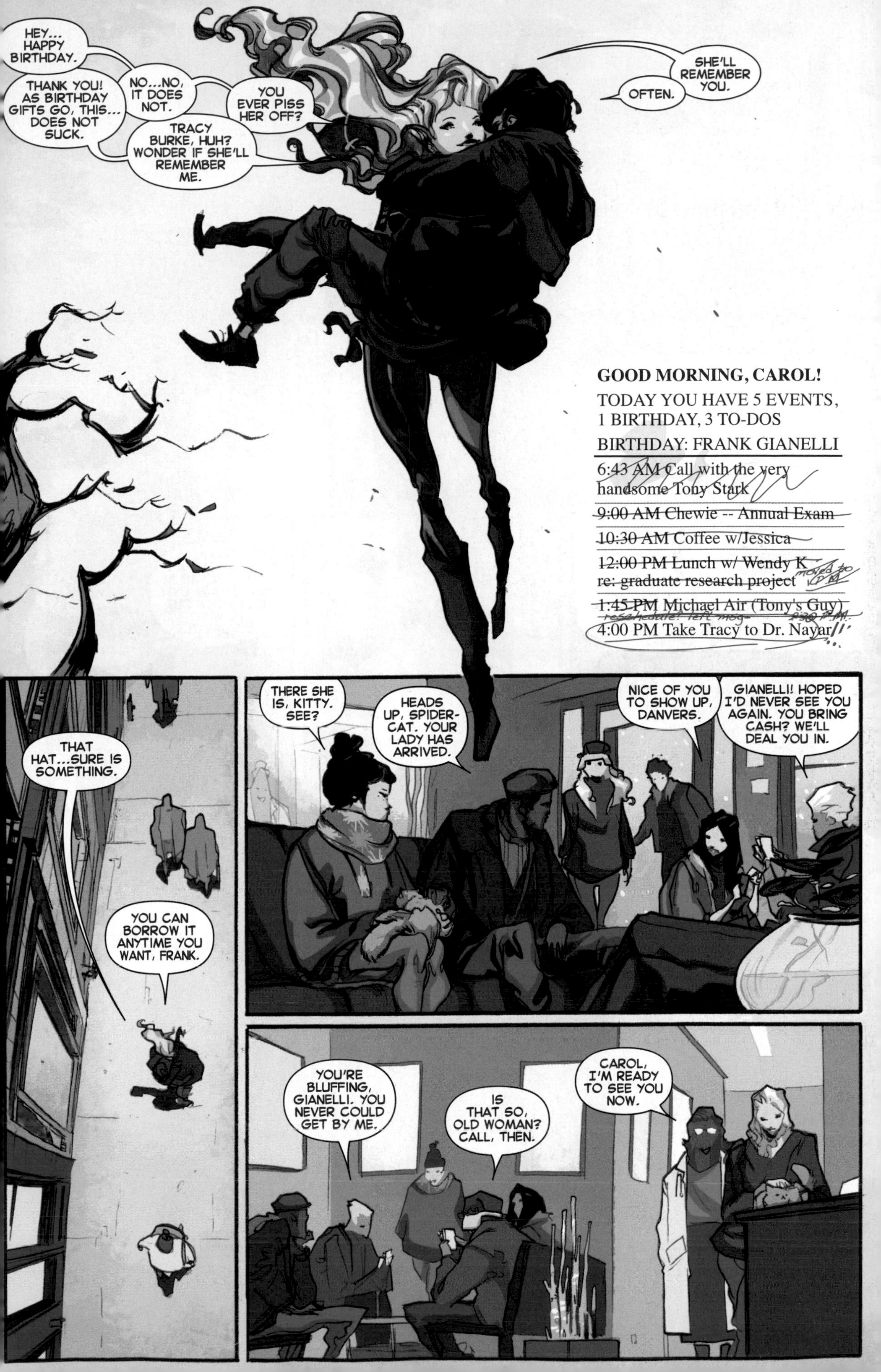
HEY... HAPPY BIRTHDAY.
THANK YOU! AS BIRTHDAY GIFTS GO, THIS... DOES NOT SUCK.
NO...NO, IT DOES NOT.
YOU EVER PISS HER OFF?
TRACY BURKE, HUH? WONDER IF SHE'LL REMEMBER ME.
OFTEN.
SHE'LL REMEMBER YOU.
GOOD MORNING, CAROL!
TODAY YOU HAVE 5 EVENTS, 1 BIRTHDAY, 3 TO-DOS
BIRTHDAY: FRANK GIANELLI
6:43 AM Call with the very handsome Tony Stark
9:00 AM Chewie -- Annual Exam
10:30 AM Coffee w/Jessica
12:00 PM Lunch w/ Wendy K re: graduate research project
1:45 PM Michael Air (Tony's Guy)
4:00 PM Take Tracy to Dr. Nayar!!
THAT HAT...SURE IS SOMETHING.
YOU CAN BORROW IT ANYTIME YOU WANT, FRANK.
THERE SHE IS, KITTY. SEE?
HEADS UP, SPIDER-CAT. YOUR LADY HAS ARRIVED.
NICE OF YOU TO SHOW UP, DANVERS.
GIANELLI! HOPED I'D NEVER SEE YOU AGAIN. YOU BRING CASH? WE'LL DEAL YOU IN.
YOU'RE BLUFFING, GIANELLI. YOU NEVER COULD GET BY ME.
IS THAT SO, OLD WOMAN? CALL, THEN.
CAROL, I'M READY TO SEE YOU NOW.

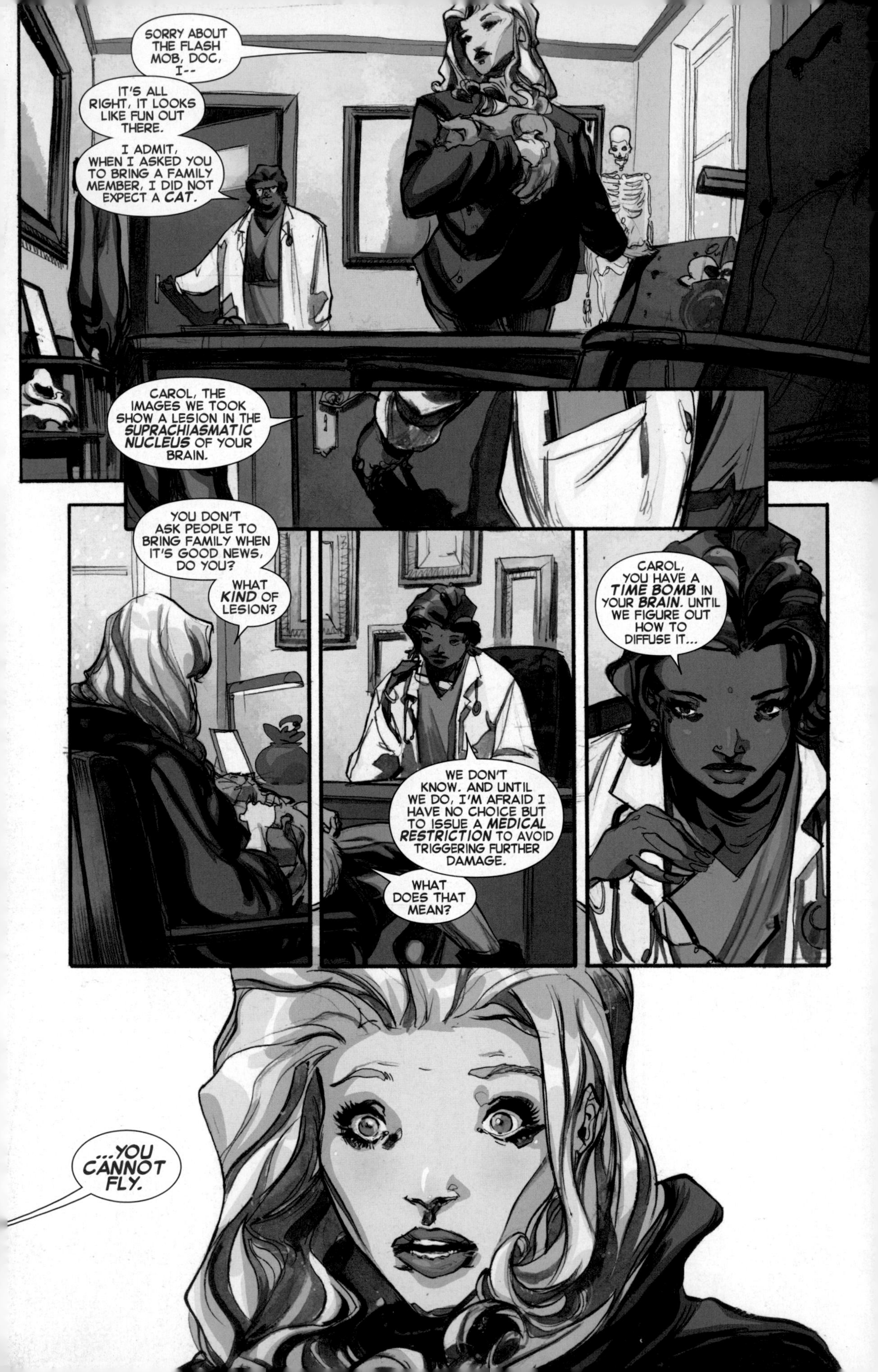
SORRY ABOUT THE FLASH MOB, DOC, I--
IT'S ALL RIGHT, IT LOOKS LIKE FUN OUT THERE.
I ADMIT, WHEN I ASKED YOU TO BRING A FAMILY MEMBER, I DID NOT EXPECT A CAT.
CAROL, THE IMAGES WE TOOK SHOW A LESION IN THE SUPRACHIASMATIC NUCLEUS OF YOUR BRAIN.
YOU DON'T ASK PEOPLE TO BRING FAMILY WHEN IT'S GOOD NEWS, DO YOU?
WHAT KIND OF LESION?
WE DON'T KNOW. AND UNTIL WE DO, I'M AFRAID I HAVE NO CHOICE BUT TO ISSUE A MEDICAL RESTRICTION TO AVOID TRIGGERING FURTHER DAMAGE.
WHAT DOES THAT MEAN?
CAROL, YOU HAVE A TIME BOMB IN YOUR BRAIN. UNTIL WE FIGURE OUT HOW TO DIFFUSE IT...
...YOU CANNOT FLY.

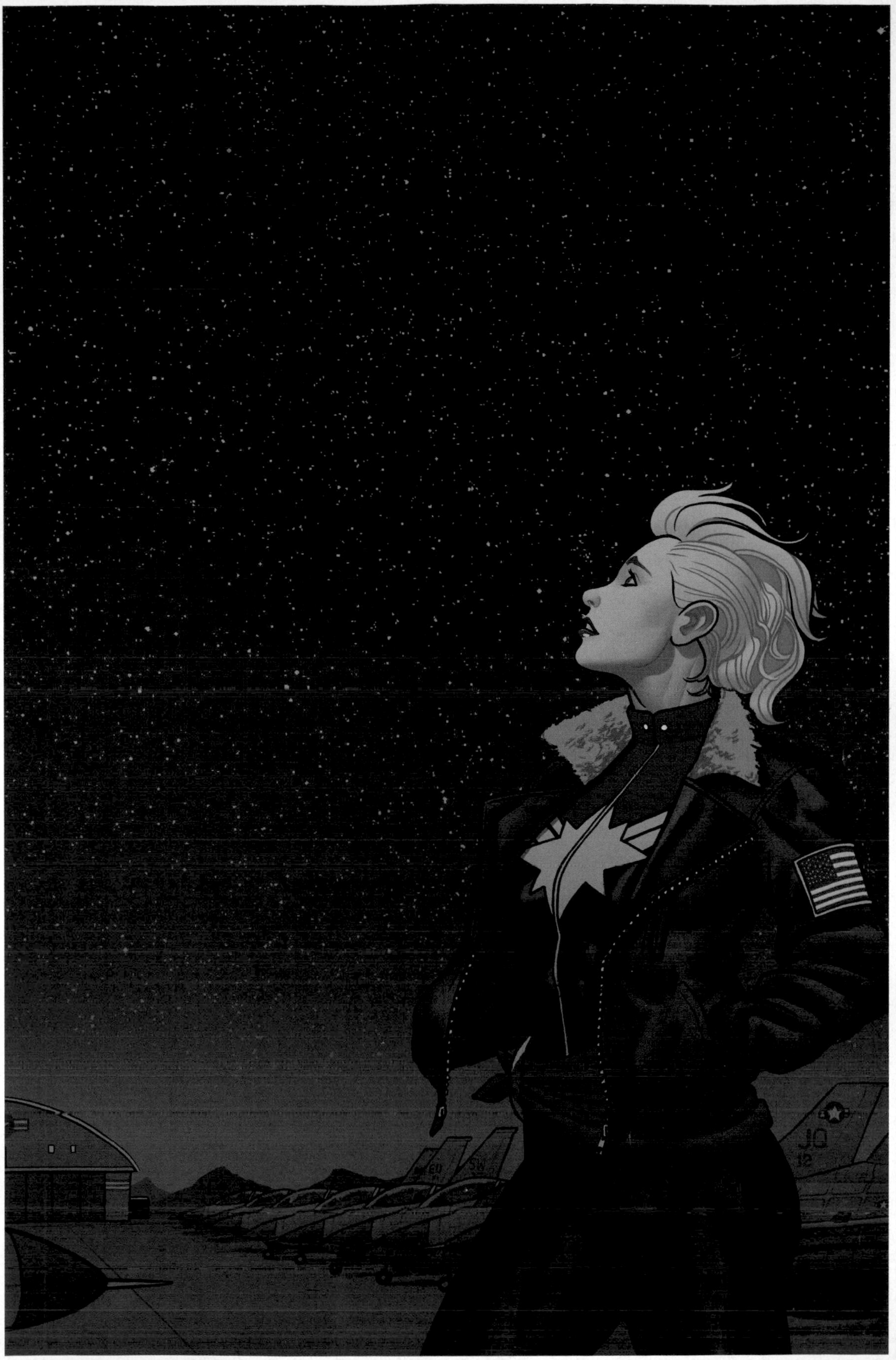
JQ
12

TEN

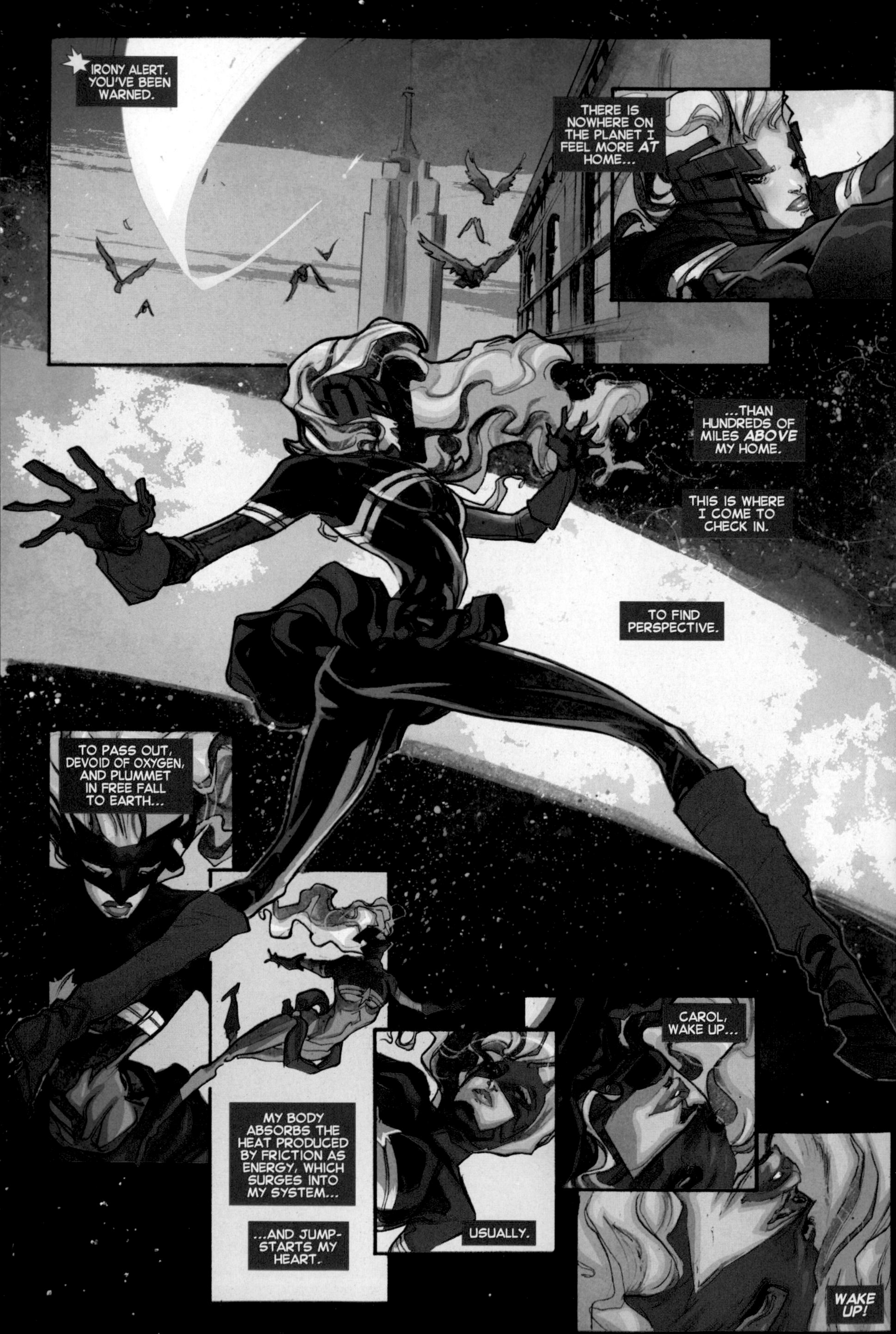
IRONY ALERT. YOU'VE BEEN WARNED.
THERE IS NOWHERE ON THE PLANET I FEEL MORE AT HOME...
...THAN HUNDREDS OF MILES ABOVE MY HOME.
THIS IS WHERE I COME TO CHECK IN.
TO FIND PERSPECTIVE.
TO PASS OUT, DEVOID OF OXYGEN, AND PLUMMET IN FREE FALL TO EARTH...
MY BODY ABSORBS THE HEAT PRODUCED BY FRICTION AS ENERGY, WHICH SURGES INTO MY SYSTEM...
...AND JUMP-STARTS MY HEART.
USUALLY.
CAROL, WAKE UP...
WAKE UP!

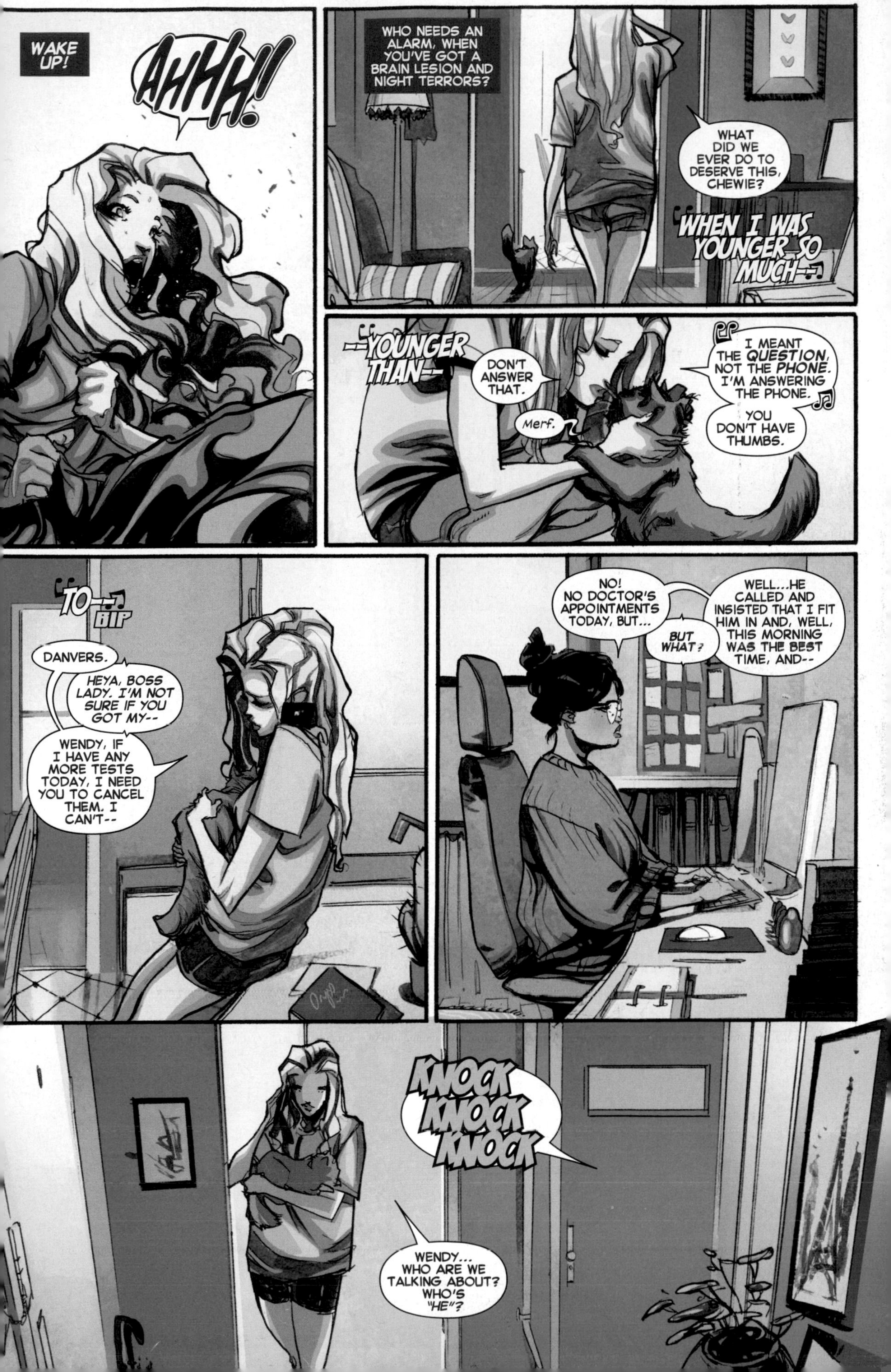
WAKE UP!
AHHH!
WHO NEEDS AN ALARM, WHEN YOU'VE GOT A BRAIN LESION AND NIGHT TERRORS?
WHAT DID WE EVER DO TO DESERVE THIS, CHEWIE?
WHEN I WAS YOUNGER SO MUCH--
--YOUNGER THAN--
DON'T ANSWER THAT.
Merf.
I MEANT THE QUESTION, NOT THE PHONE. I'M ANSWERING THE PHONE.
YOU DON'T HAVE THUMBS.
TO--
BIP
DANVERS.
HEYA, BOSS LADY. I'M NOT SURE IF YOU GOT MY--
WENDY, IF I HAVE ANY MORE TESTS TODAY, I NEED YOU TO CANCEL THEM. I CAN'T--
NO! NO DOCTOR'S APPOINTMENTS TODAY, BUT...
BUT WHAT?
WELL...HE CALLED AND INSISTED THAT I FIT HIM IN AND, WELL, THIS MORNING WAS THE BEST TIME, AND--
KNOCK KNOCK KNOCK
WENDY... WHO ARE WE TALKING ABOUT? WHO'S "HE"?

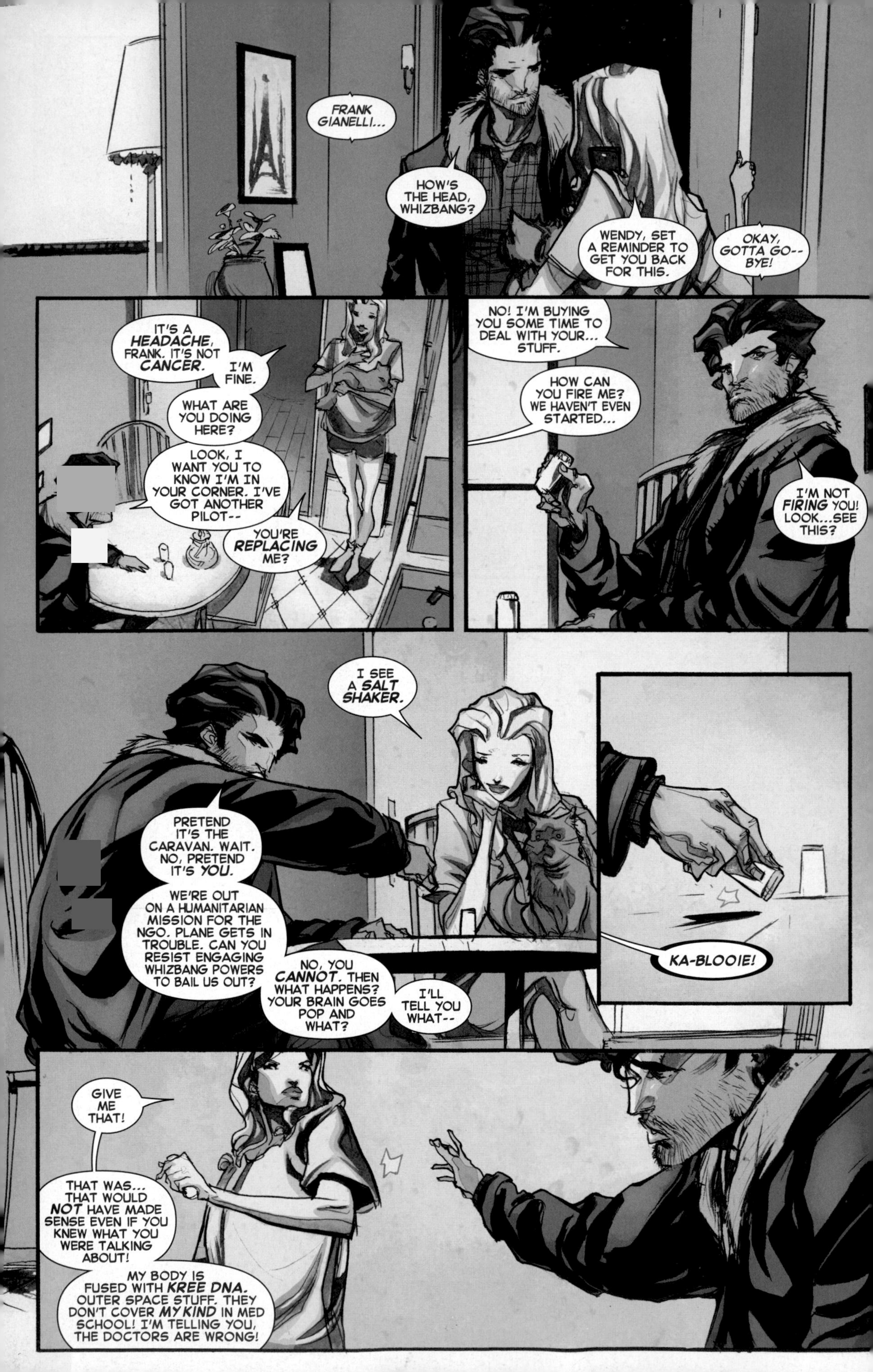

FRANK GIANELLI...
HOW'S THE HEAD, WHIZBANG?
WENDY, SET A REMINDER TO GET YOU BACK FOR THIS.
OKAY, GOTTA GO-- BYE!
IT'S A HEADACHE, FRANK. IT'S NOT CANCER.
I'M FINE.
WHAT ARE YOU DOING HERE?
LOOK, I WANT YOU TO KNOW I'M IN YOUR CORNER. I'VE GOT ANOTHER PILOT--
YOU'RE REPLACING ME?
NO! I'M BUYING YOU SOME TIME TO DEAL WITH YOUR... STUFF.
HOW CAN YOU FIRE ME? WE HAVEN'T EVEN STARTED...
I'M NOT FIRING YOU! LOOK...SEE THIS?
I SEE A SALT SHAKER.
PRETEND IT'S THE CARAVAN. WAIT. NO, PRETEND IT'S YOU.
WE'RE OUT ON A HUMANITARIAN MISSION FOR THE NGO. PLANE GETS IN TROUBLE. CAN YOU RESIST ENGAGING WHIZBANG POWERS TO BAIL US OUT?
NO, YOU CANNOT. THEN WHAT HAPPENS? YOUR BRAIN GOES POP AND WHAT?
I'LL TELL YOU WHAT--
KA-BLOOIE!
GIVE ME THAT!
THAT WAS... THAT WOULD NOT HAVE MADE SENSE EVEN IF YOU KNEW WHAT YOU WERE TALKING ABOUT!
MY BODY IS FUSED WITH KREE DNA. OUTER SPACE STUFF. THEY DON'T COVER MY KIND IN MED SCHOOL! I'M TELLING YOU, THE DOCTORS ARE WRONG!

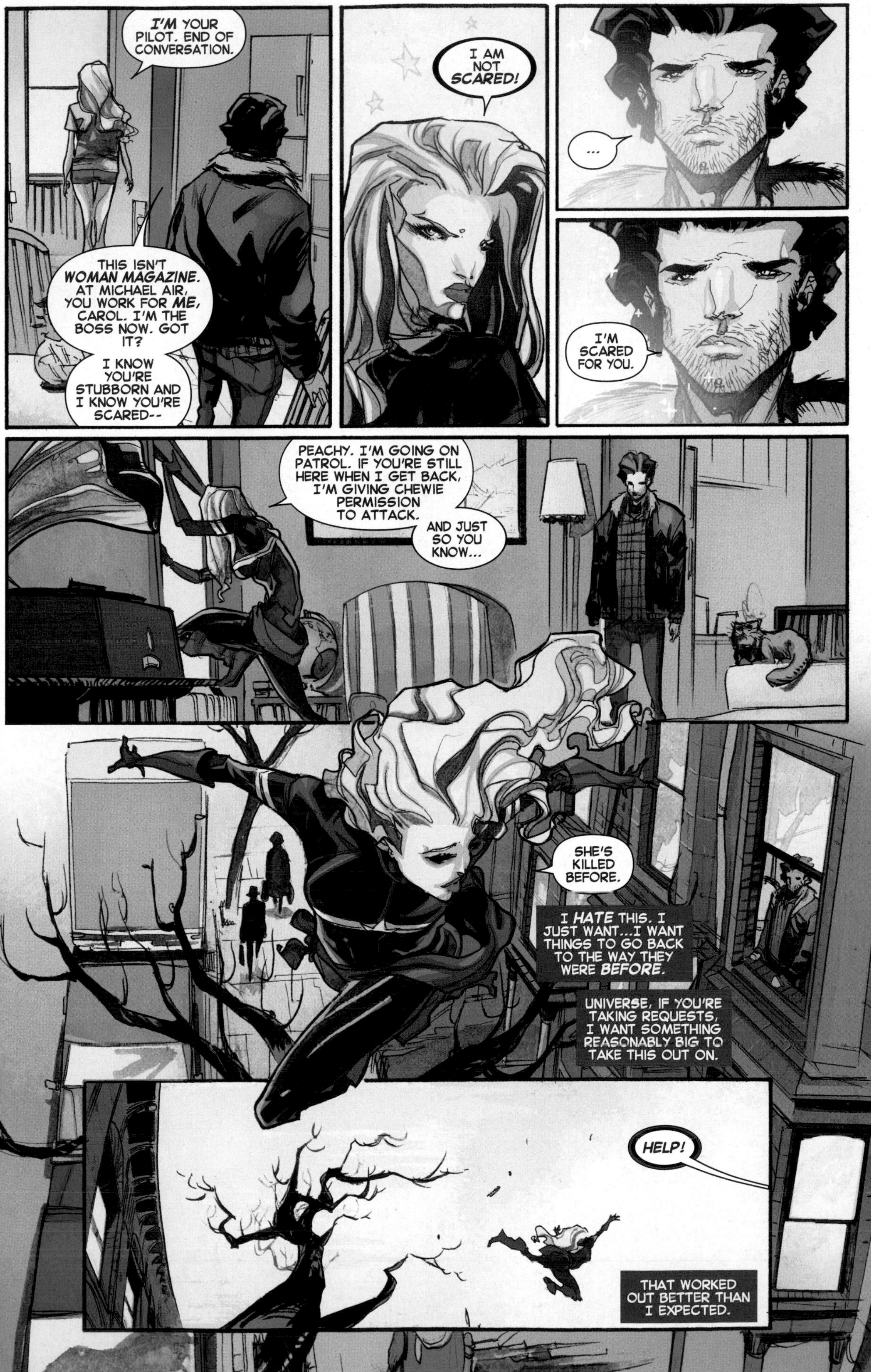
I'M YOUR PILOT. END OF CONVERSATION.
THIS ISN'T WOMAN MAGAZINE. AT MICHAEL AIR, YOU WORK FOR ME, CAROL. I'M THE BOSS NOW. GOT IT?
I KNOW YOU'RE STUBBORN AND I KNOW YOU'RE SCARED--
I AM NOT SCARED!
...
I'M SCARED FOR YOU.
PEACHY. I'M GOING ON PATROL. IF YOU'RE STILL HERE WHEN I GET BACK, I'M GIVING CHEWIE PERMISSION TO ATTACK.
AND JUST SO YOU KNOW...
SHE'S KILLED BEFORE.
I HATE THIS. I JUST WANT...I WANT THINGS TO GO BACK TO THE WAY THEY WERE BEFORE.
UNIVERSE, IF YOU'RE TAKING REQUESTS, I WANT SOMETHING REASONABLY BIG TO TAKE THIS OUT ON.
HELP!
THAT WORKED OUT BETTER THAN I EXPECTED.

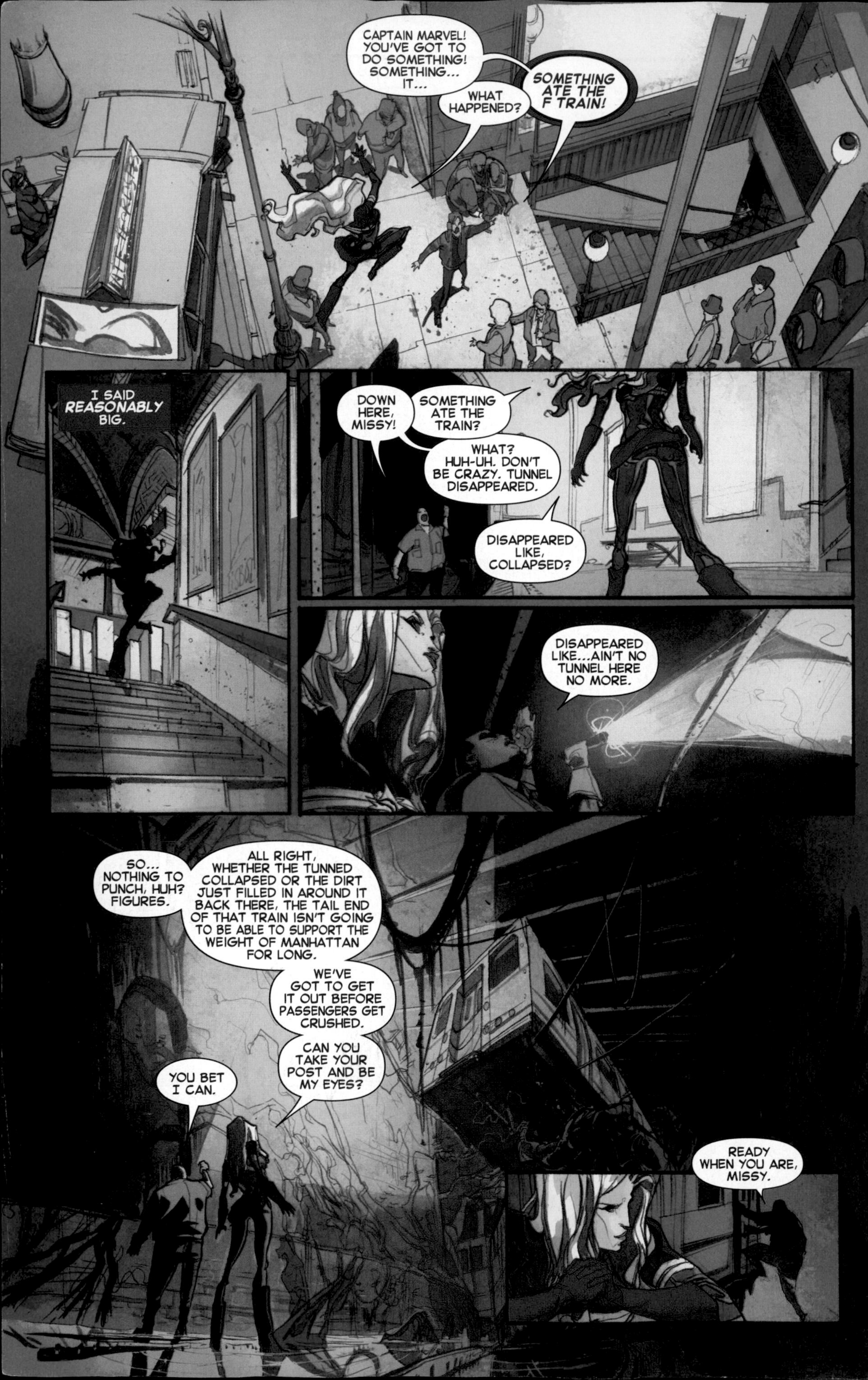

CAPTAIN MARVEL! YOU'VE GOT TO DO SOMETHING! SOMETHING... IT...
WHAT HAPPENED?
SOMETHING ATE THE F TRAIN!
I SAID REASONABLY BIG.
DOWN HERE, MISSY!
SOMETHING ATE THE TRAIN?
WHAT? HUH-UH. DON'T BE CRAZY. TUNNEL DISAPPEARED.
DISAPPEARED LIKE, COLLAPSED?
DISAPPEARED LIKE...AIN'T NO TUNNEL HERE NO MORE.
SO... NOTHING TO PUNCH, HUH? FIGURES.
ALL RIGHT, WHETHER THE TUNNED COLLAPSED OR THE DIRT JUST FILLED IN AROUND IT BACK THERE, THE TAIL END OF THAT TRAIN ISN'T GOING TO BE ABLE TO SUPPORT THE WEIGHT OF MANHATTAN FOR LONG.
WE'VE GOT TO GET IT OUT BEFORE PASSENGERS GET CRUSHED.
CAN YOU TAKE YOUR POST AND BE MY EYES?
YOU BET I CAN.
READY WHEN YOU ARE, MISSY.

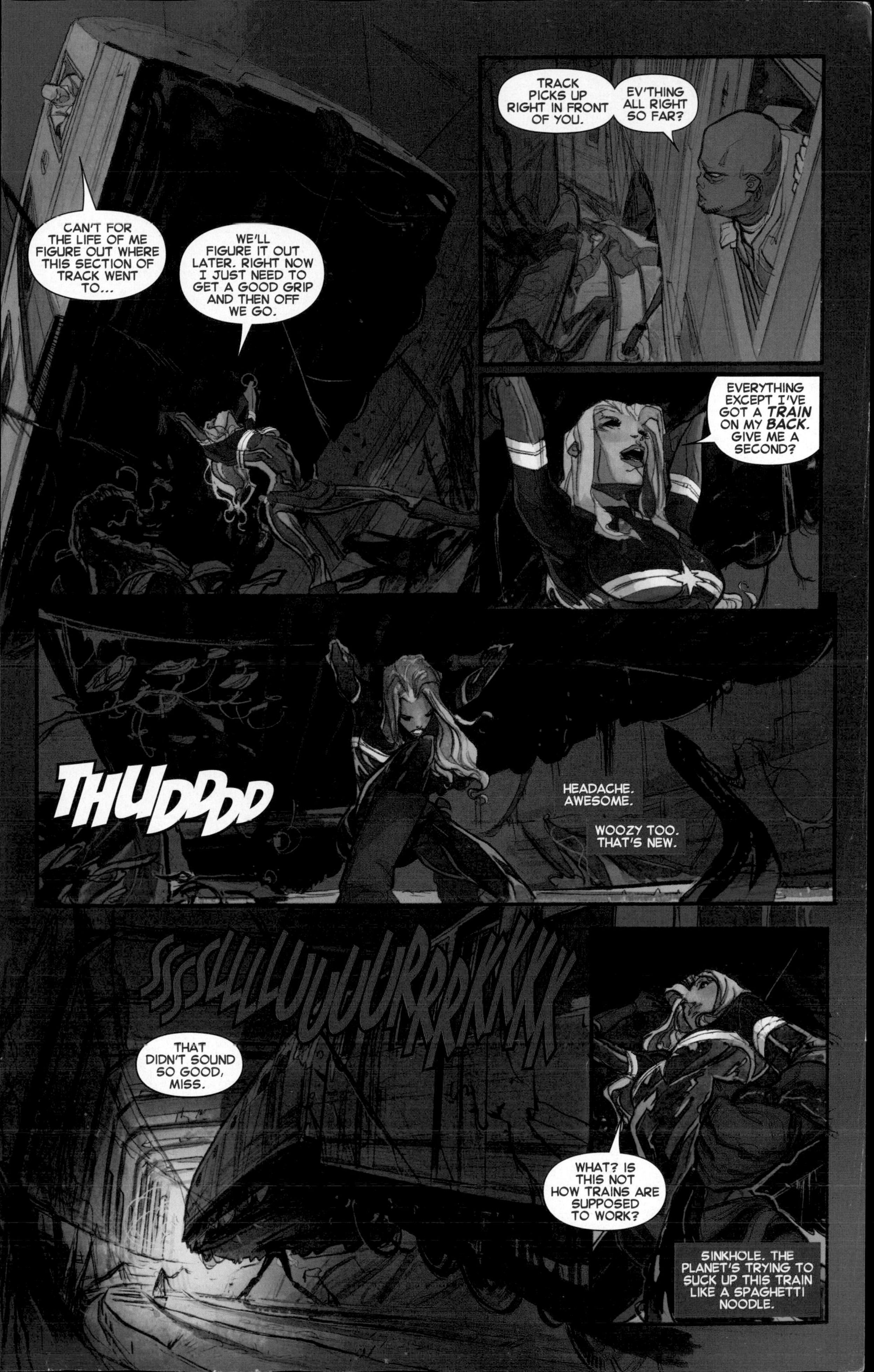
CAN'T FOR THE LIFE OF ME FIGURE OUT WHERE THIS SECTION OF TRACK WENT TO...
WE'LL FIGURE IT OUT LATER. RIGHT NOW I JUST NEED TO GET A GOOD GRIP AND THEN OFF WE GO.
TRACK PICKS UP RIGHT IN FRONT OF YOU.
EV'THING ALL RIGHT SO FAR?
EVERYTHING EXCEPT I'VE GOT A TRAIN ON MY BACK. GIVE ME A SECOND?
THUDDDD
HEADACHE. AWESOME.
WOOZY TOO. THAT'S NEW.
SSSLLLUUUURRRKKKK
THAT DIDN'T SOUND SO GOOD, MISS.
WHAT? IS THIS NOT HOW TRAINS ARE SUPPOSED TO WORK?
SINKHOLE. THE PLANET'S TRYING TO SUCK UP THIS TRAIN LIKE A SPAGHETTI NOODLE.

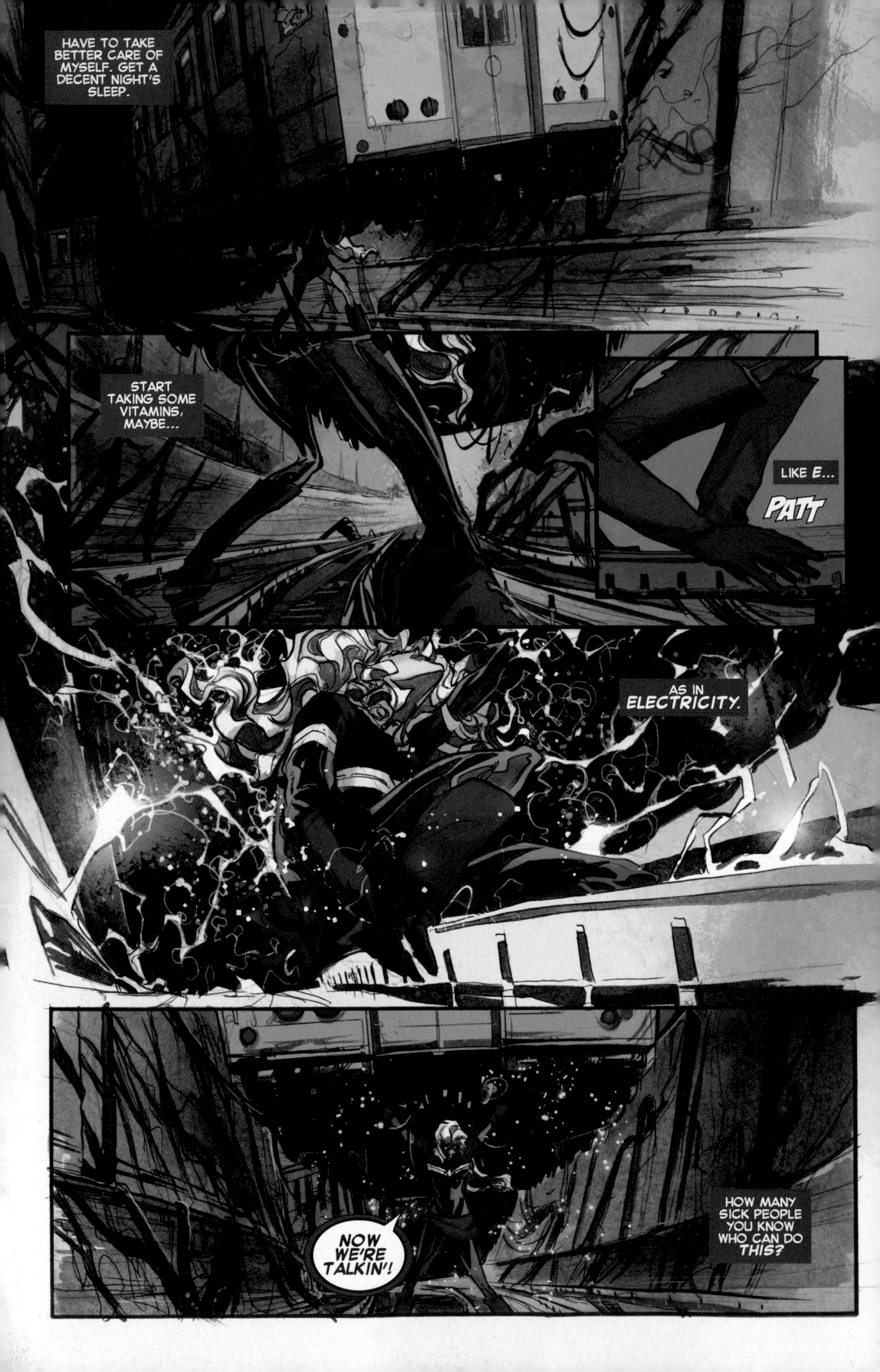
HAVE TO TAKE BETTER CARE OF MYSELF. GET A DECENT NIGHT'S SLEEP.
START TAKING SOME VITAMINS, MAYBE...
LIKE E...
PATT
AS IN *ELECTRICITY*.
NOW WE'RE TALKIN'!
HOW MANY SICK PEOPLE YOU KNOW WHO CAN DO *THIS?*

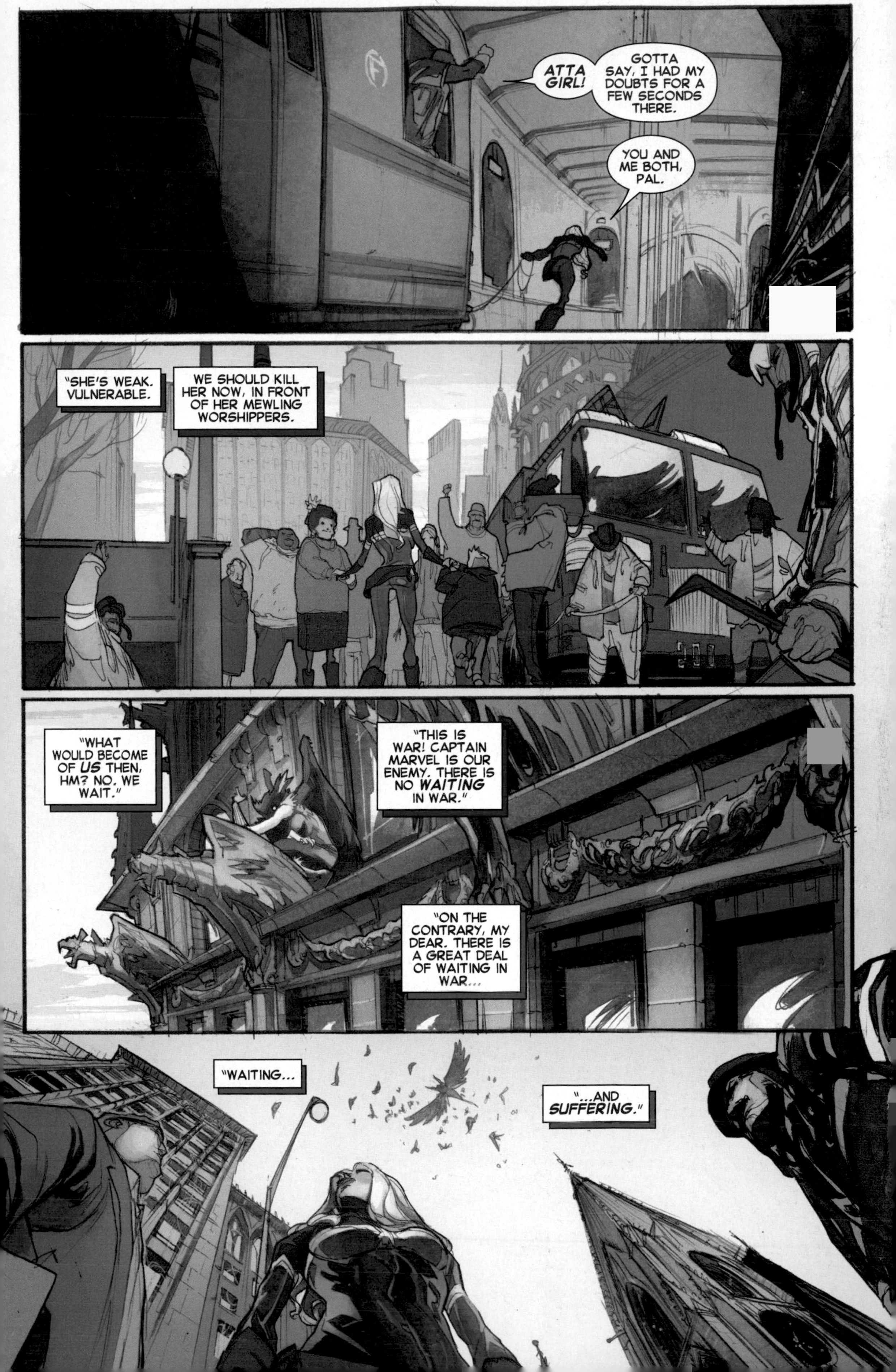

ATTA GIRL!
GOTTA SAY, I HAD MY DOUBTS FOR A FEW SECONDS THERE.
YOU AND ME BOTH, PAL.
"SHE'S WEAK. VULNERABLE.
WE SHOULD KILL HER NOW, IN FRONT OF HER MEWLING WORSHIPPERS.
"WHAT WOULD BECOME OF US THEN, HM? NO. WE WAIT."
"THIS IS WAR! CAPTAIN MARVEL IS OUR ENEMY. THERE IS NO WAITING IN WAR."
"ON THE CONTRARY, MY DEAR. THERE IS A GREAT DEAL OF WAITING IN WAR...
"WAITING...
"...AND SUFFERING."

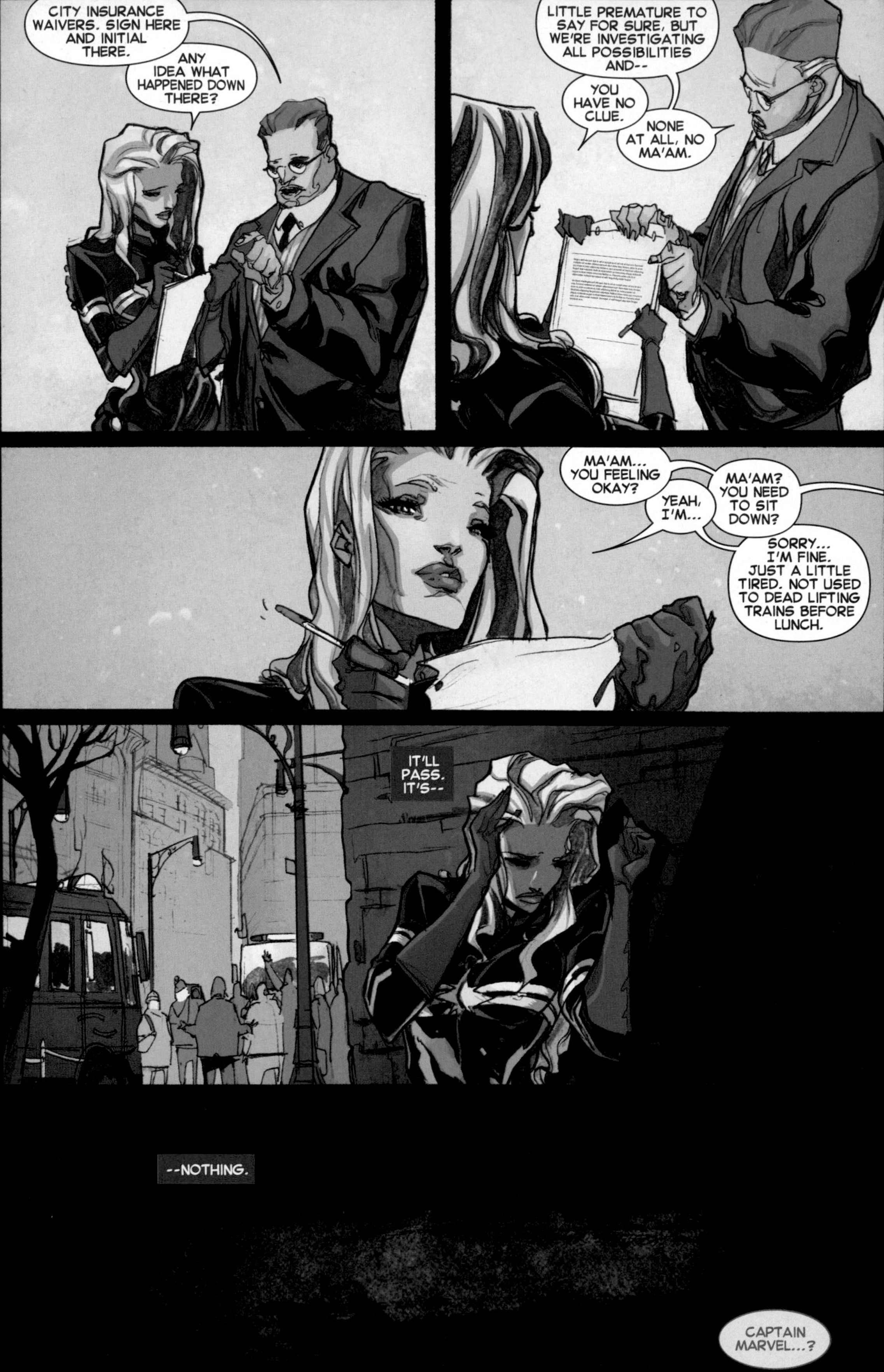
CITY INSURANCE WAIVERS. SIGN HERE AND INITIAL THERE.
ANY IDEA WHAT HAPPENED DOWN THERE?
LITTLE PREMATURE TO SAY FOR SURE, BUT WE'RE INVESTIGATING ALL POSSIBILITIES AND--
YOU HAVE NO CLUE.
NONE AT ALL, NO MA'AM.
MA'AM... YOU FEELING OKAY?
YEAH, I'M...
MA'AM? YOU NEED TO SIT DOWN?
SORRY... I'M FINE. JUST A LITTLE TIRED. NOT USED TO DEAD LIFTING TRAINS BEFORE LUNCH.
IT'LL PASS. IT'S--
--NOTHING.
CAPTAIN MARVEL...?

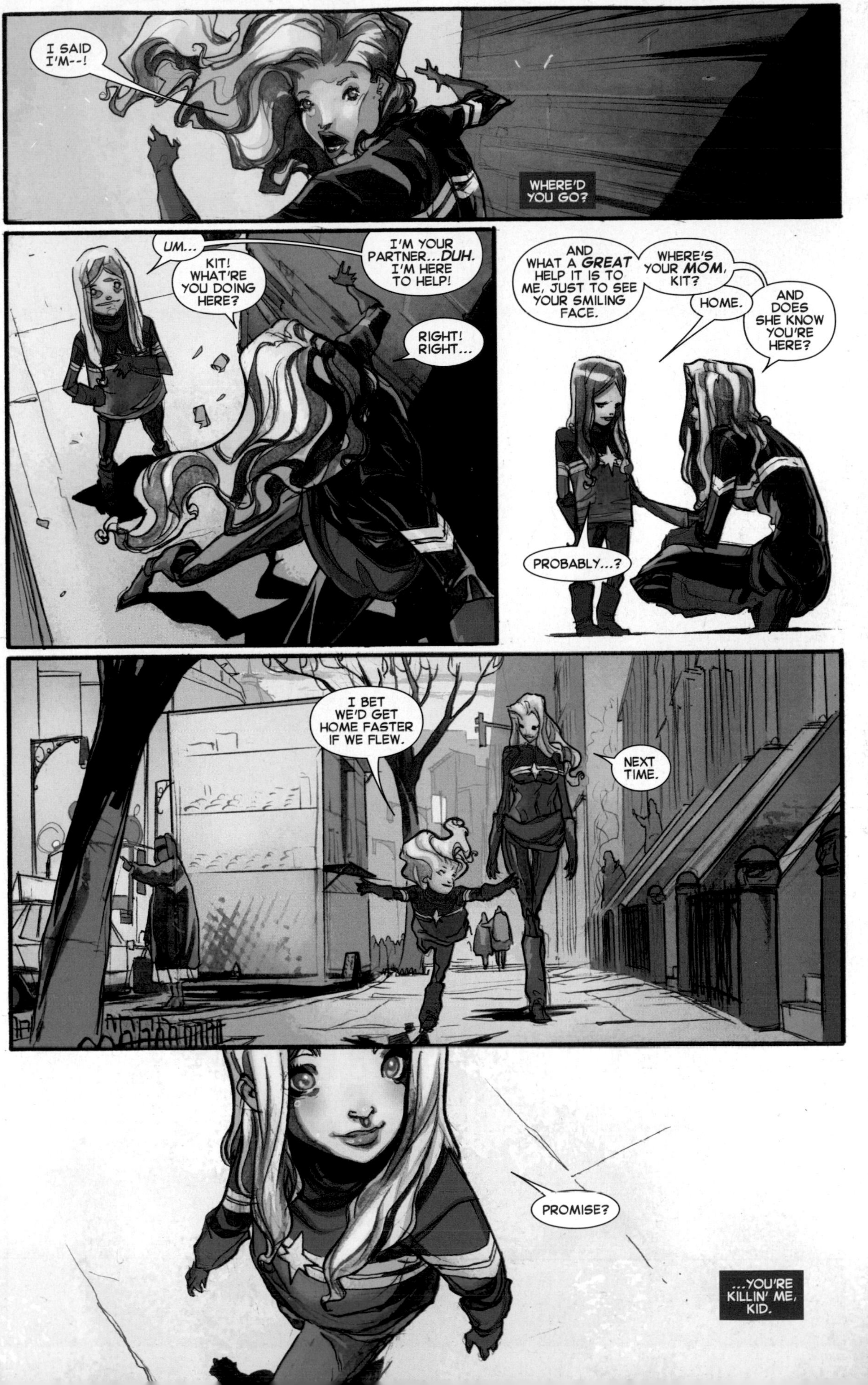
I SAID I'M--!
WHERE'D YOU GO?
UM...
I'M YOUR PARTNER...DUH. I'M HERE TO HELP!
KIT! WHAT'RE YOU DOING HERE?
RIGHT! RIGHT...
AND WHAT A GREAT HELP IT IS TO ME, JUST TO SEE YOUR SMILING FACE.
WHERE'S YOUR MOM, KIT?
HOME.
AND DOES SHE KNOW YOU'RE HERE?
PROBABLY...?
I BET WE'D GET HOME FASTER IF WE FLEW.
NEXT TIME.
PROMISE?
...YOU'RE KILLIN' ME, KID.

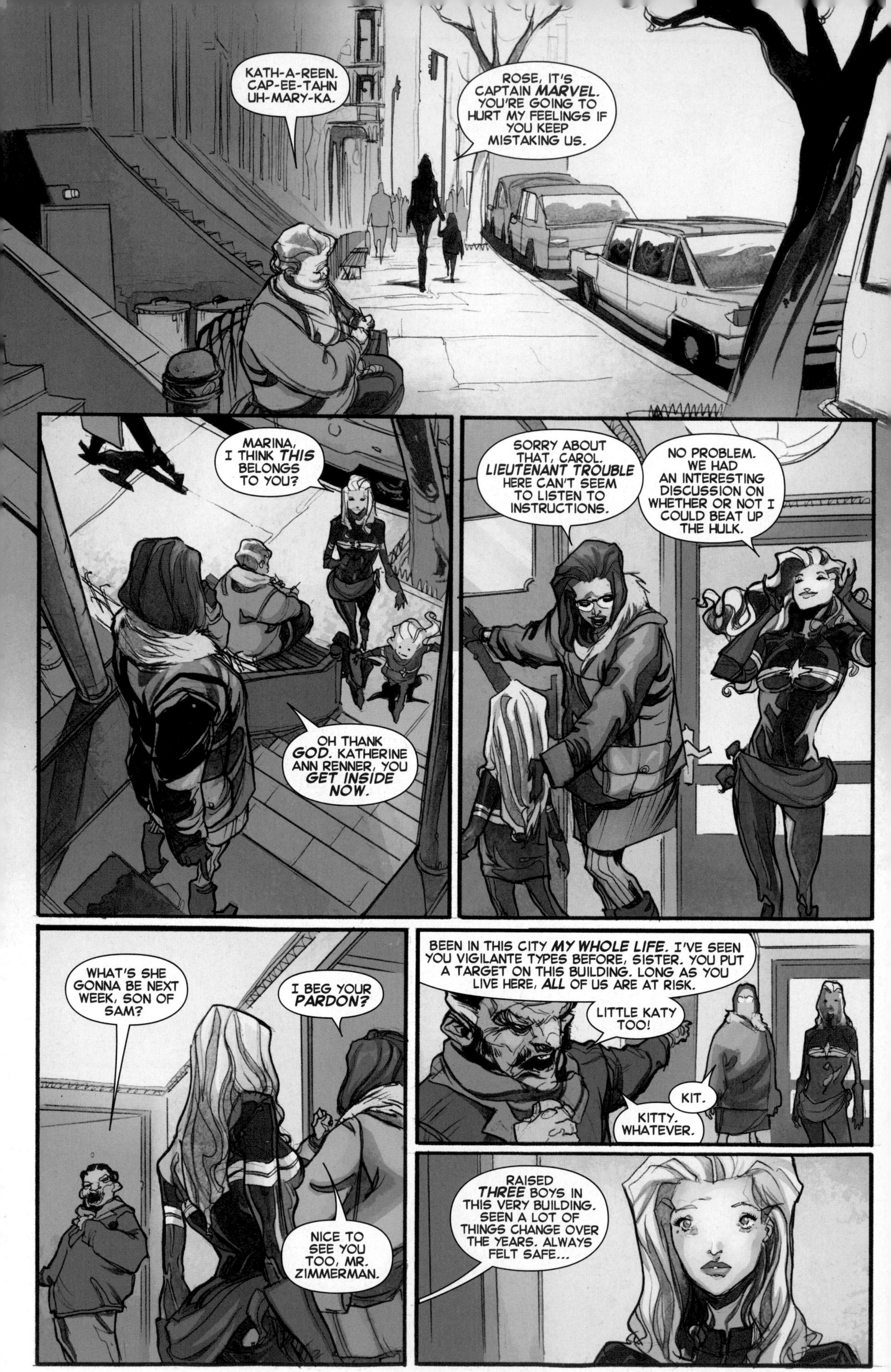
KATH-A-REEN. CAP-EE-TAHN UH-MARY-KA.
ROSE, IT'S CAPTAIN MARVEL. YOU'RE GOING TO HURT MY FEELINGS IF YOU KEEP MISTAKING US.
MARINA, I THINK THIS BELONGS TO YOU?
OH THANK GOD. KATHERINE ANN RENNER, YOU GET INSIDE NOW.
SORRY ABOUT THAT, CAROL. LIEUTENANT TROUBLE HERE CAN'T SEEM TO LISTEN TO INSTRUCTIONS.
NO PROBLEM. WE HAD AN INTERESTING DISCUSSION ON WHETHER OR NOT I COULD BEAT UP THE HULK.
WHAT'S SHE GONNA BE NEXT WEEK, SON OF SAM?
I BEG YOUR PARDON?
NICE TO SEE YOU TOO, MR. ZIMMERMAN.
BEEN IN THIS CITY MY WHOLE LIFE. I'VE SEEN YOU VIGILANTE TYPES BEFORE, SISTER. YOU PUT A TARGET ON THIS BUILDING. LONG AS YOU LIVE HERE, ALL OF US ARE AT RISK.
LITTLE KATY TOO!
KIT.
KITTY. WHATEVER.
RAISED THREE BOYS IN THIS VERY BUILDING. SEEN A LOT OF THINGS CHANGE OVER THE YEARS. ALWAYS FELT SAFE...

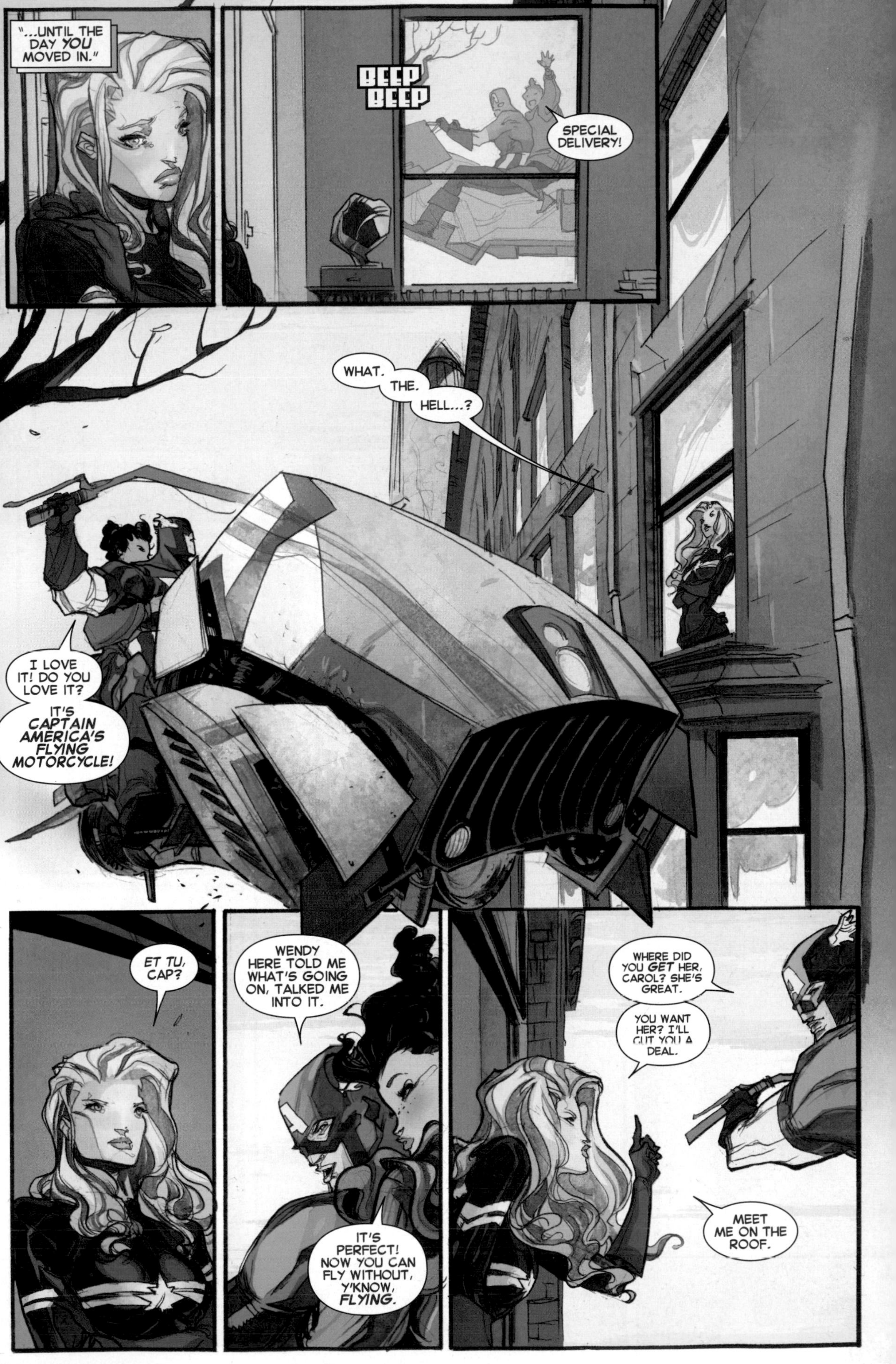
"...UNTIL THE DAY *YOU* MOVED IN."
BEEP BEEP
SPECIAL DELIVERY!
WHAT. THE. HELL...?
I LOVE IT! DO YOU LOVE IT?
IT'S *CAPTAIN AMERICA'S FLYING MOTORCYCLE!*
ET TU, CAP?
WENDY HERE TOLD ME WHAT'S GOING ON, TALKED ME INTO IT.
IT'S PERFECT! NOW YOU CAN FLY WITHOUT, Y'KNOW, *FLYING*.
WHERE DID YOU *GET* HER, CAROL? SHE'S GREAT.
YOU WANT HER? I'LL CUT YOU A DEAL.
MEET ME ON THE ROOF.

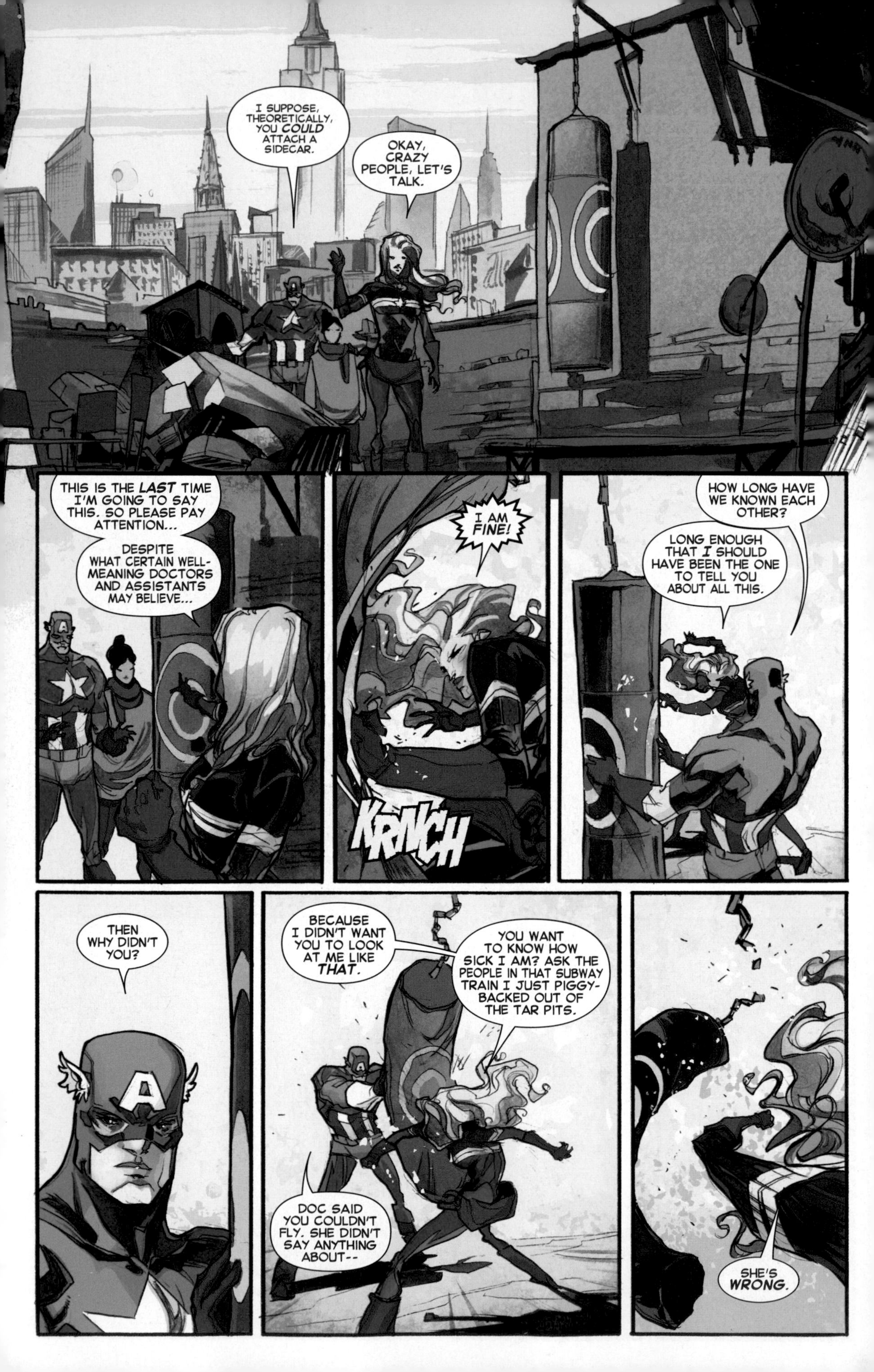

I SUPPOSE, THEORETICALLY, YOU COULD ATTACH A SIDECAR.
OKAY, CRAZY PEOPLE, LET'S TALK.
THIS IS THE LAST TIME I'M GOING TO SAY THIS. SO PLEASE PAY ATTENTION...
DESPITE WHAT CERTAIN WELL-MEANING DOCTORS AND ASSISTANTS MAY BELIEVE...
I AM FINE!
KRNCH
HOW LONG HAVE WE KNOWN EACH OTHER?
LONG ENOUGH THAT I SHOULD HAVE BEEN THE ONE TO TELL YOU ABOUT ALL THIS.
THEN WHY DIDN'T YOU?
BECAUSE I DIDN'T WANT YOU TO LOOK AT ME LIKE THAT.
YOU WANT TO KNOW HOW SICK I AM? ASK THE PEOPLE IN THAT SUBWAY TRAIN I JUST PIGGY-BACKED OUT OF THE TAR PITS.
DOC SAID YOU COULDN'T FLY. SHE DIDN'T SAY ANYTHING ABOUT--
SHE'S WRONG.

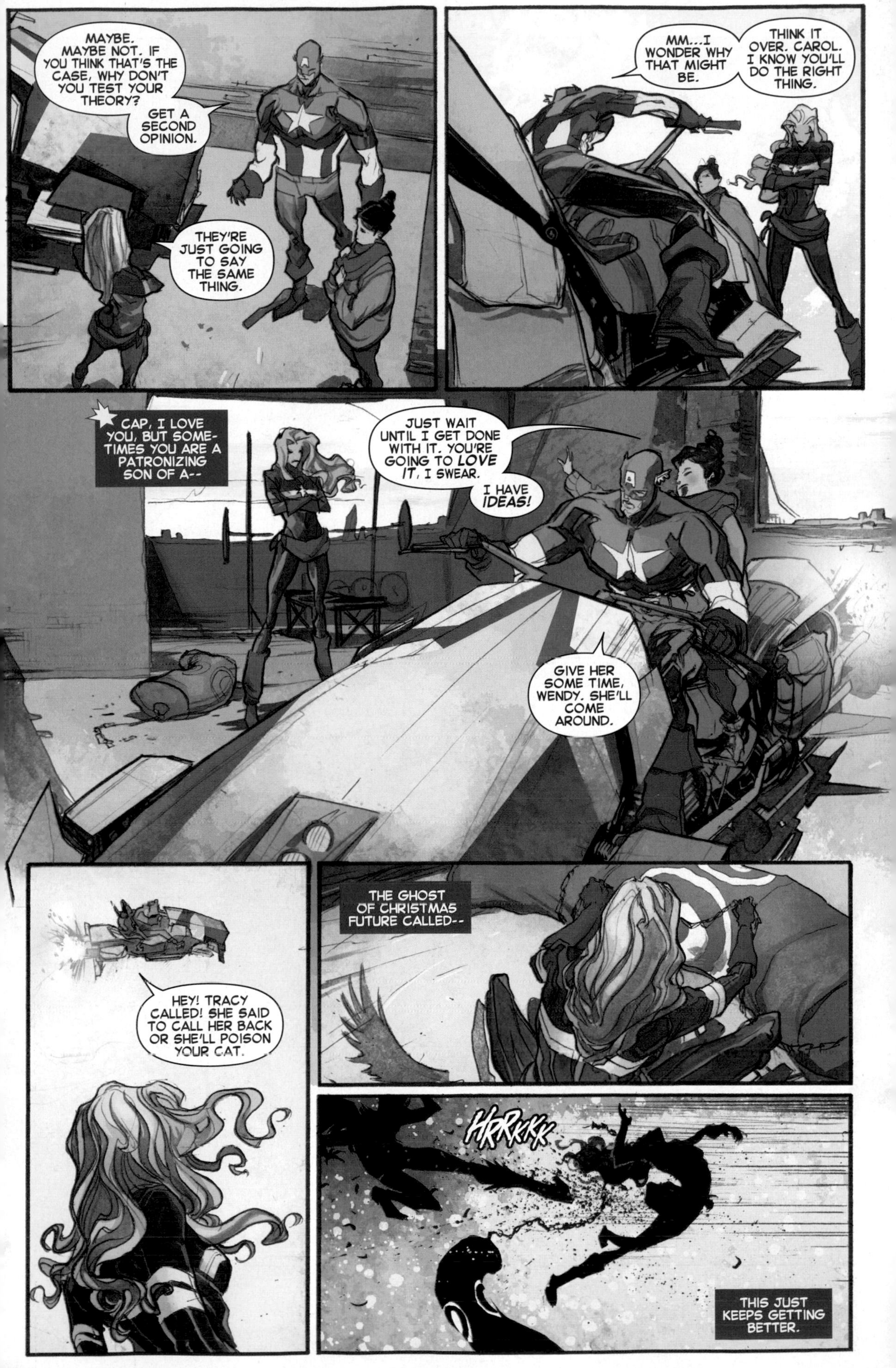
MAYBE. MAYBE NOT. IF YOU THINK THAT'S THE CASE, WHY DON'T YOU TEST YOUR THEORY?
GET A SECOND OPINION.
THEY'RE JUST GOING TO SAY THE SAME THING.
MM...I WONDER WHY THAT MIGHT BE.
THINK IT OVER. CAROL. I KNOW YOU'LL DO THE RIGHT THING.
CAP, I LOVE YOU, BUT SOME-TIMES YOU ARE A PATRONIZING SON OF A--
JUST WAIT UNTIL I GET DONE WITH IT. YOU'RE GOING TO LOVE IT, I SWEAR.
I HAVE IDEAS!
GIVE HER SOME TIME, WENDY. SHE'LL COME AROUND.
HEY! TRACY CALLED! SHE SAID TO CALL HER BACK OR SHE'LL POISON YOUR CAT.
THE GHOST OF CHRISTMAS FUTURE CALLED--
HRRKKK
THIS JUST KEEPS GETTING BETTER.

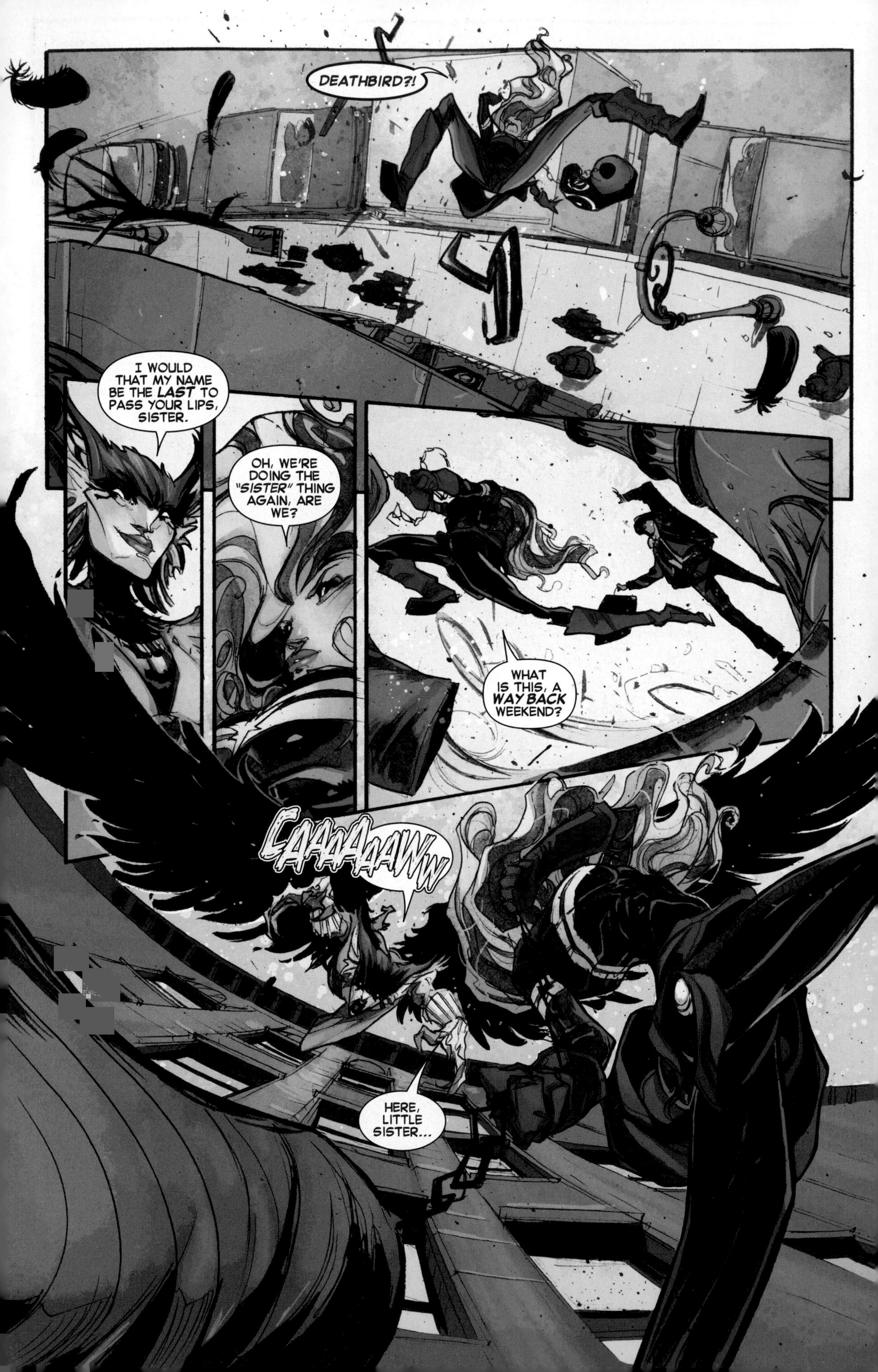

DEATHBIRD?!
I WOULD THAT MY NAME BE THE LAST TO PASS YOUR LIPS, SISTER.
OH, WE'RE DOING THE "SISTER" THING AGAIN, ARE WE?
WHAT IS THIS, A WAY BACK WEEKEND?
CAAAAAAAWW
HERE, LITTLE SISTER...

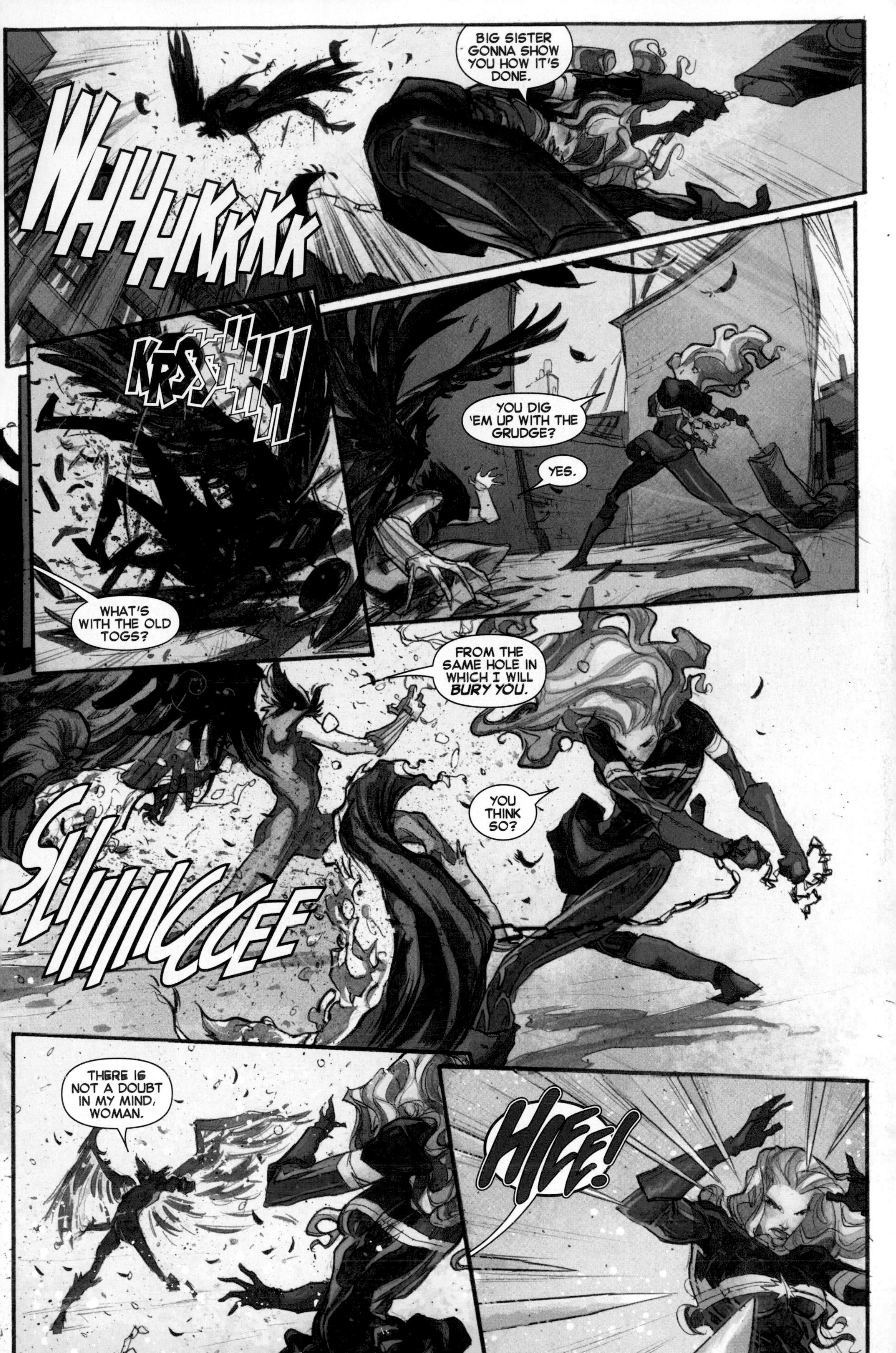
BIG SISTER GONNA SHOW YOU HOW IT'S DONE.
WHHUKKKK
KRSSHHH
YOU DIG 'EM UP WITH THE GRUDGE?
YES.
WHAT'S WITH THE OLD TOGS?
FROM THE SAME HOLE IN WHICH I WILL BURY YOU.
YOU THINK SO?
SLIIIIICCEE
THERE IS NOT A DOUBT IN MY MIND, WOMAN.
HEE!

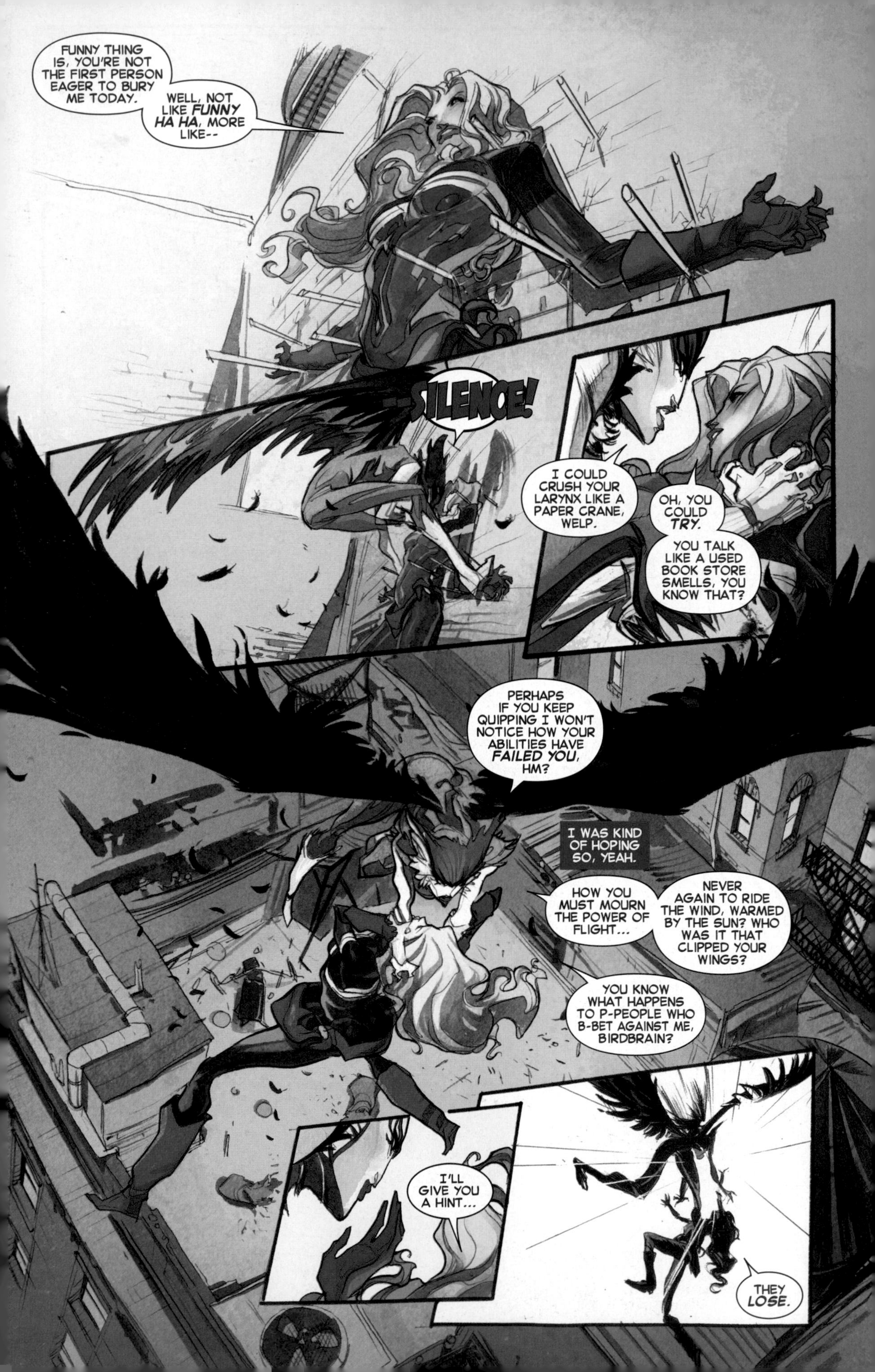

FUNNY THING IS, YOU'RE NOT THE FIRST PERSON EAGER TO BURY ME TODAY.
WELL, NOT LIKE FUNNY HA HA, MORE LIKE--
SILENCE!
I COULD CRUSH YOUR LARYNX LIKE A PAPER CRANE, WELP.
OH, YOU COULD TRY.
YOU TALK LIKE A USED BOOK STORE SMELLS, YOU KNOW THAT?
PERHAPS IF YOU KEEP QUIPPING I WON'T NOTICE HOW YOUR ABILITIES HAVE FAILED YOU, HM?
I WAS KIND OF HOPING SO, YEAH.
HOW YOU MUST MOURN THE POWER OF FLIGHT...
NEVER AGAIN TO RIDE THE WIND, WARMED BY THE SUN? WHO WAS IT THAT CLIPPED YOUR WINGS?
YOU KNOW WHAT HAPPENS TO P-PEOPLE WHO B-BET AGAINST ME, BIRDBRAIN?
I'LL GIVE YOU A HINT...
THEY LOSE.

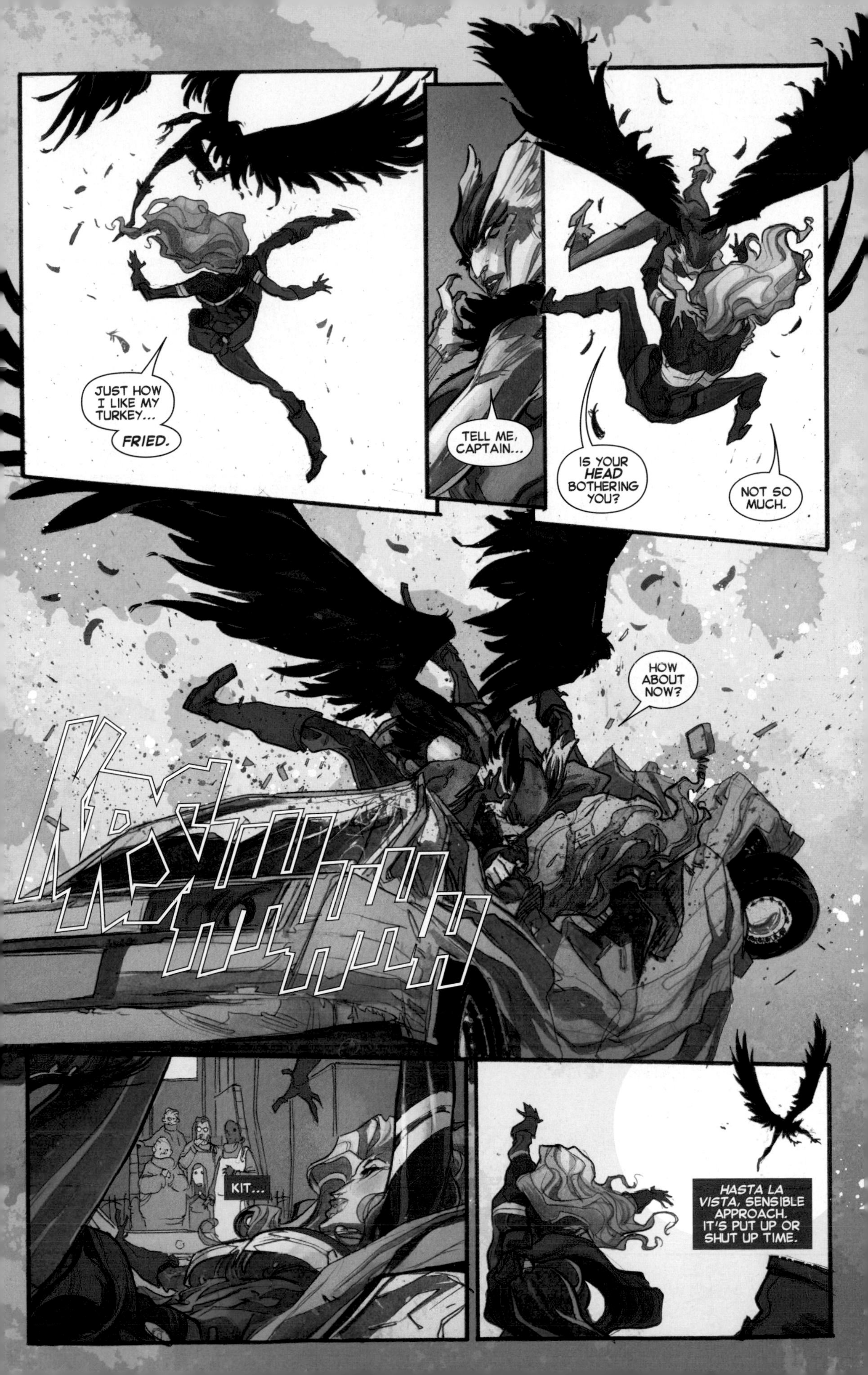
JUST HOW I LIKE MY TURKEY...
FRIED.
TELL ME, CAPTAIN...
IS YOUR HEAD BOTHERING YOU?
NOT SO MUCH.
HOW ABOUT NOW?
KRASHHHHH
KIT...
HASTA LA VISTA, SENSIBLE APPROACH. IT'S PUT UP OR SHUT UP TIME.

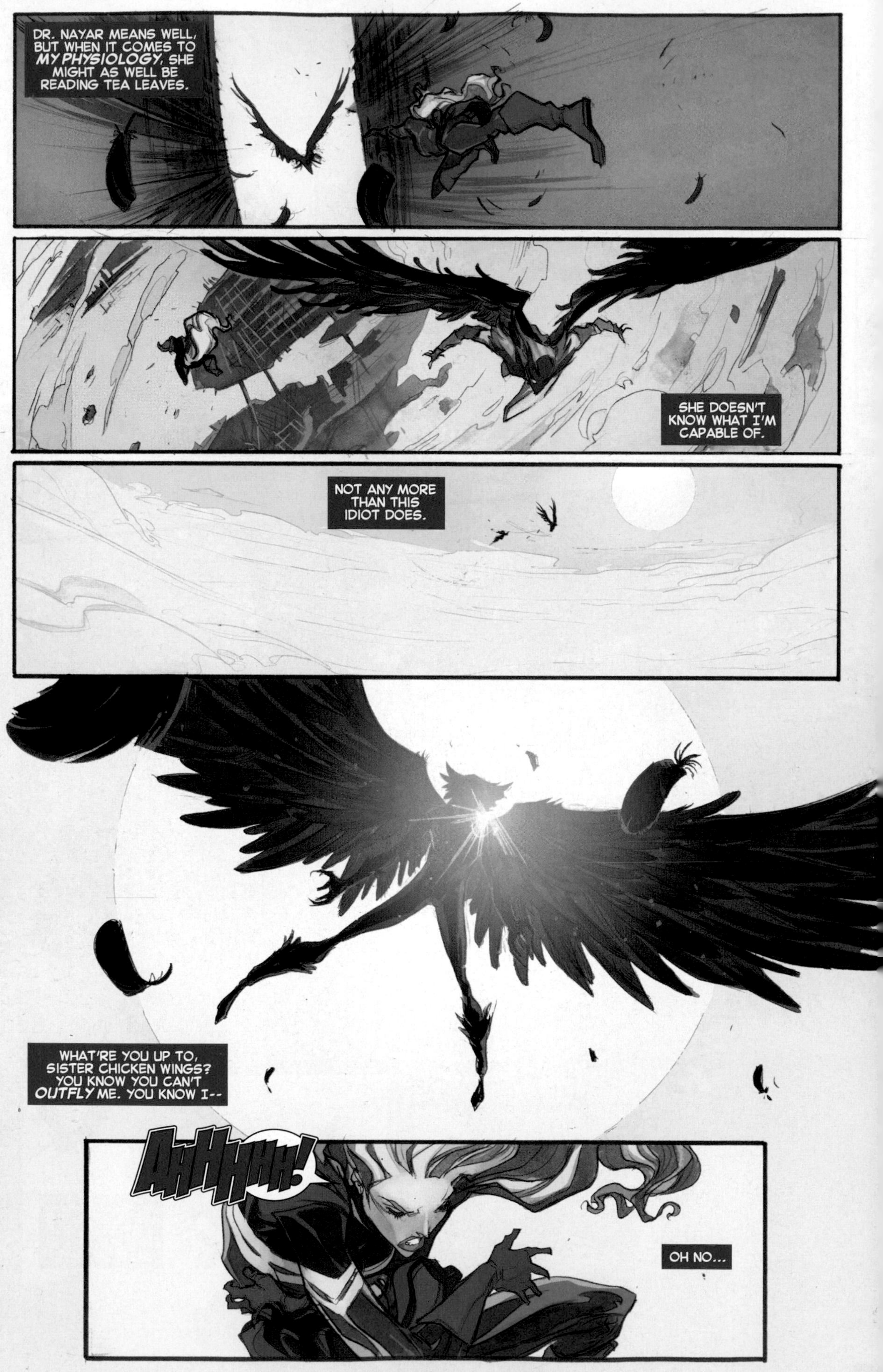
DR. NAYAR MEANS WELL, BUT WHEN IT COMES TO *MY PHYSIOLOGY*, SHE MIGHT AS WELL BE READING TEA LEAVES.
SHE DOESN'T KNOW WHAT I'M CAPABLE OF.
NOT ANY MORE THAN THIS IDIOT DOES.
WHAT'RE YOU UP TO, SISTER CHICKEN WINGS? YOU KNOW YOU CAN'T *OUTFLY* ME. YOU KNOW I--
AHHHHH!
OH NO...

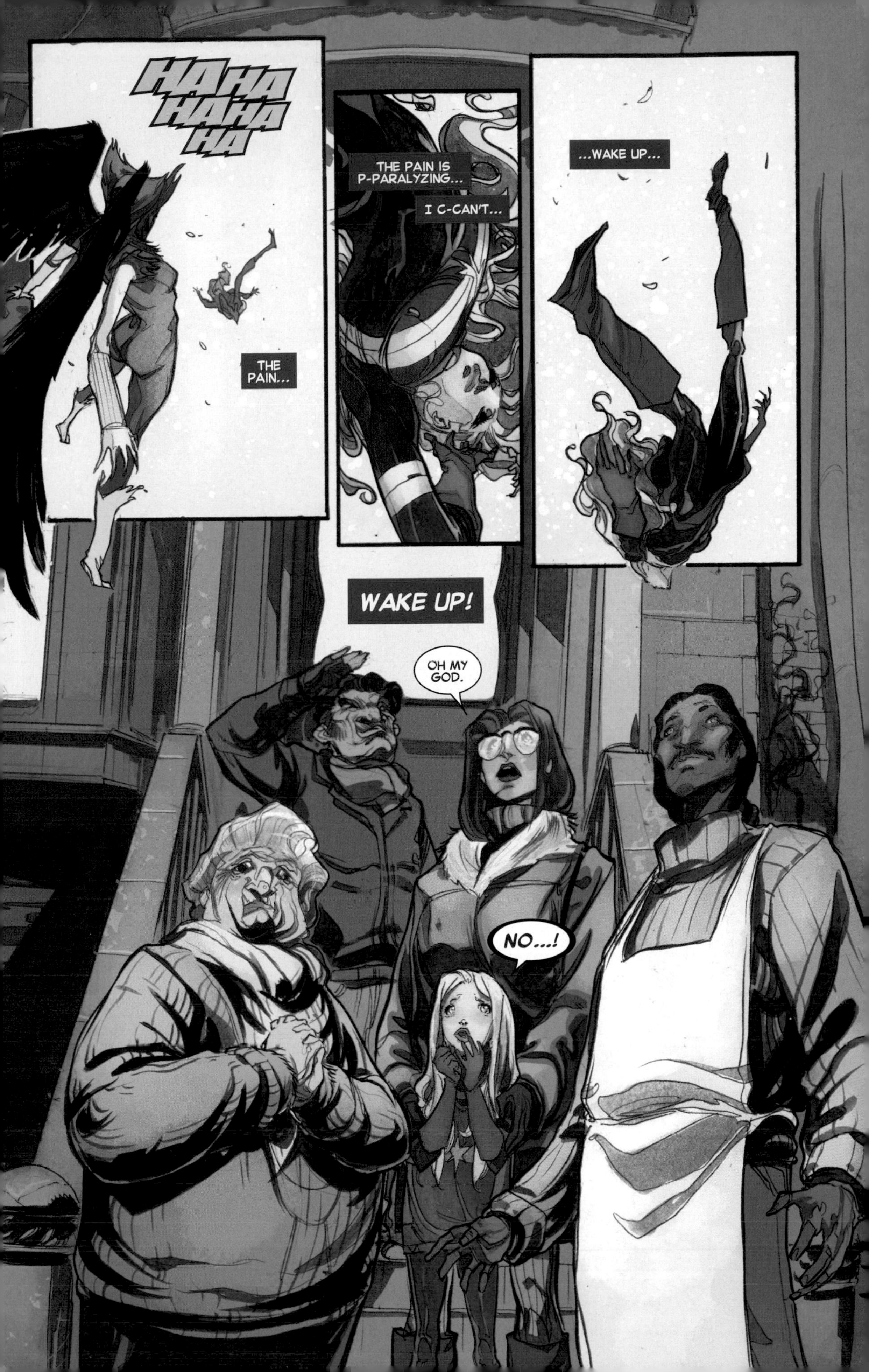
HAHA HAHA HA
THE PAIN...
THE PAIN IS P-PARALYZING...
I C-CAN'T...
...WAKE UP...
WAKE UP!
OH MY GOD.
NO...!

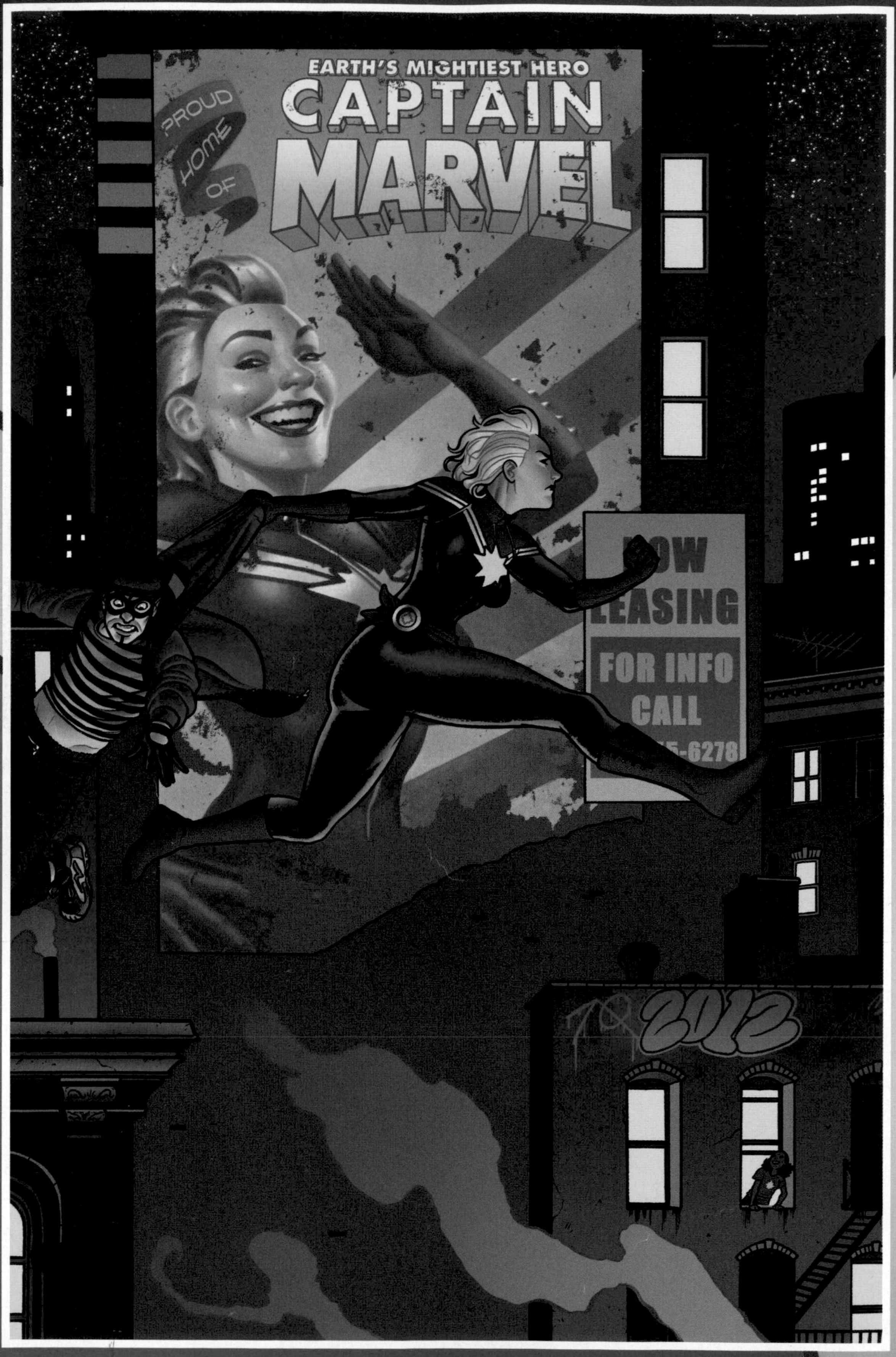
EARTH'S MIGHTIEST HERO
CAPTAIN MARVEL
PROUD HOME OF
LEASING
FOR INFO
CALL

ELEVEN

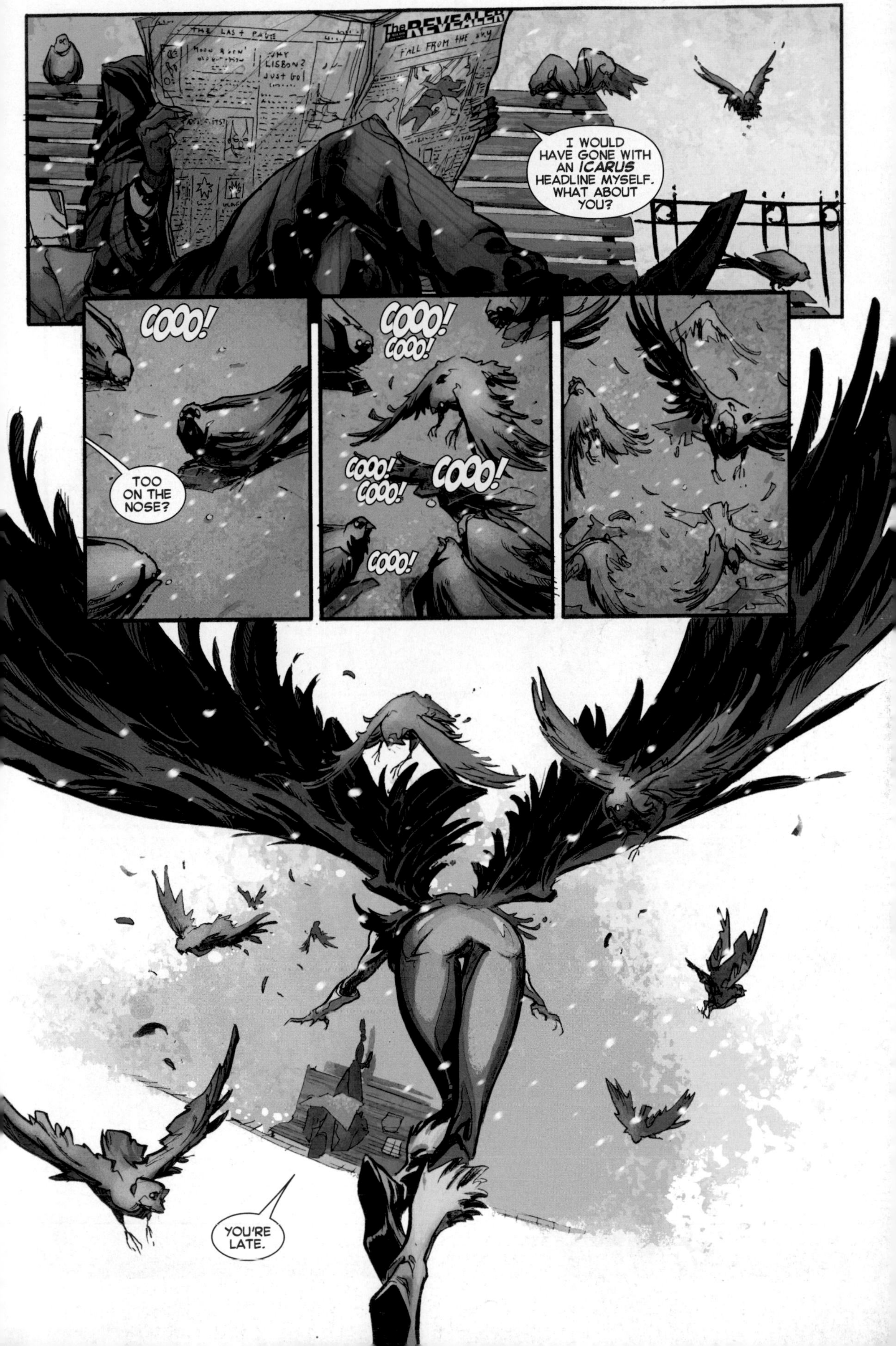
The REVEALER
FALL FROM THE SKY
I WOULD HAVE GONE WITH AN ICARUS HEADLINE MYSELF. WHAT ABOUT YOU?
COOO!
TOO ON THE NOSE?
COOO! COOO!
COOO! COOO!
COOO!
COOO!
YOU'RE LATE.

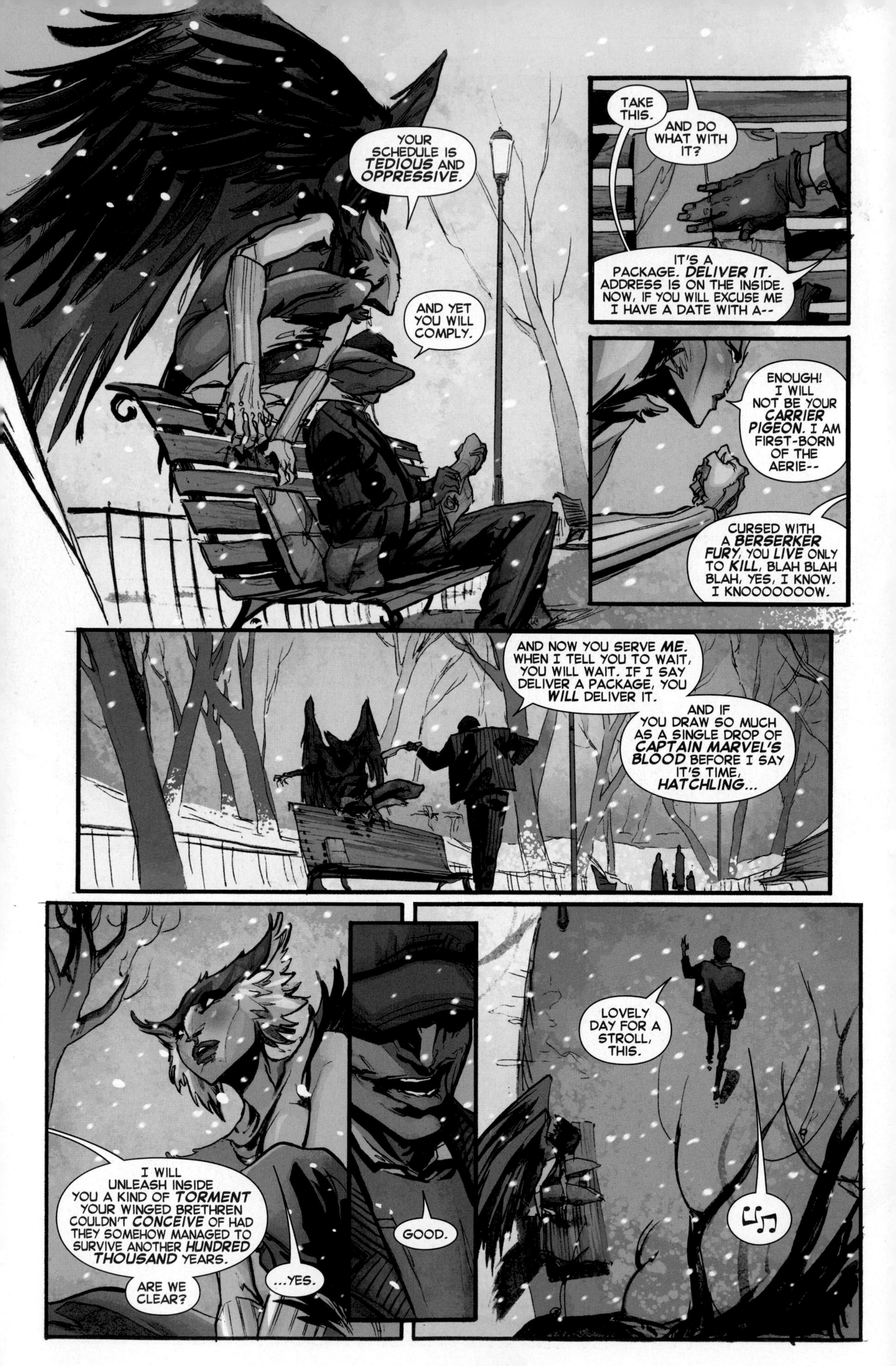
YOUR SCHEDULE IS TEDIOUS AND OPPRESSIVE.
AND YET YOU WILL COMPLY.
TAKE THIS.
AND DO WHAT WITH IT?
IT'S A PACKAGE. DELIVER IT. ADDRESS IS ON THE INSIDE. NOW, IF YOU WILL EXCUSE ME I HAVE A DATE WITH A--
ENOUGH! I WILL NOT BE YOUR CARRIER PIGEON. I AM FIRST-BORN OF THE AERIE--
CURSED WITH A BERSERKER FURY, YOU LIVE ONLY TO KILL, BLAH BLAH BLAH, YES, I KNOW. I KNOOOOOOOW.
AND NOW YOU SERVE ME. WHEN I TELL YOU TO WAIT, YOU WILL WAIT. IF I SAY DELIVER A PACKAGE, YOU WILL DELIVER IT.
AND IF YOU DRAW SO MUCH AS A SINGLE DROP OF CAPTAIN MARVEL'S BLOOD BEFORE I SAY IT'S TIME, HATCHLING...
I WILL UNLEASH INSIDE YOU A KIND OF TORMENT YOUR WINGED BRETHREN COULDN'T CONCEIVE OF HAD THEY SOMEHOW MANAGED TO SURVIVE ANOTHER HUNDRED THOUSAND YEARS.
ARE WE CLEAR?
...YES.
GOOD.
LOVELY DAY FOR A STROLL, THIS.

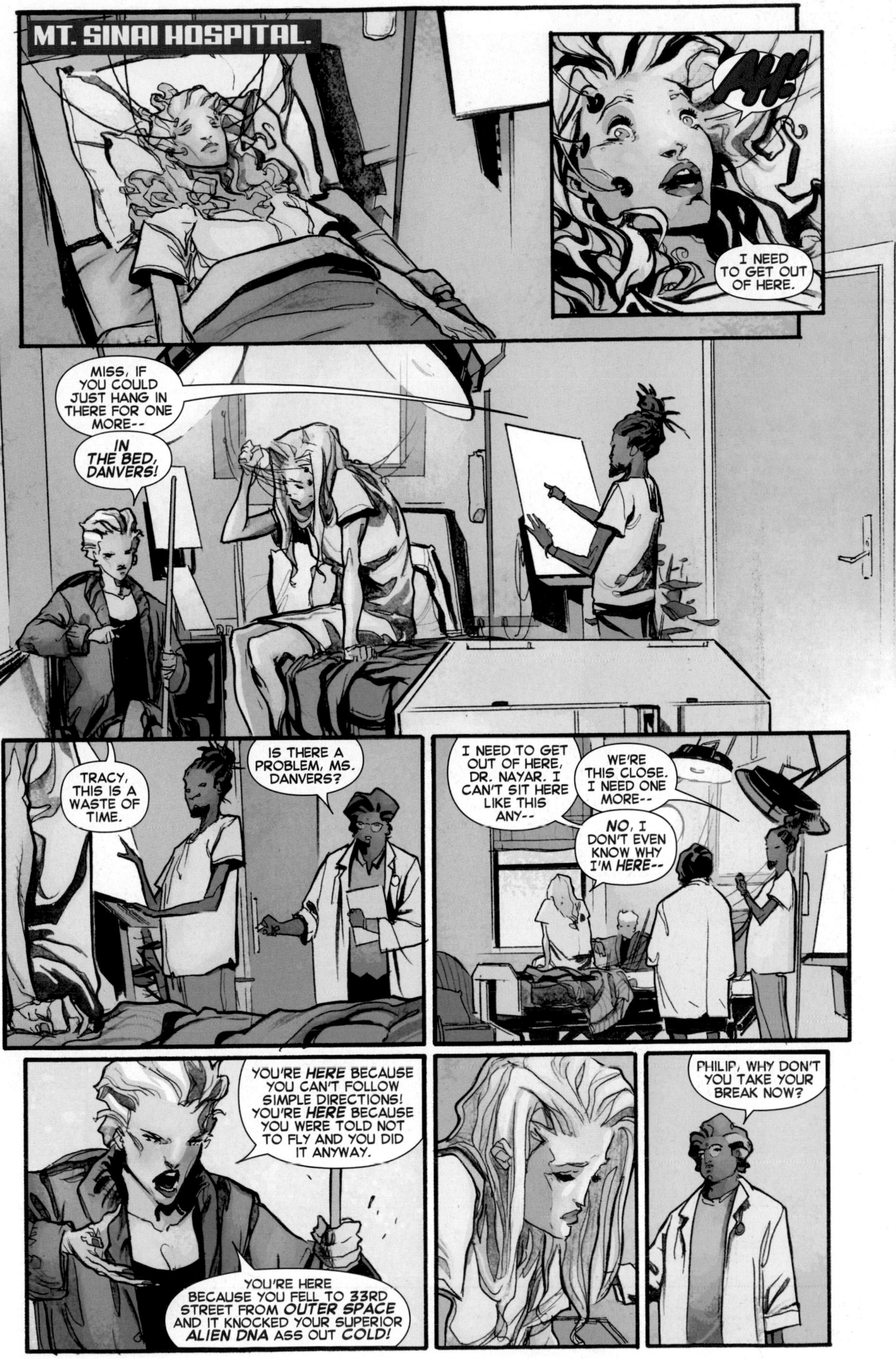
MT. SINAI HOSPITAL.
AH!
I NEED TO GET OUT OF HERE.
MISS, IF YOU COULD JUST HANG IN THERE FOR ONE MORE--
IN THE BED, DANVERS!
TRACY, THIS IS A WASTE OF TIME.
IS THERE A PROBLEM, MS. DANVERS?
I NEED TO GET OUT OF HERE, DR. NAYAR. I CAN'T SIT HERE LIKE THIS ANY--
WE'RE THIS CLOSE. I NEED ONE MORE--
NO, I DON'T EVEN KNOW WHY I'M HERE--
YOU'RE HERE BECAUSE YOU CAN'T FOLLOW SIMPLE DIRECTIONS! YOU'RE HERE BECAUSE YOU WERE TOLD NOT TO FLY AND YOU DID IT ANYWAY.
YOU'RE HERE BECAUSE YOU FELL TO 33RD STREET FROM OUTER SPACE AND IT KNOCKED YOUR SUPERIOR ALIEN DNA ASS OUT COLD!
PHILIP, WHY DON'T YOU TAKE YOUR BREAK NOW?

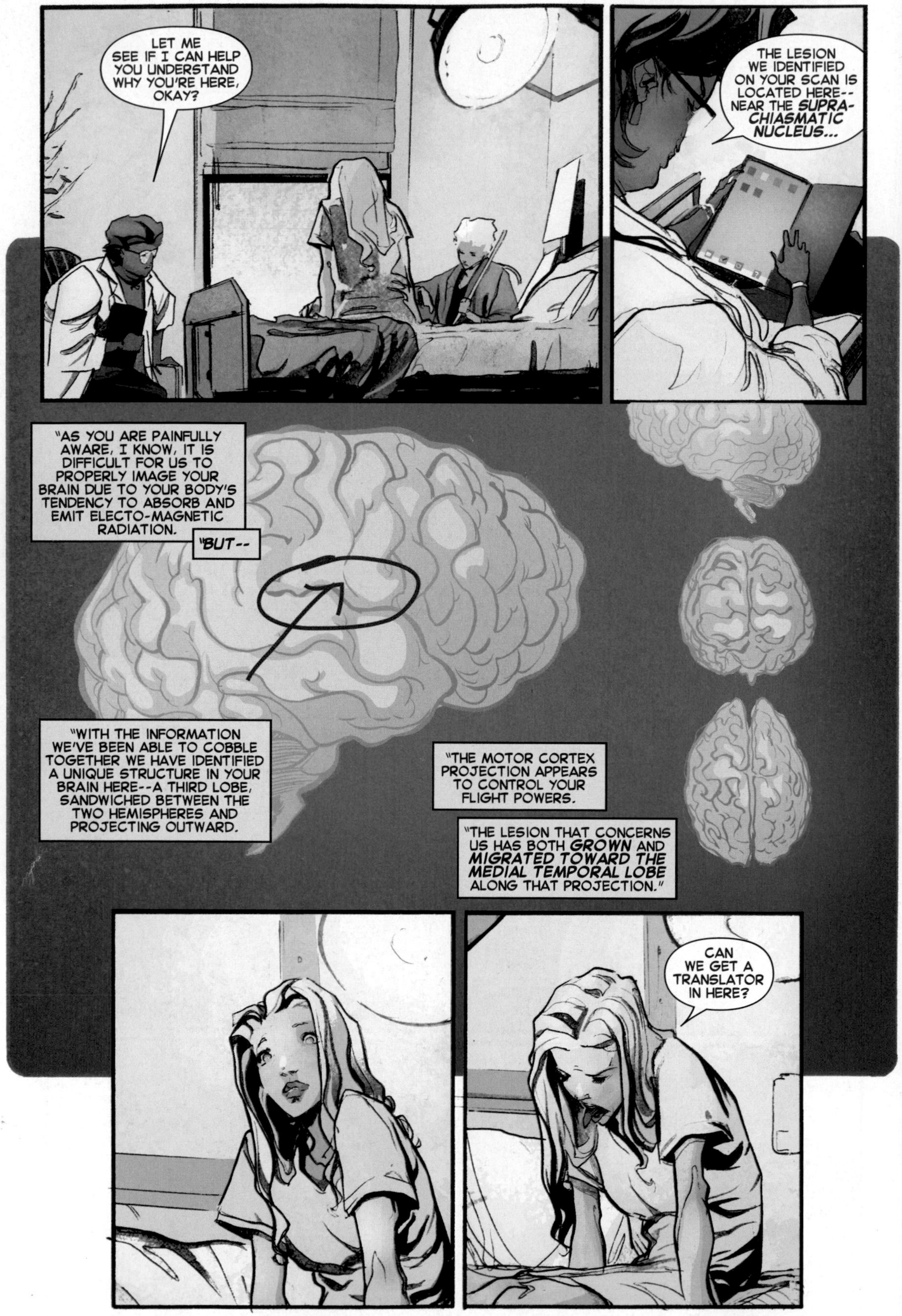
LET ME SEE IF I CAN HELP YOU UNDERSTAND WHY YOU'RE HERE, OKAY?
THE LESION WE IDENTIFIED ON YOUR SCAN IS LOCATED HERE-- NEAR THE *SUPRA-CHIASMATIC NUCLEUS...*
"AS YOU ARE PAINFULLY AWARE, I KNOW, IT IS DIFFICULT FOR US TO PROPERLY IMAGE YOUR BRAIN DUE TO YOUR BODY'S TENDENCY TO ABSORB AND EMIT ELECTO-MAGNETIC RADIATION.
"*BUT--*
"WITH THE INFORMATION WE'VE BEEN ABLE TO COBBLE TOGETHER WE HAVE IDENTIFIED A UNIQUE STRUCTURE IN YOUR BRAIN HERE--A THIRD LOBE, SANDWICHED BETWEEN THE TWO HEMISPHERES AND PROJECTING OUTWARD.
"THE MOTOR CORTEX PROJECTION APPEARS TO CONTROL YOUR FLIGHT POWERS.
"THE LESION THAT CONCERNS US HAS BOTH *GROWN* AND *MIGRATED TOWARD THE MEDIAL TEMPORAL LOBE* ALONG THAT PROJECTION."
CAN WE GET A TRANSLATOR IN HERE?

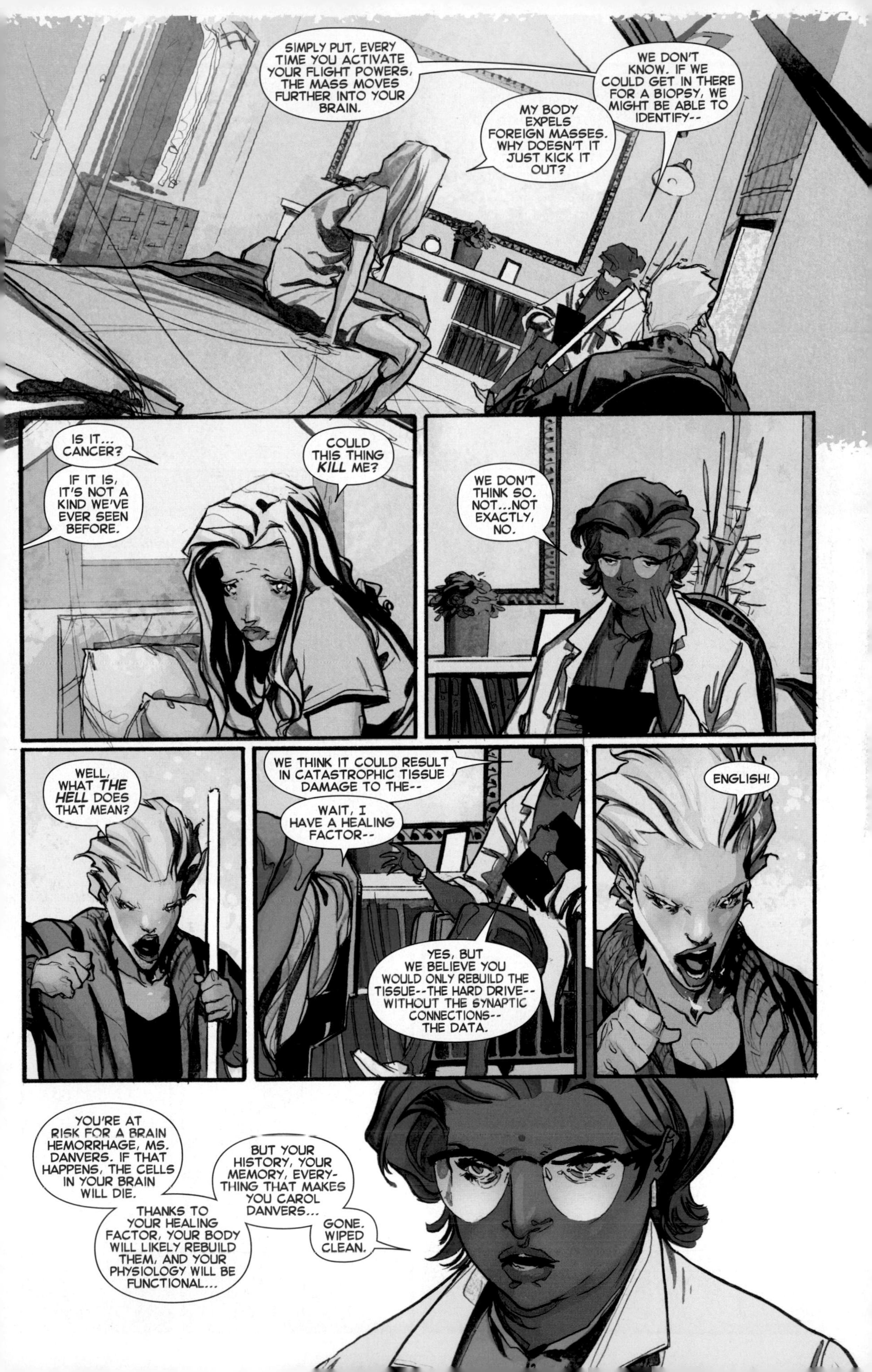
SIMPLY PUT, EVERY TIME YOU ACTIVATE YOUR FLIGHT POWERS, THE MASS MOVES FURTHER INTO YOUR BRAIN.
MY BODY EXPELS FOREIGN MASSES. WHY DOESN'T IT JUST KICK IT OUT?
WE DON'T KNOW. IF WE COULD GET IN THERE FOR A BIOPSY, WE MIGHT BE ABLE TO IDENTIFY--
IS IT... CANCER?
IF IT IS, IT'S NOT A KIND WE'VE EVER SEEN BEFORE.
COULD THIS THING *KILL* ME?
WE DON'T THINK SO. NOT...NOT EXACTLY, NO.
WELL, WHAT ***THE HELL*** DOES THAT MEAN?
WE THINK IT COULD RESULT IN CATASTROPHIC TISSUE DAMAGE TO THE--
WAIT, I HAVE A HEALING FACTOR--
YES, BUT WE BELIEVE YOU WOULD ONLY REBUILD THE TISSUE--THE HARD DRIVE--WITHOUT THE SYNAPTIC CONNECTIONS--THE DATA.
ENGLISH!
YOU'RE AT RISK FOR A BRAIN HEMORRHAGE, MS. DANVERS. IF THAT HAPPENS, THE CELLS IN YOUR BRAIN WILL DIE.
THANKS TO YOUR HEALING FACTOR, YOUR BODY WILL LIKELY REBUILD THEM, AND YOUR PHYSIOLOGY WILL BE FUNCTIONAL...
BUT YOUR HISTORY, YOUR MEMORY, EVERYTHING THAT MAKES YOU CAROL DANVERS...
GONE. WIPED CLEAN.

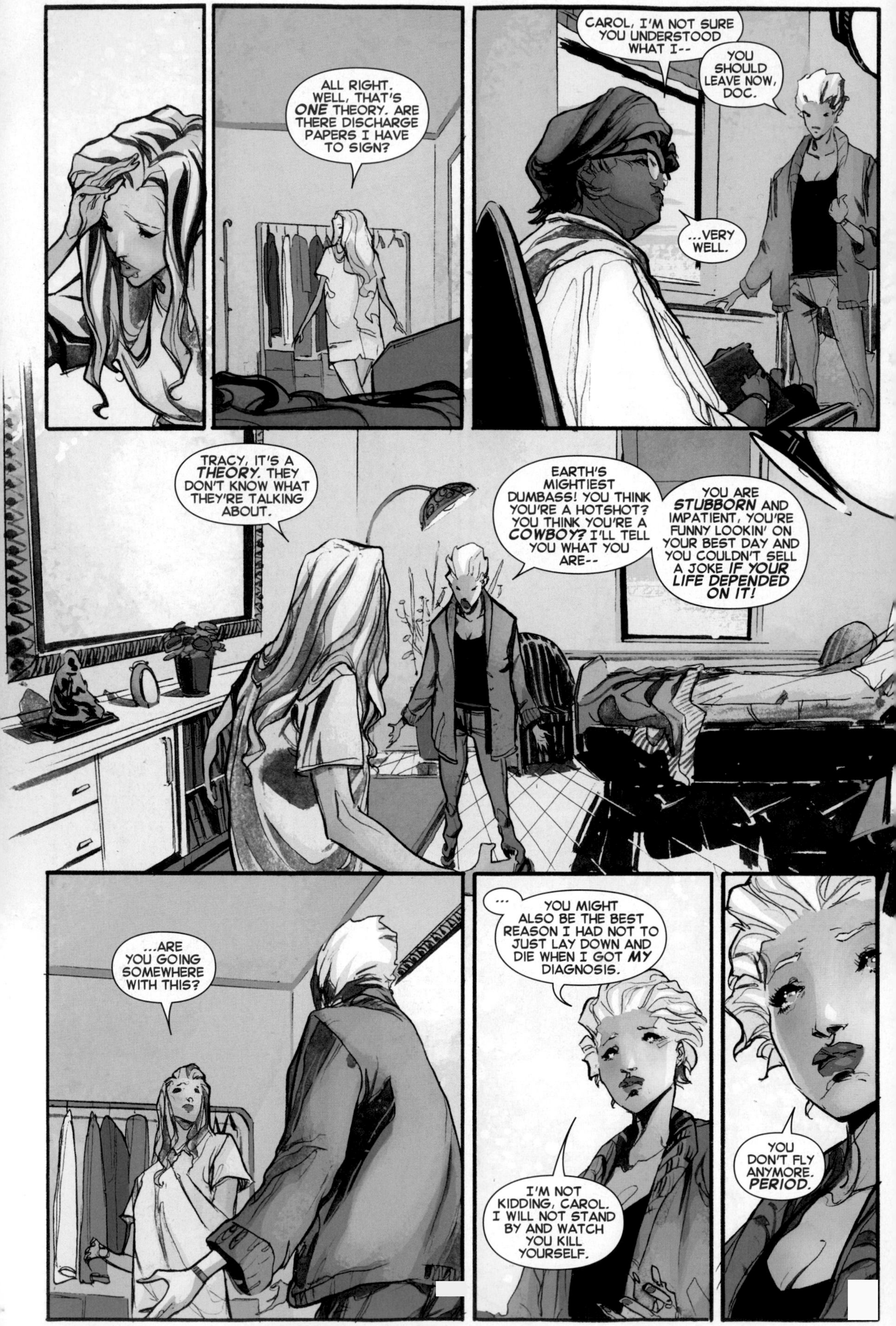
ALL RIGHT. WELL, THAT'S ONE THEORY. ARE THERE DISCHARGE PAPERS I HAVE TO SIGN?
CAROL, I'M NOT SURE YOU UNDERSTOOD WHAT I--
YOU SHOULD LEAVE NOW, DOC.
...VERY WELL.
TRACY, IT'S A THEORY. THEY DON'T KNOW WHAT THEY'RE TALKING ABOUT.
EARTH'S MIGHTIEST DUMBASS! YOU THINK YOU'RE A HOTSHOT? YOU THINK YOU'RE A COWBOY? I'LL TELL YOU WHAT YOU ARE--
YOU ARE STUBBORN AND IMPATIENT, YOU'RE FUNNY LOOKIN' ON YOUR BEST DAY AND YOU COULDN'T SELL A JOKE IF YOUR LIFE DEPENDED ON IT!
...ARE YOU GOING SOMEWHERE WITH THIS?
...
YOU MIGHT ALSO BE THE BEST REASON I HAD NOT TO JUST LAY DOWN AND DIE WHEN I GOT MY DIAGNOSIS.
I'M NOT KIDDING, CAROL. I WILL NOT STAND BY AND WATCH YOU KILL YOURSELF.
YOU DON'T FLY ANYMORE. PERIOD.

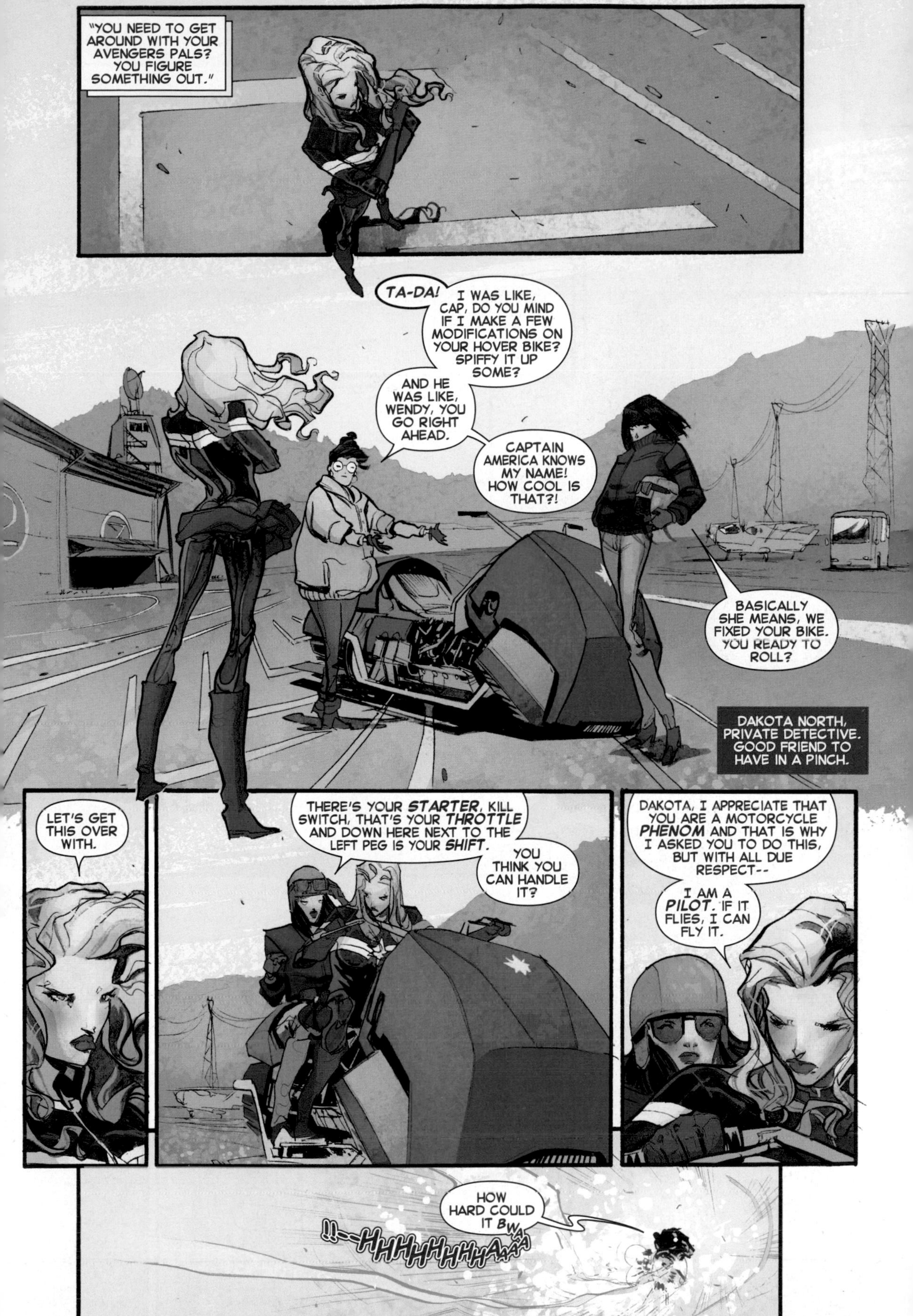
"YOU NEED TO GET AROUND WITH YOUR AVENGERS PALS? YOU FIGURE SOMETHING OUT."
TA-DA!
I WAS LIKE, CAP, DO YOU MIND IF I MAKE A FEW MODIFICATIONS ON YOUR HOVER BIKE? SPIFFY IT UP SOME?
AND HE WAS LIKE, WENDY, YOU GO RIGHT AHEAD.
CAPTAIN AMERICA KNOWS MY NAME! HOW COOL IS THAT?!
BASICALLY SHE MEANS, WE FIXED YOUR BIKE. YOU READY TO ROLL?
DAKOTA NORTH, PRIVATE DETECTIVE. GOOD FRIEND TO HAVE IN A PINCH.
LET'S GET THIS OVER WITH.
THERE'S YOUR STARTER, KILL SWITCH, THAT'S YOUR THROTTLE AND DOWN HERE NEXT TO THE LEFT PEG IS YOUR SHIFT.
YOU THINK YOU CAN HANDLE IT?
DAKOTA, I APPRECIATE THAT YOU ARE A MOTORCYCLE PHENOM AND THAT IS WHY I ASKED YOU TO DO THIS, BUT WITH ALL DUE RESPECT--
I AM A PILOT. IF IT FLIES, I CAN FLY IT.
HOW HARD COULD IT BWAAA
!!--HHHHHHHHHAAAA

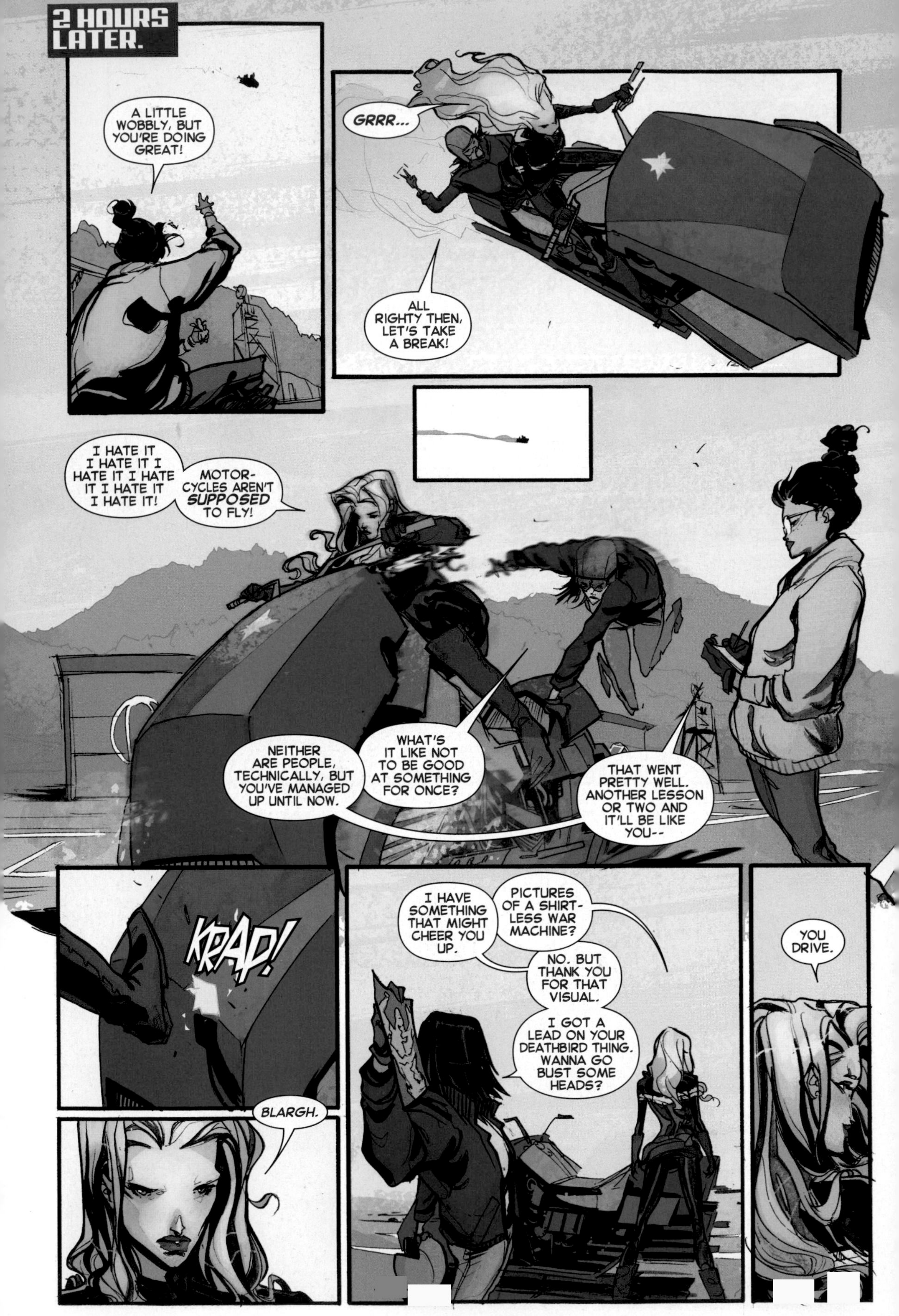
2 HOURS LATER.
A LITTLE WOBBLY, BUT YOU'RE DOING GREAT!
GRRR...
ALL RIGHTY THEN, LET'S TAKE A BREAK!
I HATE IT I HATE IT I HATE IT I HATE IT I HATE IT I HATE IT!
MOTOR-CYCLES AREN'T SUPPOSED TO FLY!
NEITHER ARE PEOPLE, TECHNICALLY, BUT YOU'VE MANAGED UP UNTIL NOW.
WHAT'S IT LIKE NOT TO BE GOOD AT SOMETHING FOR ONCE?
THAT WENT PRETTY WELL. ANOTHER LESSON OR TWO AND IT'LL BE LIKE YOU--
KRAP!
BLARGH.
I HAVE SOMETHING THAT MIGHT CHEER YOU UP.
PICTURES OF A SHIRT-LESS WAR MACHINE?
NO. BUT THANK YOU FOR THAT VISUAL.
I GOT A LEAD ON YOUR DEATHBIRD THING. WANNA GO BUST SOME HEADS?
YOU DRIVE.

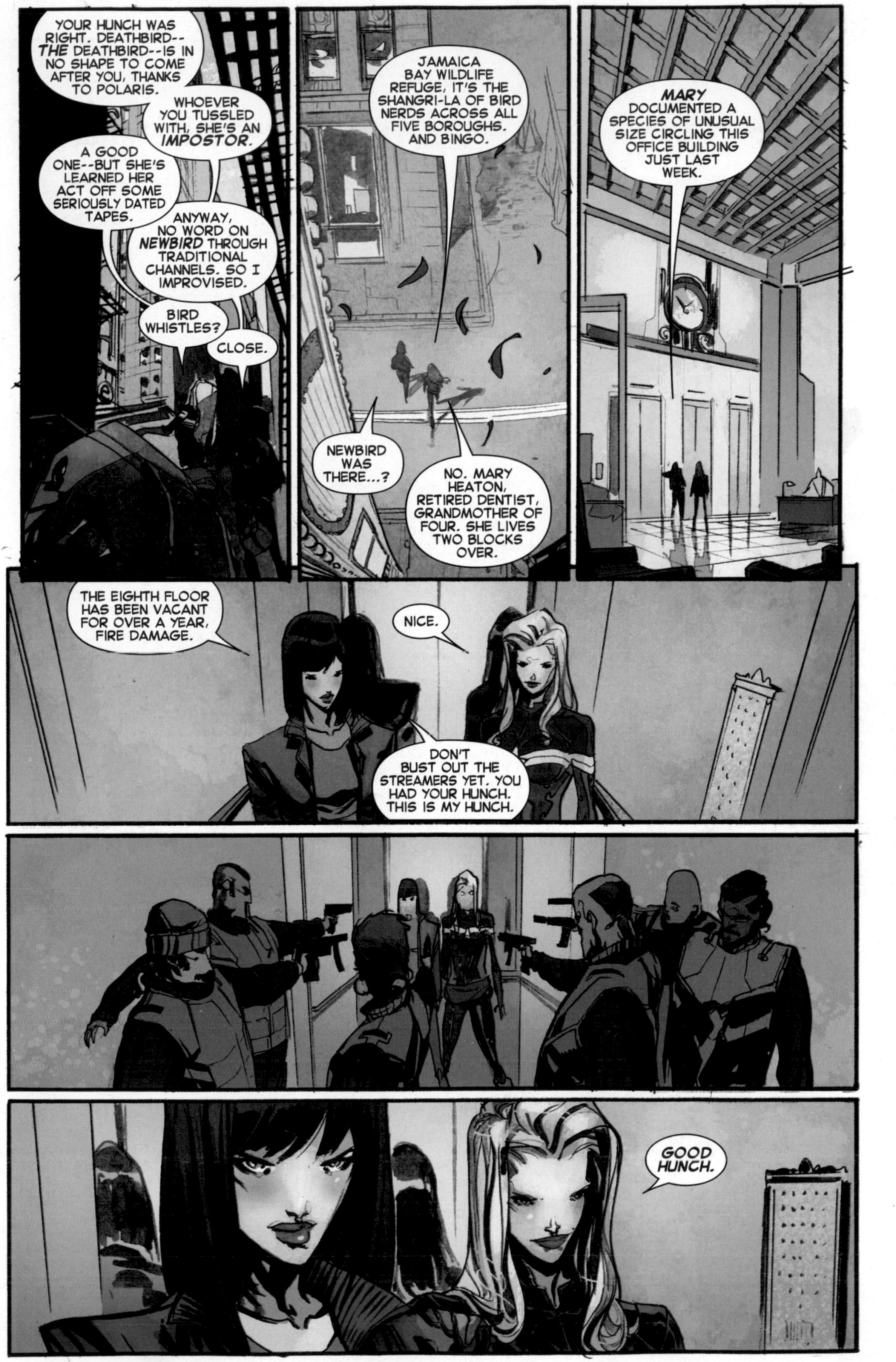
YOUR HUNCH WAS RIGHT. DEATHBIRD-- THE DEATHBIRD--IS IN NO SHAPE TO COME AFTER YOU, THANKS TO POLARIS.
WHOEVER YOU TUSSLED WITH, SHE'S AN IMPOSTOR.
A GOOD ONE--BUT SHE'S LEARNED HER ACT OFF SOME SERIOUSLY DATED TAPES.
ANYWAY, NO WORD ON NEWBIRD THROUGH TRADITIONAL CHANNELS. SO I IMPROVISED.
BIRD WHISTLES?
CLOSE.
JAMAICA BAY WILDLIFE REFUGE, IT'S THE SHANGRI-LA OF BIRD NERDS ACROSS ALL FIVE BOROUGHS. AND BINGO.
NEWBIRD WAS THERE...?
NO. MARY HEATON, RETIRED DENTIST, GRANDMOTHER OF FOUR. SHE LIVES TWO BLOCKS OVER.
MARY DOCUMENTED A SPECIES OF UNUSUAL SIZE CIRCLING THIS OFFICE BUILDING JUST LAST WEEK.
THE EIGHTH FLOOR HAS BEEN VACANT FOR OVER A YEAR, FIRE DAMAGE.
NICE.
DON'T BUST OUT THE STREAMERS YET. YOU HAD YOUR HUNCH. THIS IS MY HUNCH.
GOOD HUNCH.

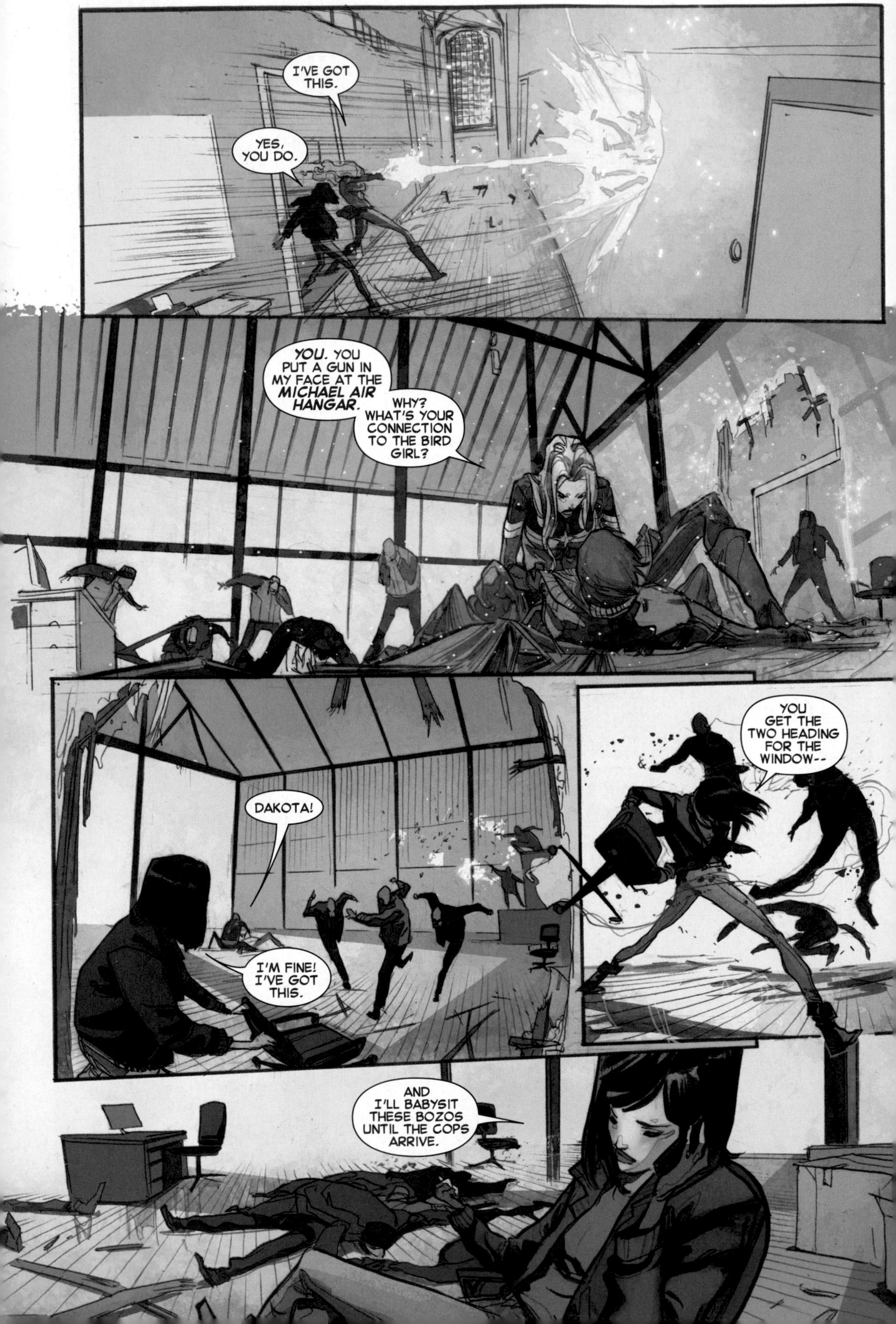
I'VE GOT THIS.
YES, YOU DO.
YOU. YOU PUT A GUN IN MY FACE AT THE *MICHAEL AIR HANGAR*.
WHY? WHAT'S YOUR CONNECTION TO THE BIRD GIRL?
DAKOTA!
I'M FINE! I'VE GOT THIS.
YOU GET THE TWO HEADING FOR THE WINDOW--
AND I'LL BABYSIT THESE BOZOS UNTIL THE COPS ARRIVE.

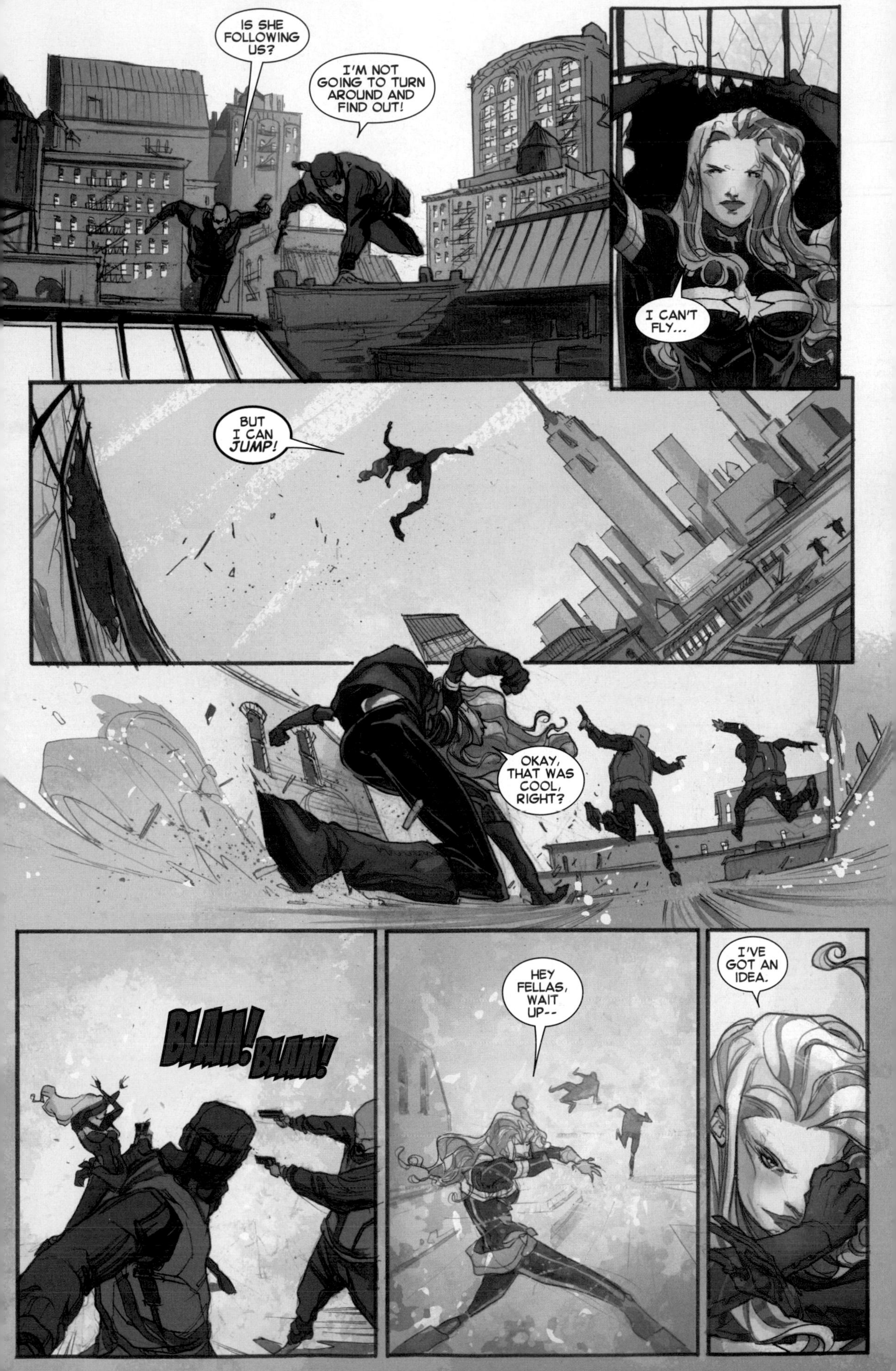
IS SHE FOLLOWING US?
I'M NOT GOING TO TURN AROUND AND FIND OUT!
I CAN'T FLY...
BUT I CAN JUMP!
OKAY, THAT WAS COOL, RIGHT?
BLAM! BLAM!
HEY FELLAS, WAIT UP--
I'VE GOT AN IDEA.

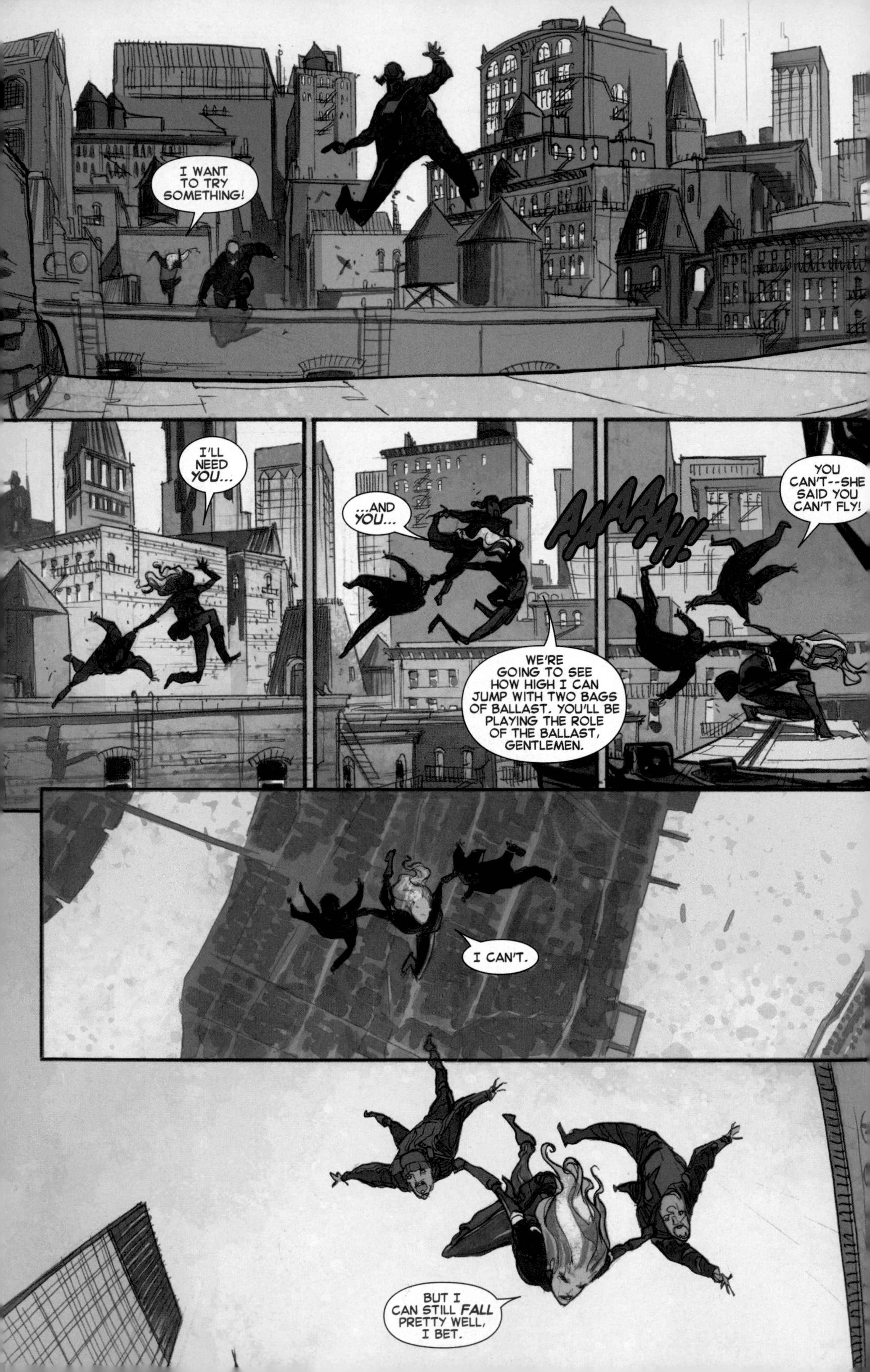
I WANT TO TRY SOMETHING!
I'LL NEED *YOU*...
...AND *YOU*...
WE'RE GOING TO SEE HOW HIGH I CAN JUMP WITH TWO BAGS OF BALLAST. YOU'LL BE PLAYING THE ROLE OF THE BALLAST, GENTLEMEN.
AAAAAH!
YOU CAN'T--SHE SAID YOU CAN'T FLY!
I CAN'T.
BUT I CAN STILL *FALL* PRETTY WELL, I BET.

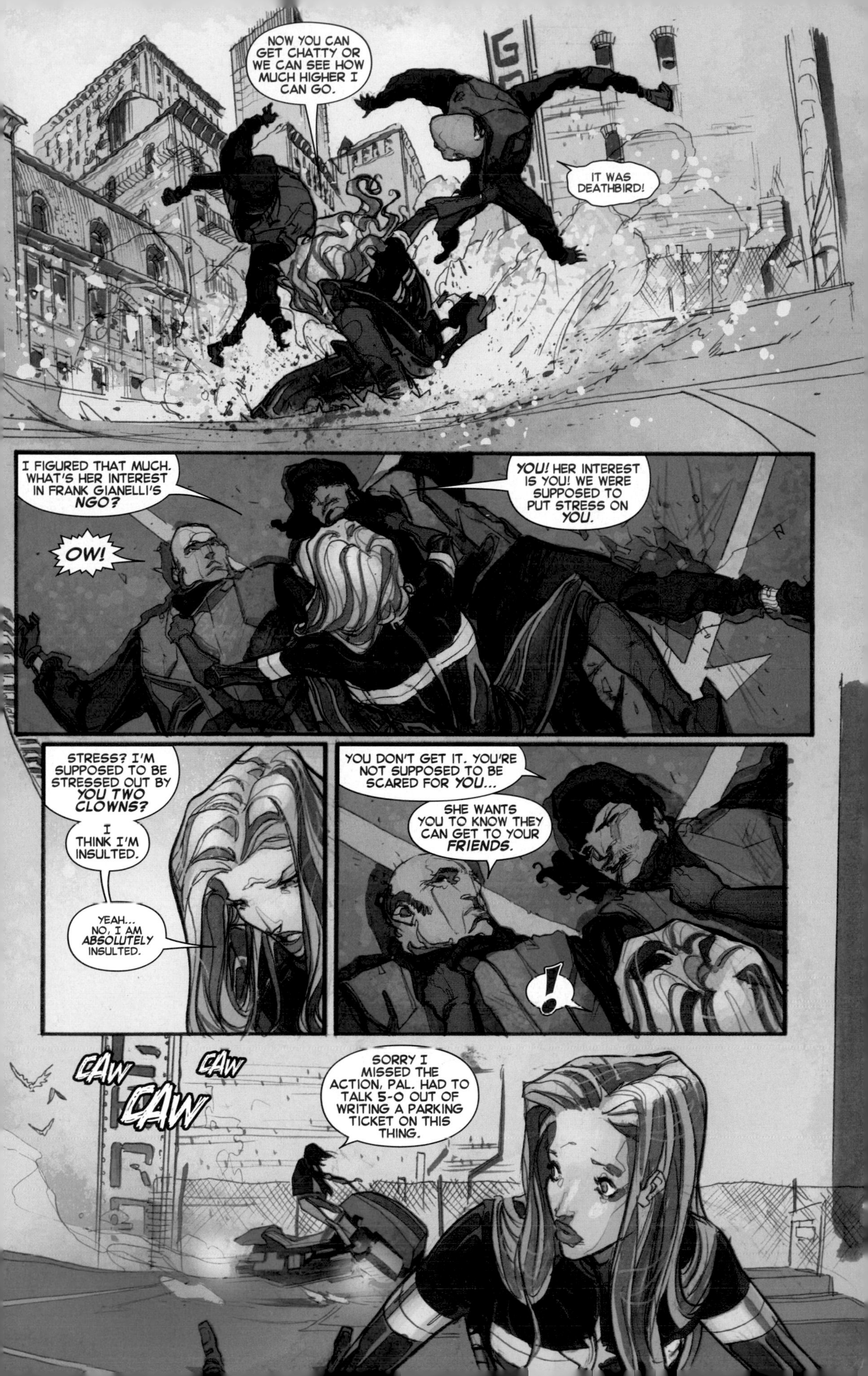
NOW YOU CAN GET CHATTY OR WE CAN SEE HOW MUCH HIGHER I CAN GO.
IT WAS DEATHBIRD!
I FIGURED THAT MUCH. WHAT'S HER INTEREST IN FRANK GIANELLI'S NGO?
YOU! HER INTEREST IS YOU! WE WERE SUPPOSED TO PUT STRESS ON YOU.
OW!
STRESS? I'M SUPPOSED TO BE STRESSED OUT BY YOU TWO CLOWNS?
I THINK I'M INSULTED.
YEAH... NO, I AM ABSOLUTELY INSULTED.
YOU DON'T GET IT. YOU'RE NOT SUPPOSED TO BE SCARED FOR YOU...
SHE WANTS YOU TO KNOW THEY CAN GET TO YOUR FRIENDS.
!
CAW
CAW
CAW
SORRY I MISSED THE ACTION, PAL. HAD TO TALK 5-O OUT OF WRITING A PARKING TICKET ON THIS THING.

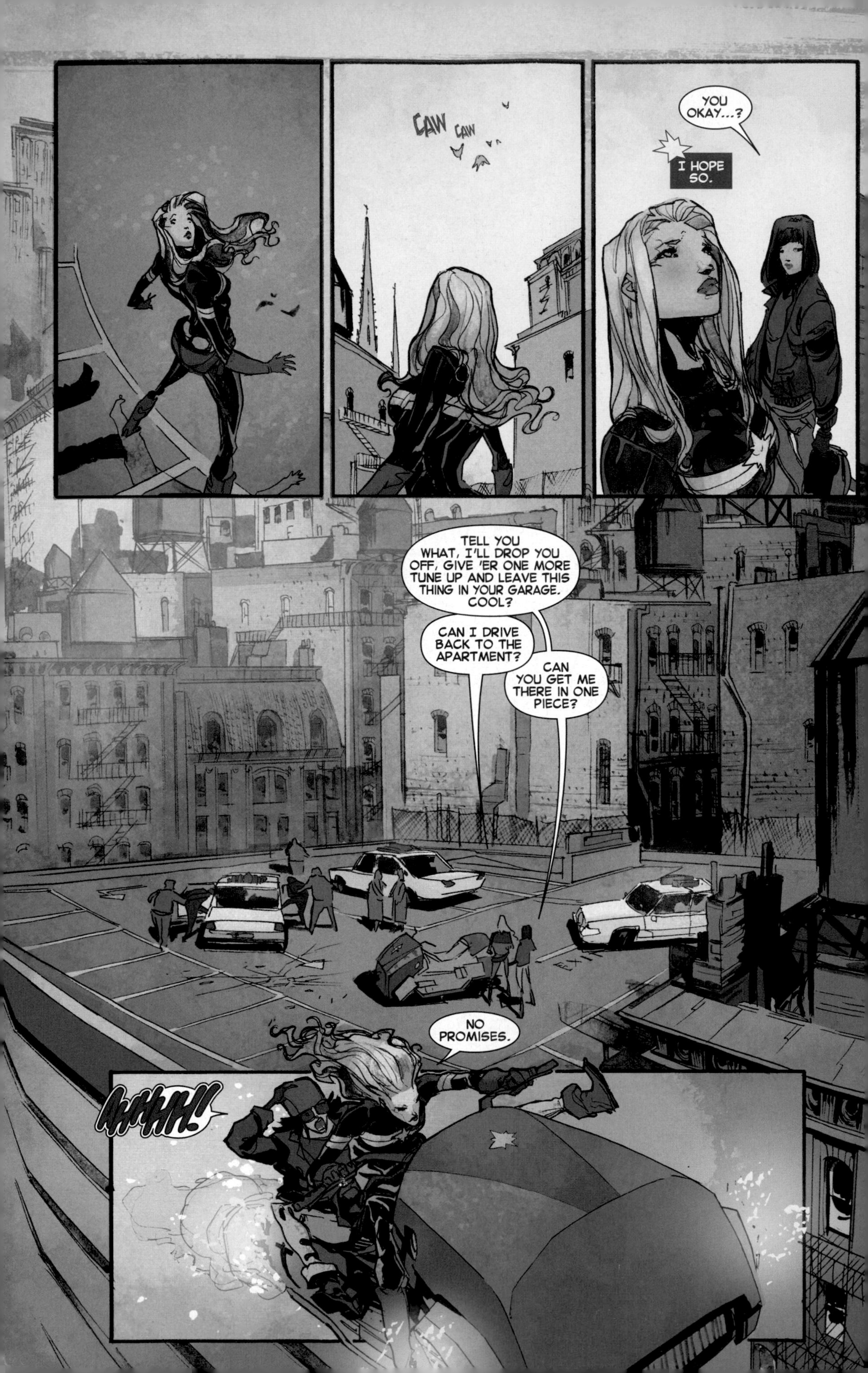
CAW CAW
YOU OKAY...?
I HOPE SO.
TELL YOU WHAT, I'LL DROP YOU OFF, GIVE 'ER ONE MORE TUNE UP AND LEAVE THIS THING IN YOUR GARAGE. COOL?
CAN I DRIVE BACK TO THE APARTMENT?
CAN YOU GET ME THERE IN ONE PIECE?
NO PROMISES.
AHHHH!

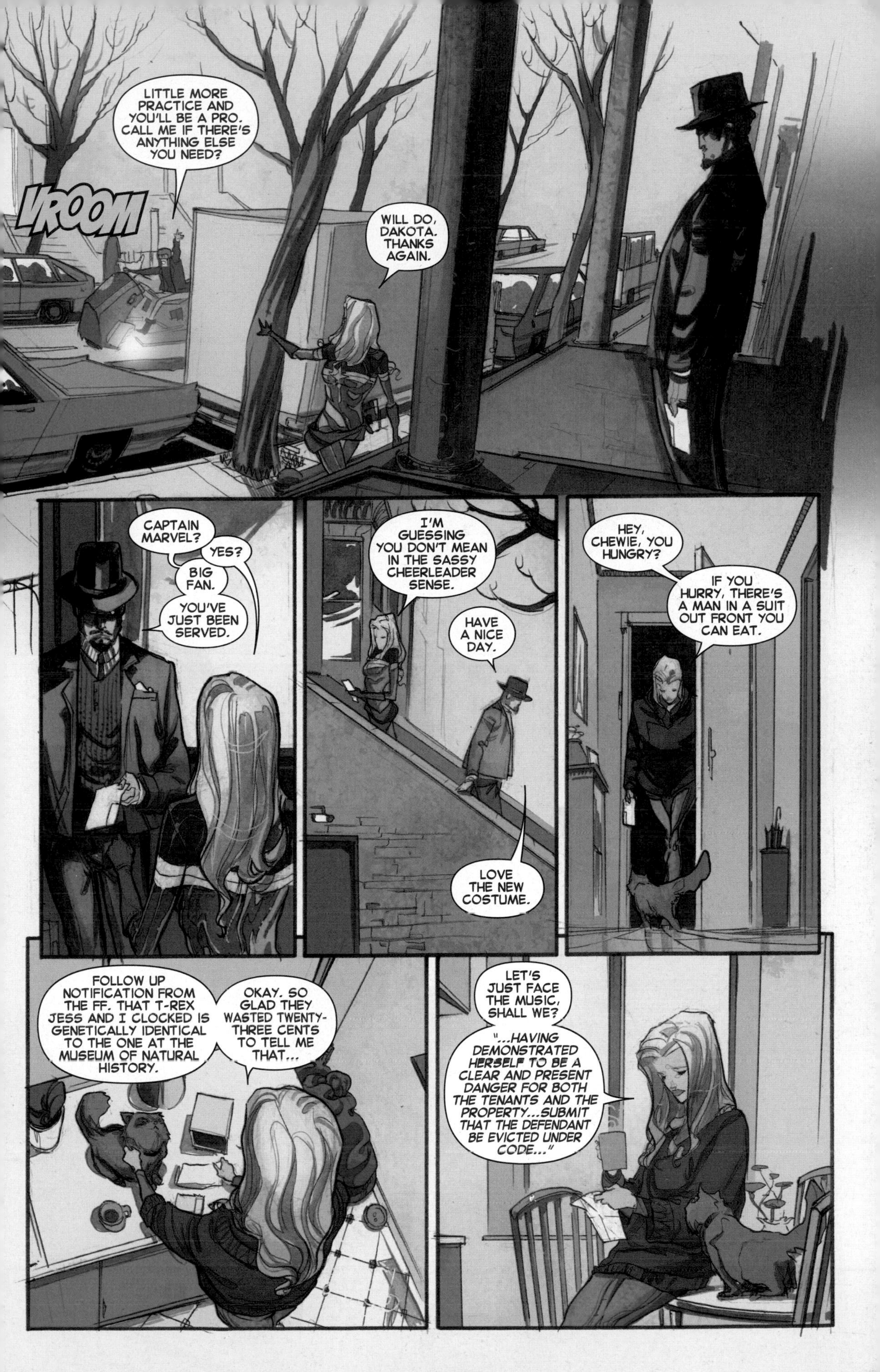
LITTLE MORE PRACTICE AND YOU'LL BE A PRO. CALL ME IF THERE'S ANYTHING ELSE YOU NEED?
VROOM
WILL DO, DAKOTA. THANKS AGAIN.
CAPTAIN MARVEL?
YES?
BIG FAN.
YOU'VE JUST BEEN SERVED.
I'M GUESSING YOU DON'T MEAN IN THE SASSY CHEERLEADER SENSE.
HAVE A NICE DAY.
LOVE THE NEW COSTUME.
HEY, CHEWIE, YOU HUNGRY?
IF YOU HURRY, THERE'S A MAN IN A SUIT OUT FRONT YOU CAN EAT.
FOLLOW UP NOTIFICATION FROM THE FF. THAT T-REX JESS AND I CLOCKED IS GENETICALLY IDENTICAL TO THE ONE AT THE MUSEUM OF NATURAL HISTORY.
OKAY. SO GLAD THEY WASTED TWENTY-THREE CENTS TO TELL ME THAT...
LET'S JUST FACE THE MUSIC, SHALL WE?
"...HAVING DEMONSTRATED HERSELF TO BE A CLEAR AND PRESENT DANGER FOR BOTH THE TENANTS AND THE PROPERTY...SUBMIT THAT THE DEFENDANT BE EVICTED UNDER CODE..."

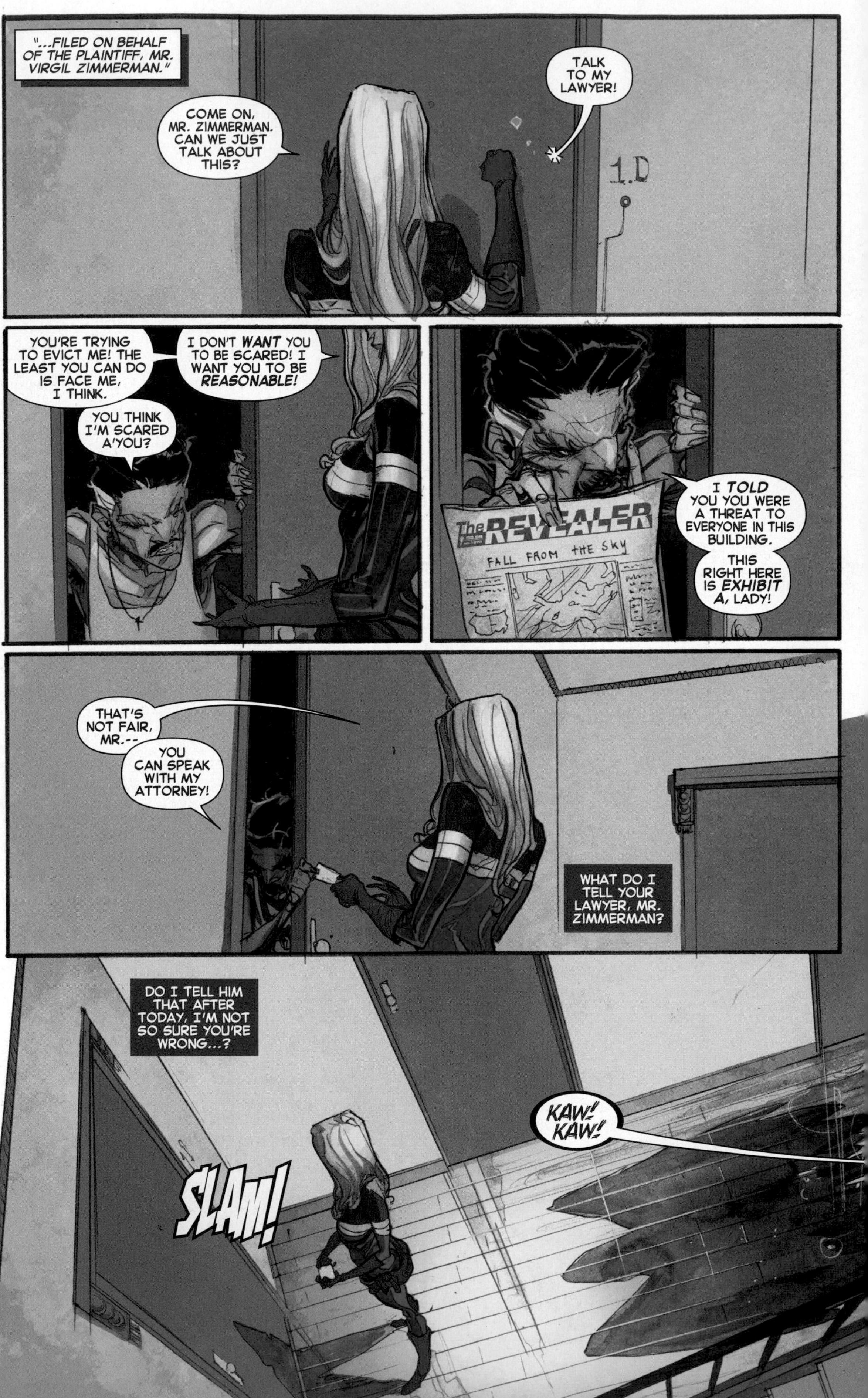
"...FILED ON BEHALF OF THE PLAINTIFF, MR. VIRGIL ZIMMERMAN."
COME ON, MR. ZIMMERMAN. CAN WE JUST TALK ABOUT THIS?
TALK TO MY LAWYER!
1.D
YOU'RE TRYING TO EVICT ME! THE LEAST YOU CAN DO IS FACE ME, I THINK.
I DON'T WANT YOU TO BE SCARED! I WANT YOU TO BE REASONABLE!
YOU THINK I'M SCARED A'YOU?
The REVEALER
FALL FROM THE SKY
I TOLD YOU YOU WERE A THREAT TO EVERYONE IN THIS BUILDING.
THIS RIGHT HERE IS EXHIBIT A, LADY!
THAT'S NOT FAIR, MR.--
YOU CAN SPEAK WITH MY ATTORNEY!
WHAT DO I TELL YOUR LAWYER, MR. ZIMMERMAN?
DO I TELL HIM THAT AFTER TODAY, I'M NOT SO SURE YOU'RE WRONG...?
KAW! KAW!
SLAM!

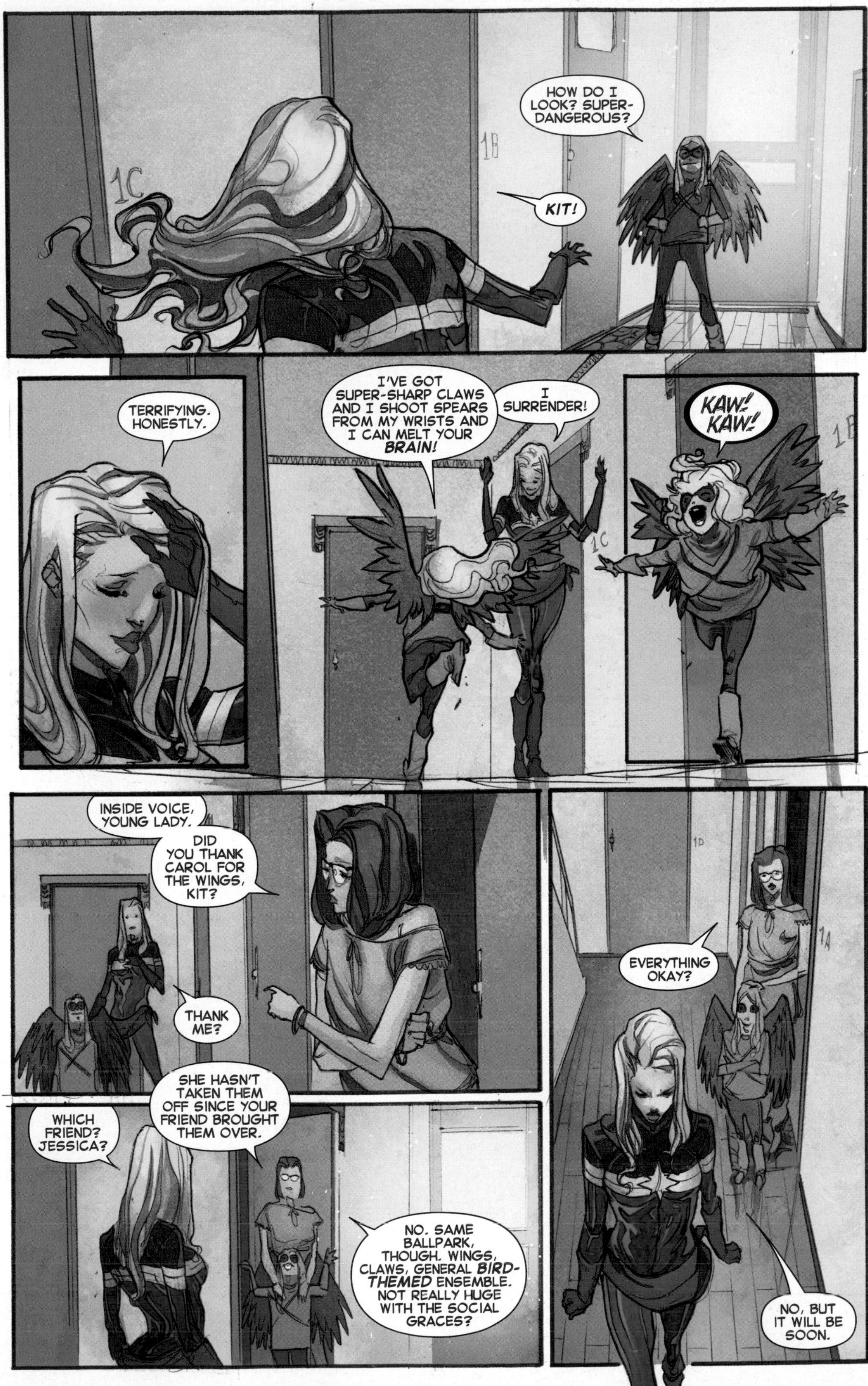

HOW DO I LOOK? SUPER-DANGEROUS?
KIT!
TERRIFYING. HONESTLY.
I'VE GOT SUPER-SHARP CLAWS AND I SHOOT SPEARS FROM MY WRISTS AND I CAN MELT YOUR BRAIN!
I SURRENDER!
KAW! KAW!
INSIDE VOICE, YOUNG LADY.
DID YOU THANK CAROL FOR THE WINGS, KIT?
THANK ME?
SHE HASN'T TAKEN THEM OFF SINCE YOUR FRIEND BROUGHT THEM OVER.
WHICH FRIEND? JESSICA?
NO. SAME BALLPARK, THOUGH. WINGS, CLAWS, GENERAL BIRD-THEMED ENSEMBLE. NOT REALLY HUGE WITH THE SOCIAL GRACES?
EVERYTHING OKAY?
NO, BUT IT WILL BE SOON.

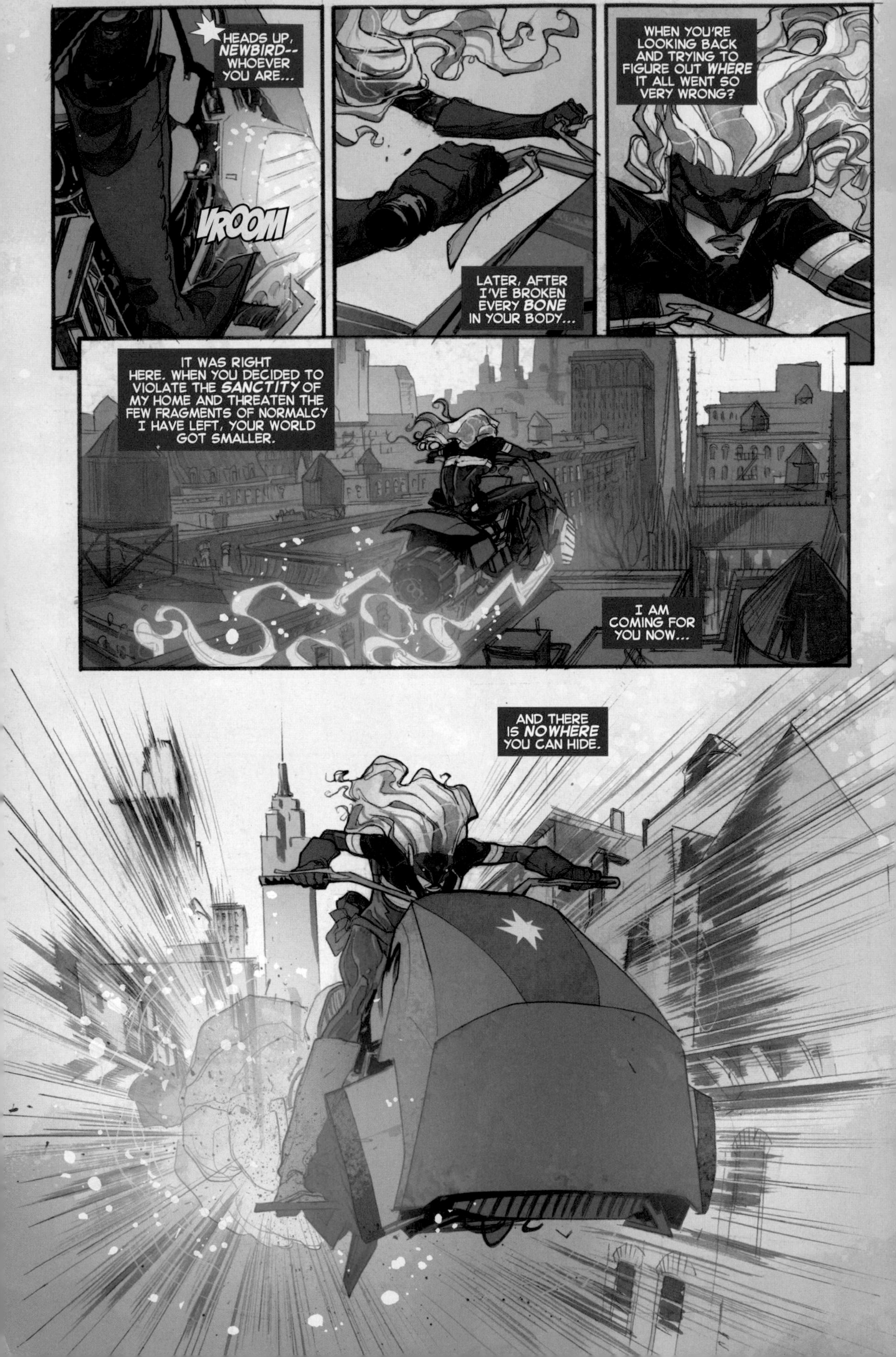
HEADS UP, NEWBIRD-- WHOEVER YOU ARE...
VROOM
LATER, AFTER I'VE BROKEN EVERY BONE IN YOUR BODY...
WHEN YOU'RE LOOKING BACK AND TRYING TO FIGURE OUT WHERE IT ALL WENT SO VERY WRONG?
IT WAS RIGHT HERE. WHEN YOU DECIDED TO VIOLATE THE SANCTITY OF MY HOME AND THREATEN THE FEW FRAGMENTS OF NORMALCY I HAVE LEFT, YOUR WORLD GOT SMALLER.
I AM COMING FOR YOU NOW...
AND THERE IS NOWHERE YOU CAN HIDE.

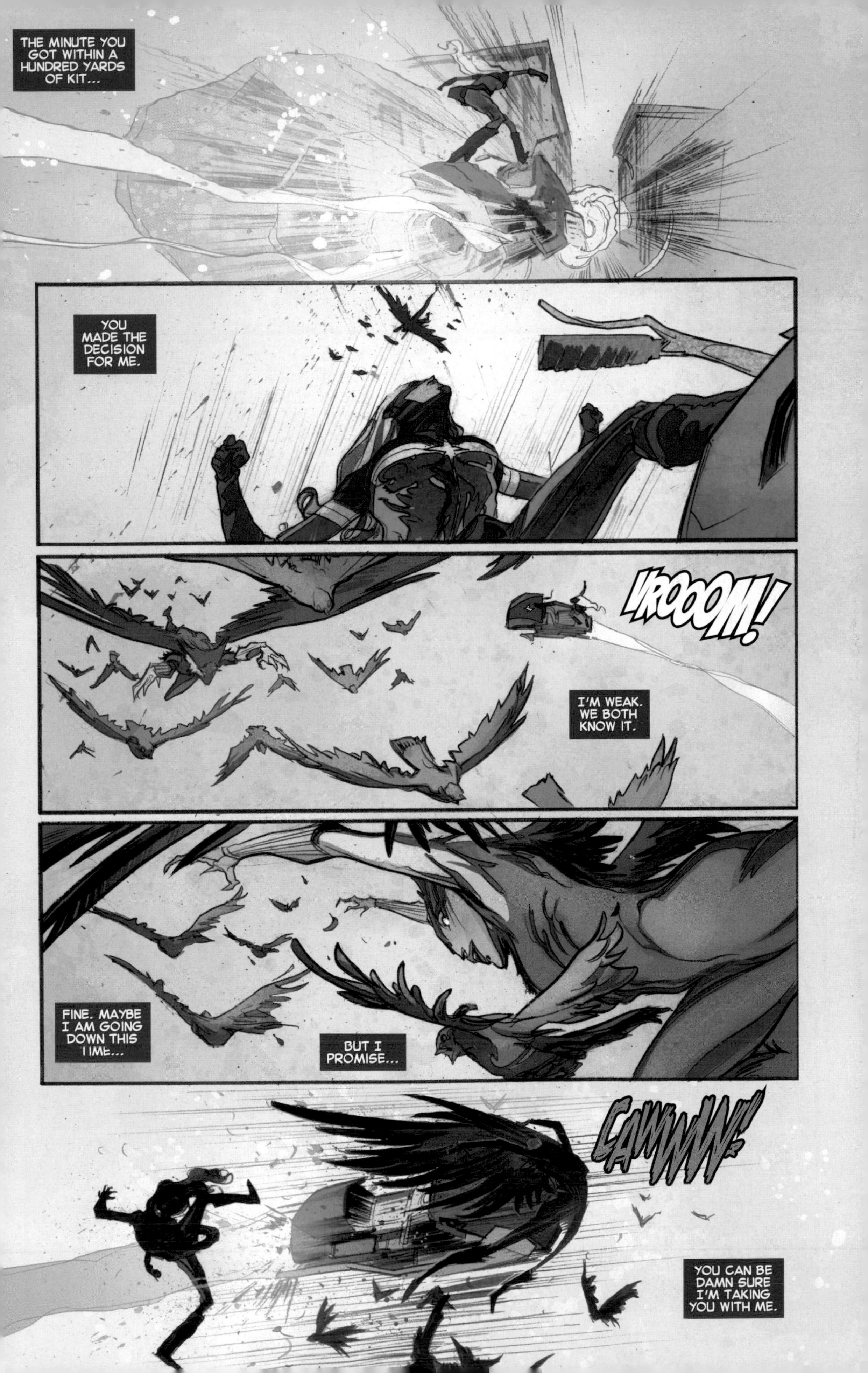
THE MINUTE YOU GOT WITHIN A HUNDRED YARDS OF KIT...
YOU MADE THE DECISION FOR ME.
VROOOM!
I'M WEAK. WE BOTH KNOW IT.
FINE. MAYBE I AM GOING DOWN THIS TIME...
BUT I PROMISE...
CAWWW!
YOU CAN BE DAMN SURE I'M TAKING YOU WITH ME.

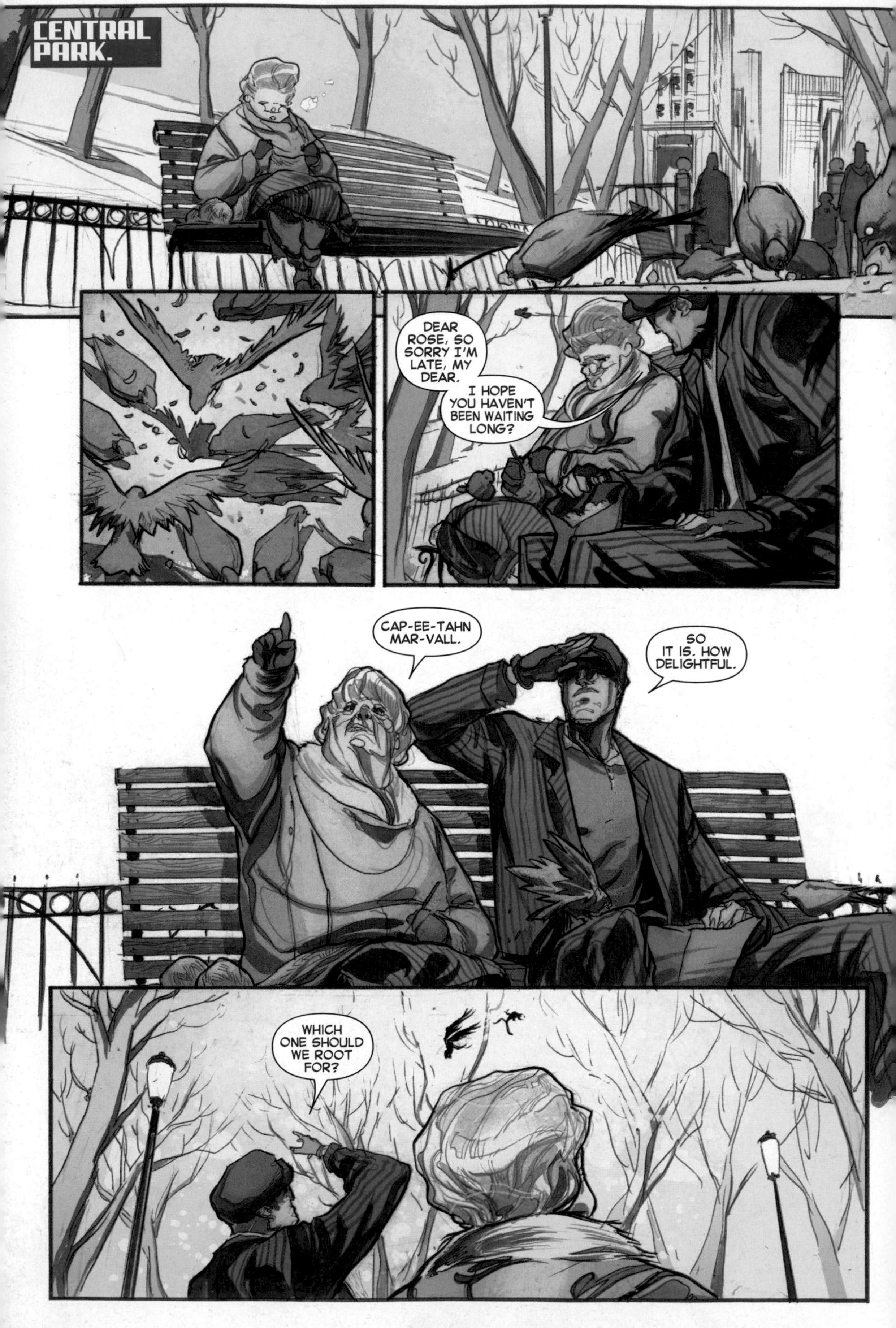
CENTRAL PARK.
DEAR ROSE, SO SORRY I'M LATE, MY DEAR.
I HOPE YOU HAVEN'T BEEN WAITING LONG?
CAP-EE-TAHN MAR-VALL.
SO IT IS. HOW DELIGHTFUL.
WHICH ONE SHOULD WE ROOT FOR?

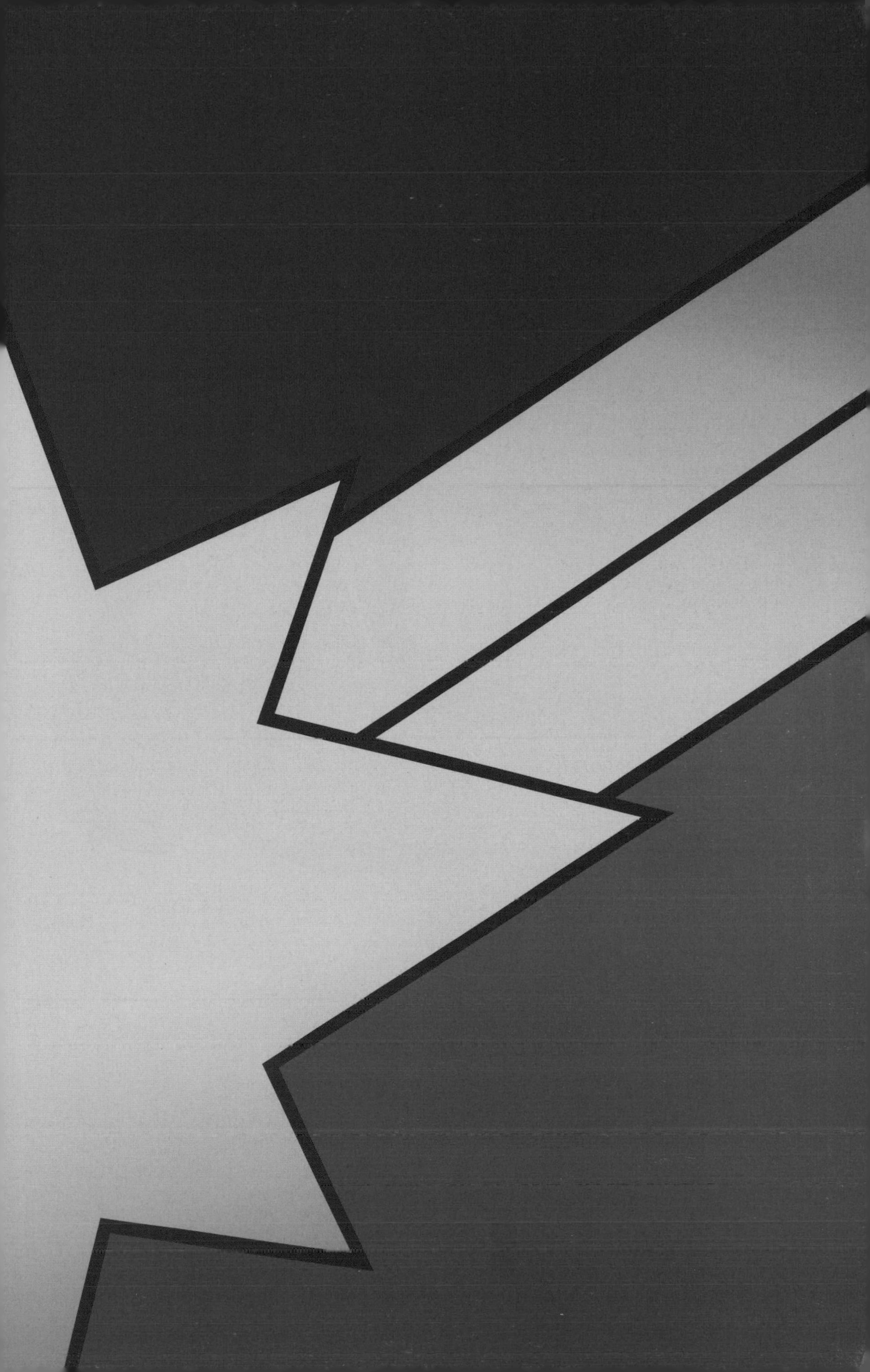

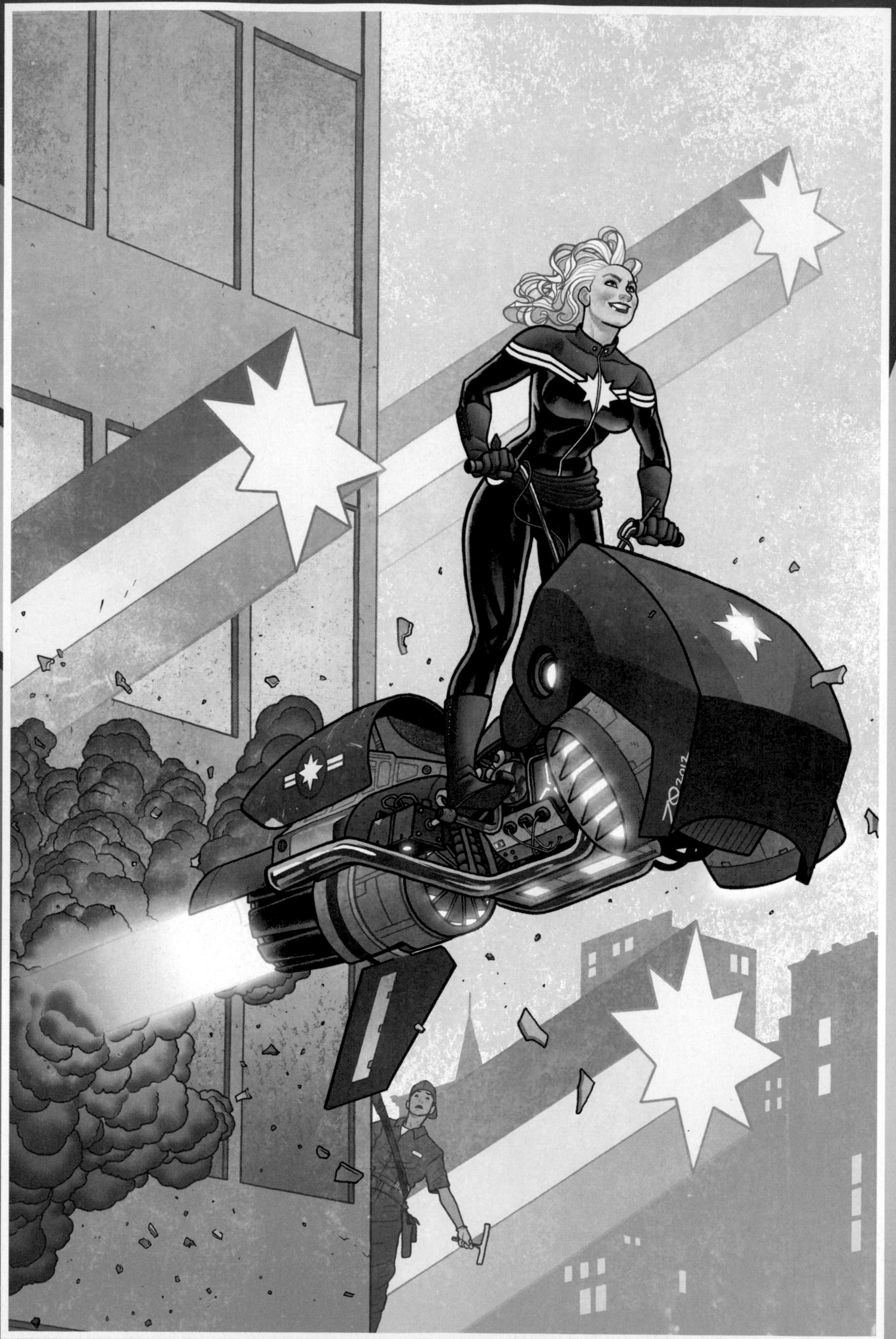

TWELVE

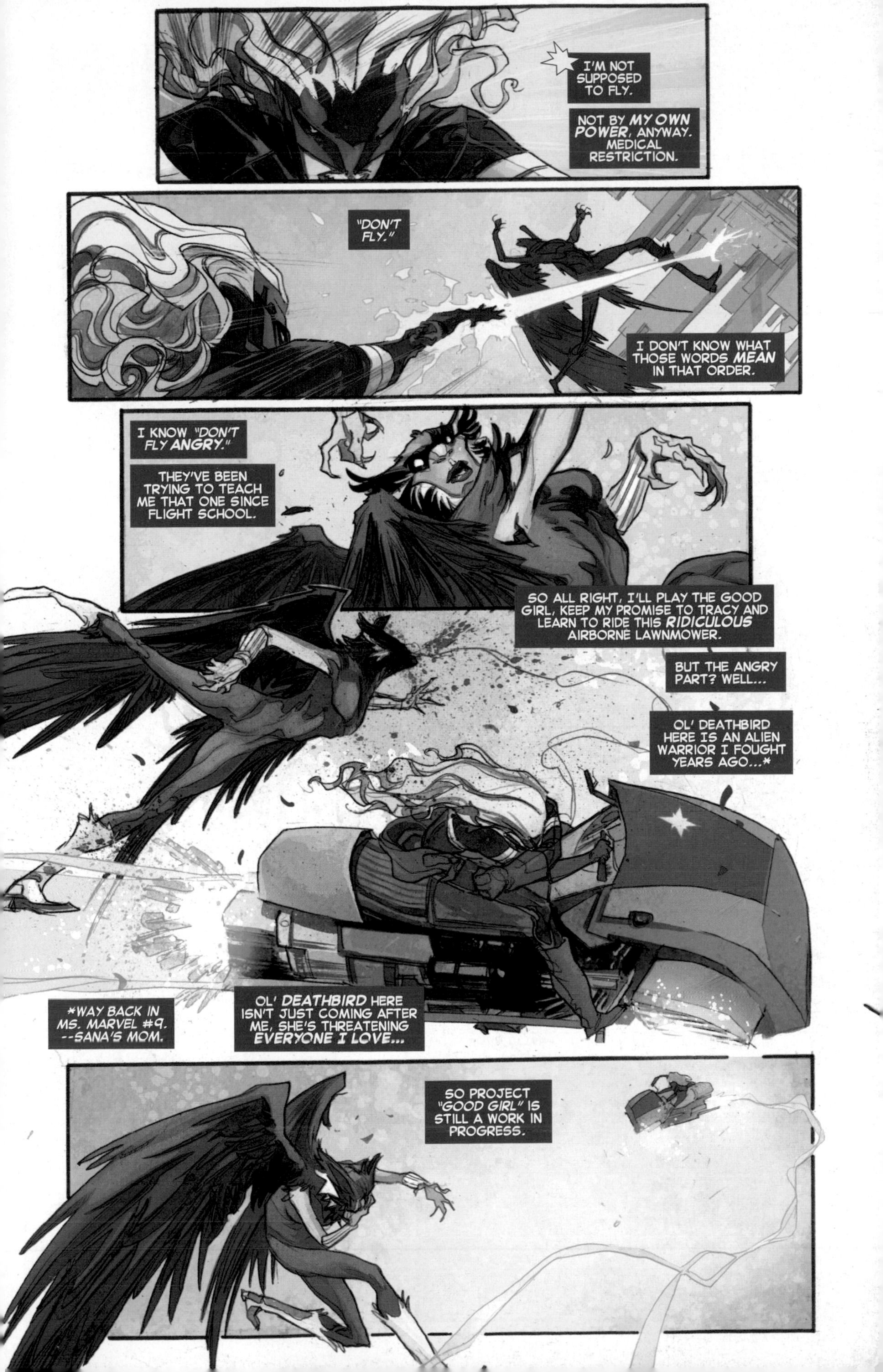
I'M NOT SUPPOSED TO FLY.
NOT BY MY OWN POWER, ANYWAY. MEDICAL RESTRICTION.
"DON'T FLY."
I DON'T KNOW WHAT THOSE WORDS MEAN IN THAT ORDER.
I KNOW "DON'T FLY ANGRY."
THEY'VE BEEN TRYING TO TEACH ME THAT ONE SINCE FLIGHT SCHOOL.
SO ALL RIGHT, I'LL PLAY THE GOOD GIRL, KEEP MY PROMISE TO TRACY AND LEARN TO RIDE THIS RIDICULOUS AIRBORNE LAWNMOWER.
BUT THE ANGRY PART? WELL...
OL' DEATHBIRD HERE IS AN ALIEN WARRIOR I FOUGHT YEARS AGO...*
*WAY BACK IN MS. MARVEL #9. --SANA'S MOM.
OL' DEATHBIRD HERE ISN'T JUST COMING AFTER ME, SHE'S THREATENING EVERYONE I LOVE...
SO PROJECT "GOOD GIRL" IS STILL A WORK IN PROGRESS.

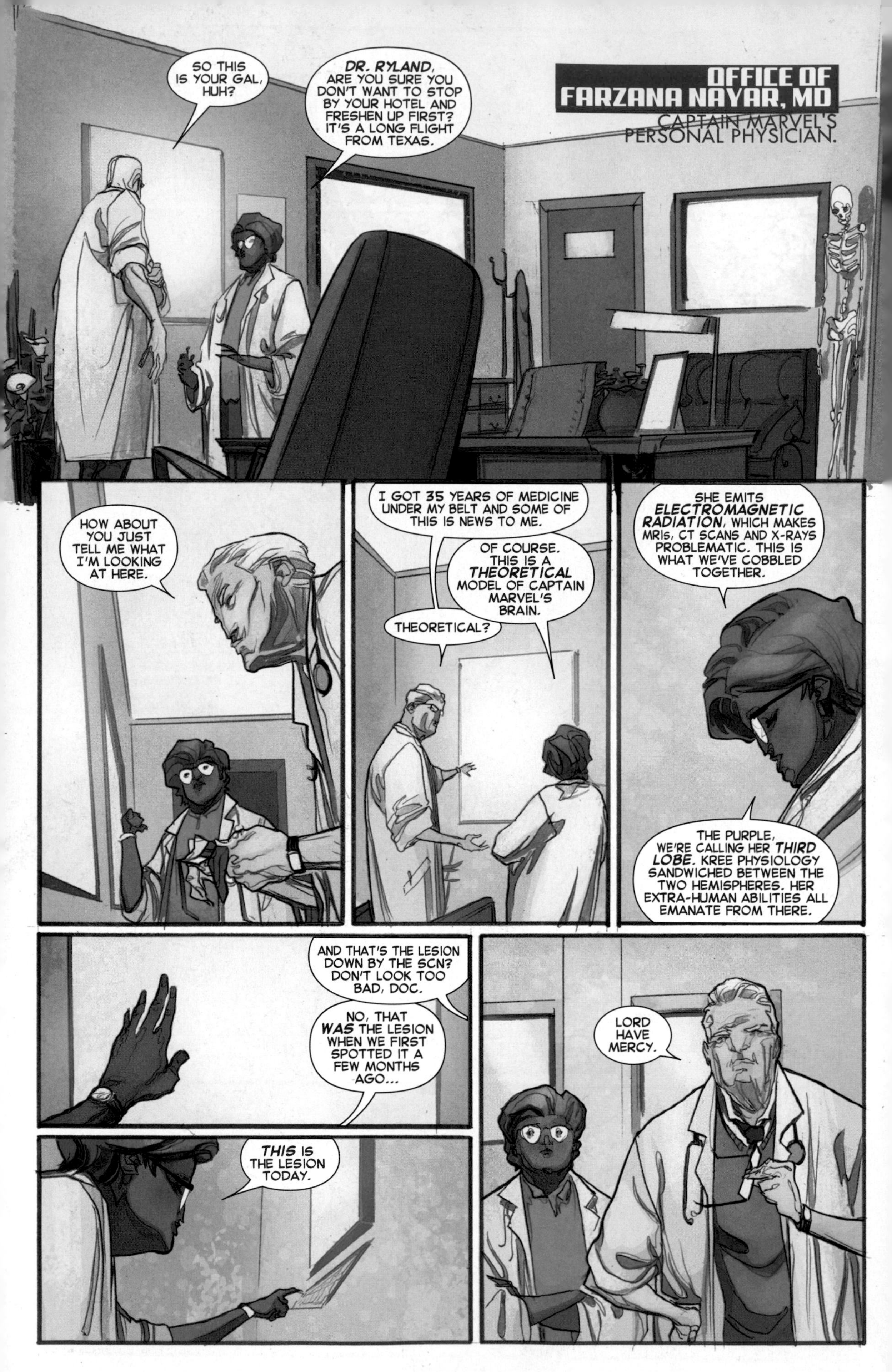
OFFICE OF FARZANA NAYAR, MD
CAPTAIN MARVEL'S PERSONAL PHYSICIAN.
SO THIS IS YOUR GAL, HUH?
DR. RYLAND, ARE YOU SURE YOU DON'T WANT TO STOP BY YOUR HOTEL AND FRESHEN UP FIRST? IT'S A LONG FLIGHT FROM TEXAS.
HOW ABOUT YOU JUST TELL ME WHAT I'M LOOKING AT HERE.
I GOT 35 YEARS OF MEDICINE UNDER MY BELT AND SOME OF THIS IS NEWS TO ME.
OF COURSE. THIS IS A THEORETICAL MODEL OF CAPTAIN MARVEL'S BRAIN.
THEORETICAL?
SHE EMITS ELECTROMAGNETIC RADIATION, WHICH MAKES MRIs, CT SCANS AND X-RAYS PROBLEMATIC. THIS IS WHAT WE'VE COBBLED TOGETHER.
THE PURPLE, WE'RE CALLING HER THIRD LOBE. KREE PHYSIOLOGY SANDWICHED BETWEEN THE TWO HEMISPHERES. HER EXTRA-HUMAN ABILITIES ALL EMANATE FROM THERE.
AND THAT'S THE LESION DOWN BY THE SCN? DON'T LOOK TOO BAD, DOC.
NO, THAT WAS THE LESION WHEN WE FIRST SPOTTED IT A FEW MONTHS AGO...
THIS IS THE LESION TODAY.
LORD HAVE MERCY.

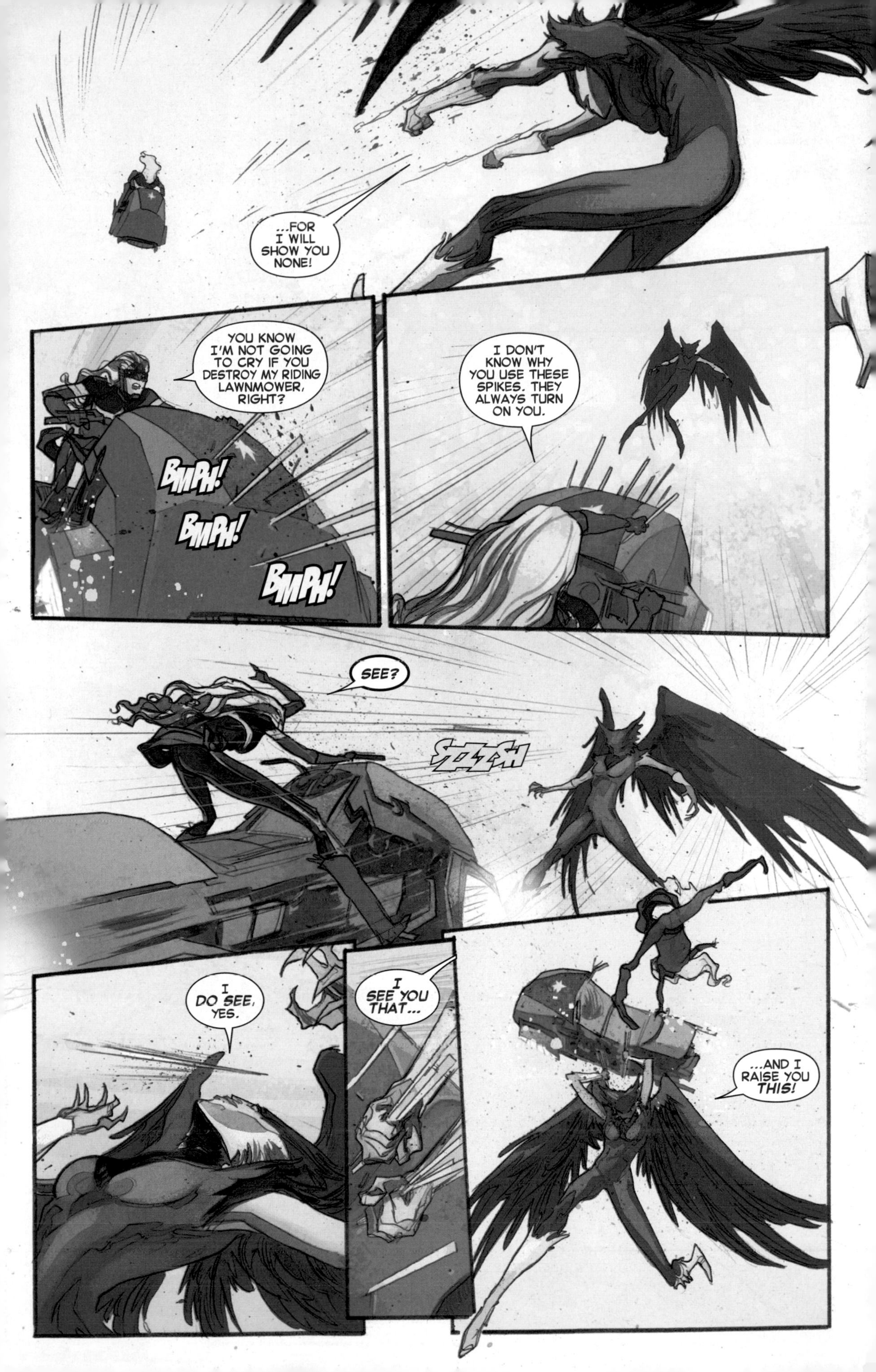
...FOR I WILL SHOW YOU NONE!
YOU KNOW I'M NOT GOING TO CRY IF YOU DESTROY MY RIDING LAWNMOWER, RIGHT?
BMPH!
BMPH!
BMPH!
I DON'T KNOW WHY YOU USE THESE SPIKES. THEY ALWAYS TURN ON YOU.
SEE?
SHZSH
I DO SEE, YES.
I SEE YOU THAT...
...AND I RAISE YOU THIS!

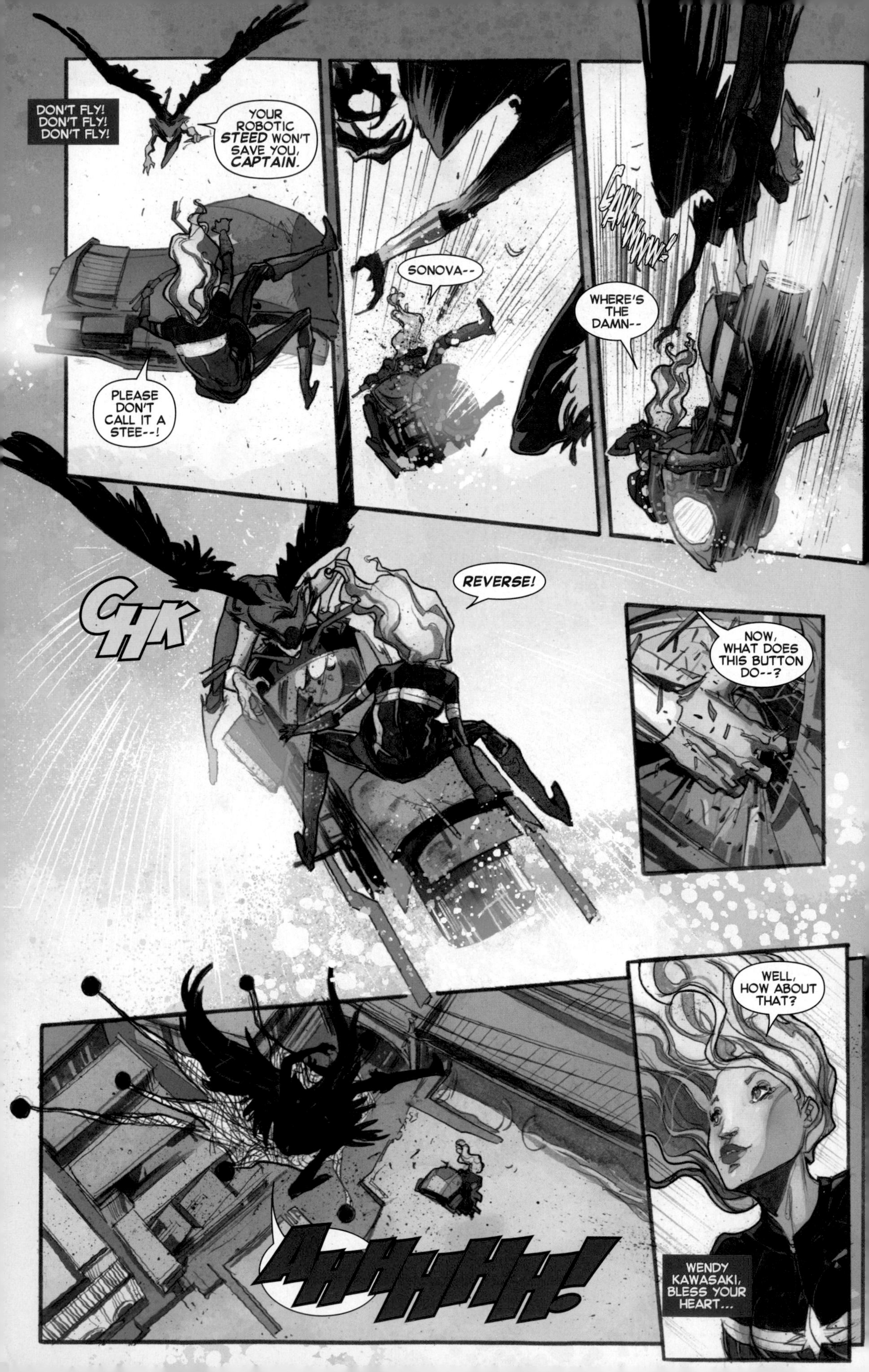

DON'T FLY! DON'T FLY! DON'T FLY!
YOUR ROBOTIC STEED WON'T SAVE YOU, CAPTAIN.
PLEASE DON'T CALL IT A STEE--!
SONOVA--
CAWWWW!
WHERE'S THE DAMN--
CHK
REVERSE!
NOW, WHAT DOES THIS BUTTON DO--?
AHHHHHH!
WELL, HOW ABOUT THAT?
WENDY KAWASAKI, BLESS YOUR HEART...

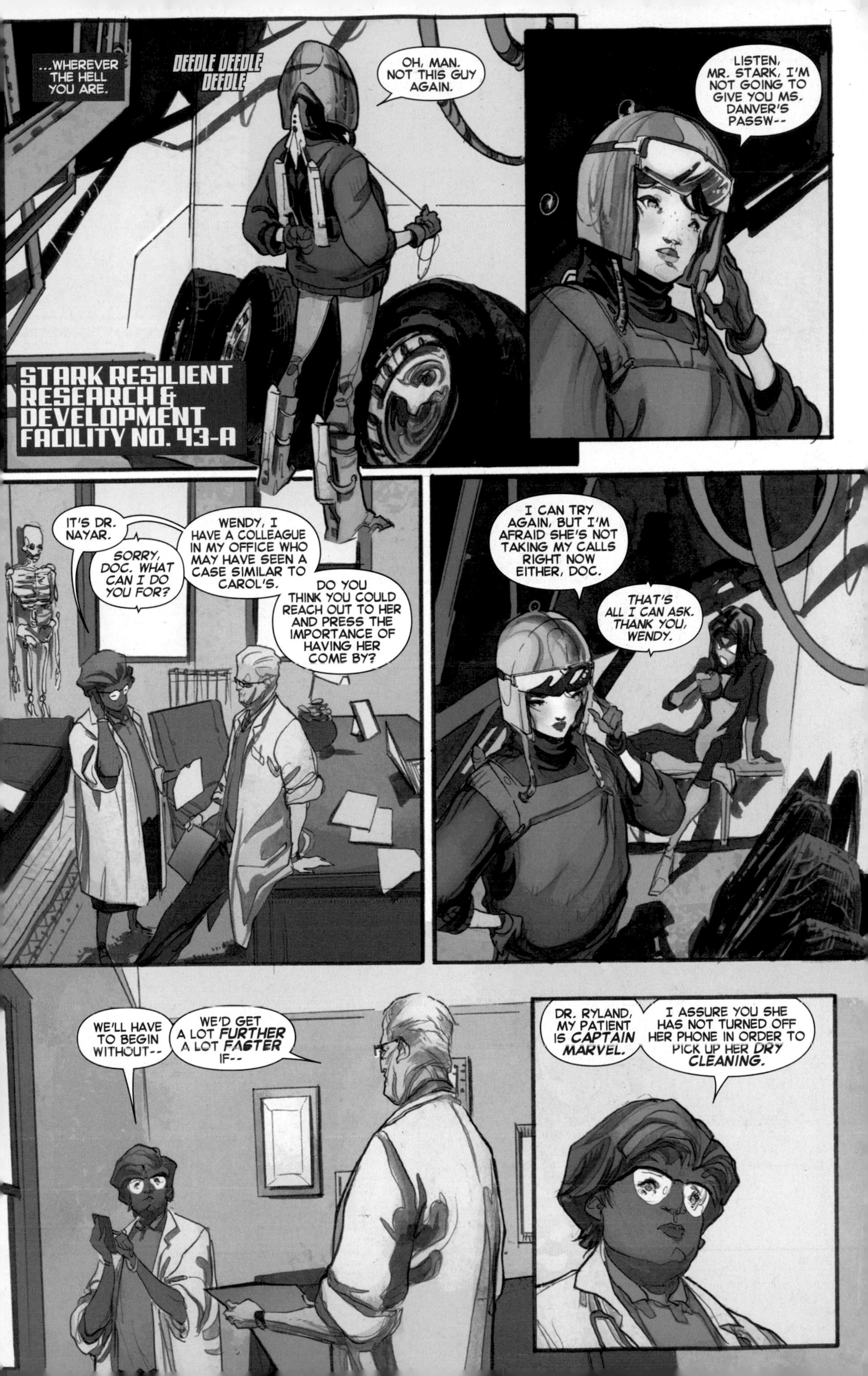
...WHEREVER THE HELL YOU ARE.
DEEDLE DEEDLE DEEDLE
OH, MAN. NOT THIS GUY AGAIN.
STARK RESILIENT RESEARCH & DEVELOPMENT FACILITY NO. 43-A
LISTEN, MR. STARK, I'M NOT GOING TO GIVE YOU MS. DANVER'S PASSW--
IT'S DR. NAYAR.
SORRY, DOC. WHAT CAN I DO YOU FOR?
WENDY, I HAVE A COLLEAGUE IN MY OFFICE WHO MAY HAVE SEEN A CASE SIMILAR TO CAROL'S.
DO YOU THINK YOU COULD REACH OUT TO HER AND PRESS THE IMPORTANCE OF HAVING HER COME BY?
I CAN TRY AGAIN, BUT I'M AFRAID SHE'S NOT TAKING MY CALLS RIGHT NOW EITHER, DOC.
THAT'S ALL I CAN ASK. THANK YOU, WENDY.
WE'LL HAVE TO BEGIN WITHOUT--
WE'D GET A LOT FURTHER A LOT FASTER IF--
DR. RYLAND, MY PATIENT IS CAPTAIN MARVEL.
I ASSURE YOU SHE HAS NOT TURNED OFF HER PHONE IN ORDER TO PICK UP HER DRY CLEANING.

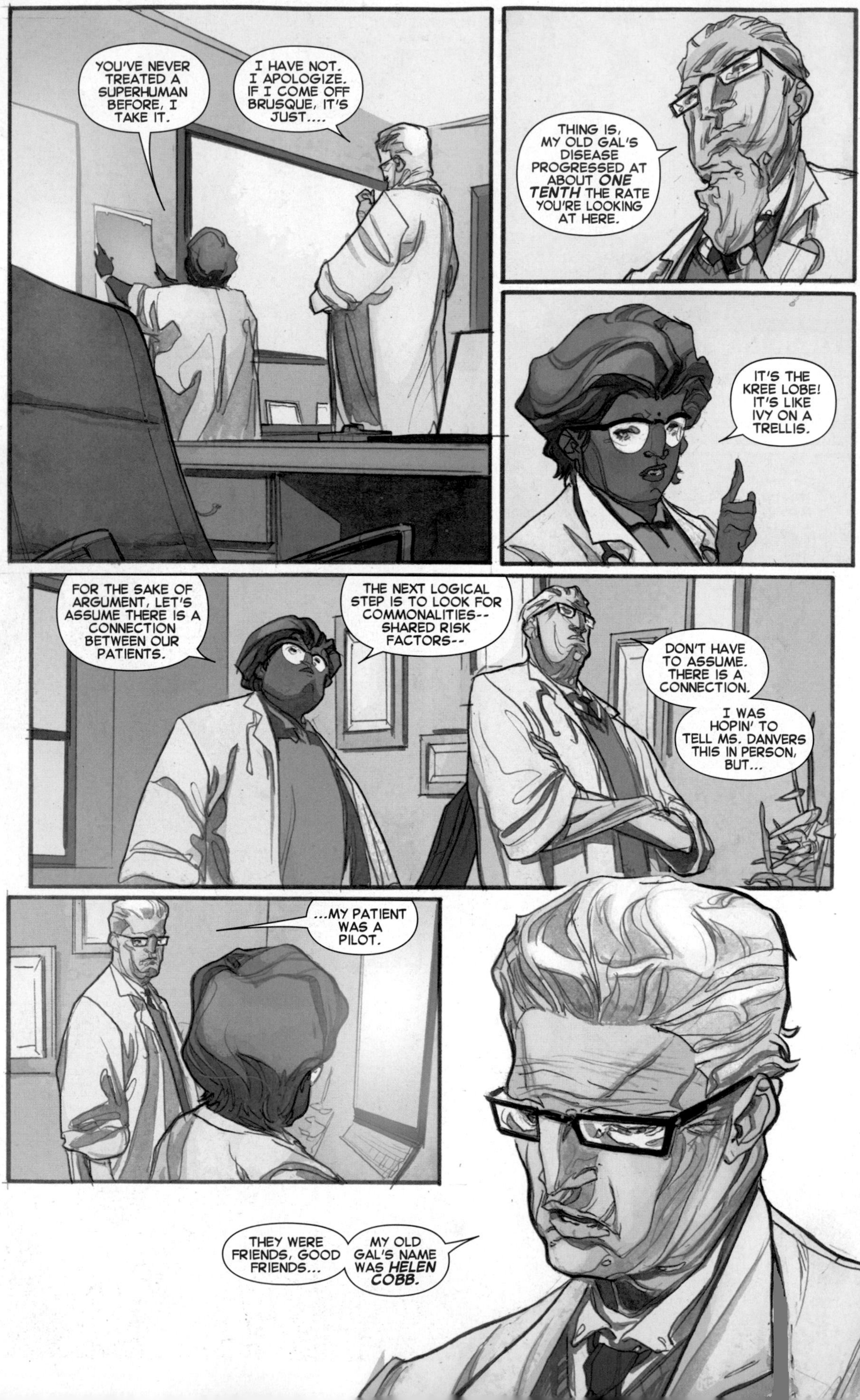
YOU'VE NEVER TREATED A SUPERHUMAN BEFORE, I TAKE IT.
I HAVE NOT. I APOLOGIZE. IF I COME OFF BRUSQUE, IT'S JUST....
THING IS, MY OLD GAL'S DISEASE PROGRESSED AT ABOUT ONE TENTH THE RATE YOU'RE LOOKING AT HERE.
IT'S THE KREE LOBE! IT'S LIKE IVY ON A TRELLIS.
FOR THE SAKE OF ARGUMENT, LET'S ASSUME THERE IS A CONNECTION BETWEEN OUR PATIENTS.
THE NEXT LOGICAL STEP IS TO LOOK FOR COMMONALITIES-- SHARED RISK FACTORS--
DON'T HAVE TO ASSUME. THERE IS A CONNECTION.
I WAS HOPIN' TO TELL MS. DANVERS THIS IN PERSON, BUT...
...MY PATIENT WAS A PILOT.
THEY WERE FRIENDS, GOOD FRIENDS...
MY OLD GAL'S NAME WAS HELEN COBB.

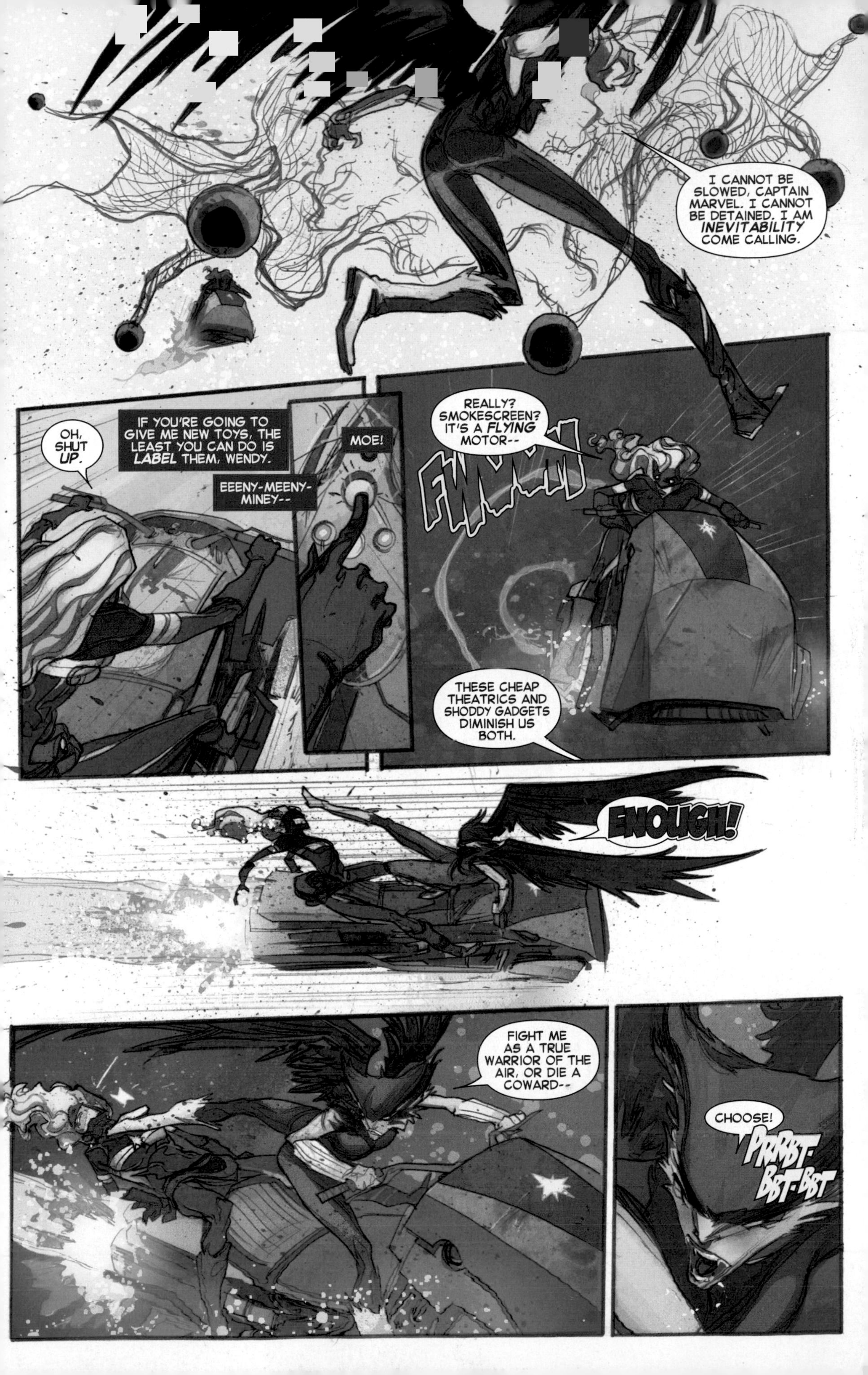
I CANNOT BE SLOWED, CAPTAIN MARVEL. I CANNOT BE DETAINED. I AM INEVITABILITY COME CALLING.
OH, SHUT UP.
IF YOU'RE GOING TO GIVE ME NEW TOYS, THE LEAST YOU CAN DO IS LABEL THEM, WENDY.
EEENY-MEENY-MINEY--
MOE!
REALLY? SMOKESCREEN? IT'S A FLYING MOTOR--
FWOOM
THESE CHEAP THEATRICS AND SHODDY GADGETS DIMINISH US BOTH.
ENOUGH!
FIGHT ME AS A TRUE WARRIOR OF THE AIR, OR DIE A COWARD--
CHOOSE!
PRRRBT-BBT-BBT

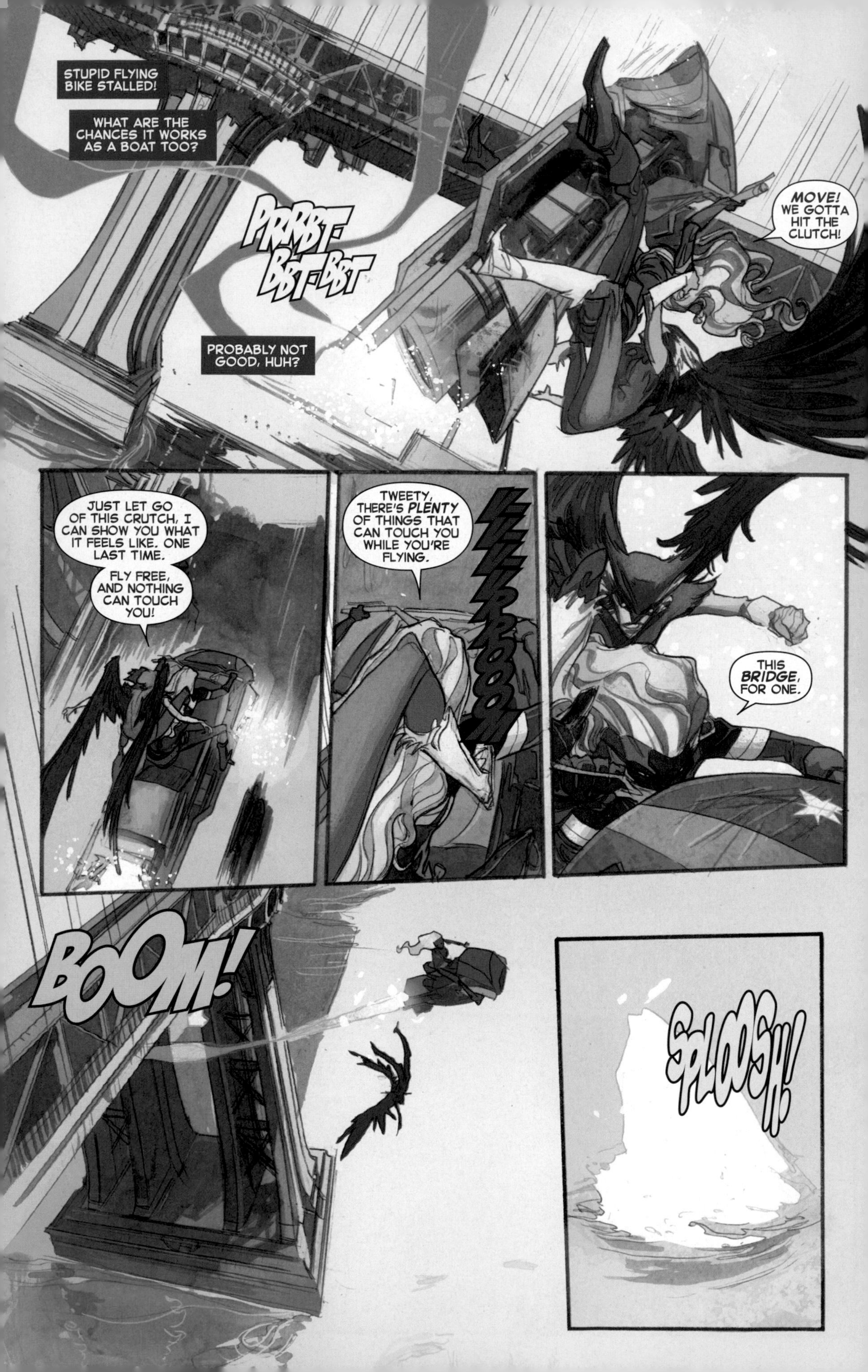
STUPID FLYING BIKE STALLED!
WHAT ARE THE CHANCES IT WORKS AS A BOAT TOO?
PRRBT-BBT-BBT
PROBABLY NOT GOOD, HUH?
MOVE! WE GOTTA HIT THE CLUTCH!
JUST LET GO OF THIS CRUTCH, I CAN SHOW YOU WHAT IT FEELS LIKE. ONE LAST TIME.
FLY FREE, AND NOTHING CAN TOUCH YOU!
TWEETY, THERE'S PLENTY OF THINGS THAT CAN TOUCH YOU WHILE YOU'RE FLYING.
THIS BRIDGE, FOR ONE.
BOOM!
SPLOOSH!

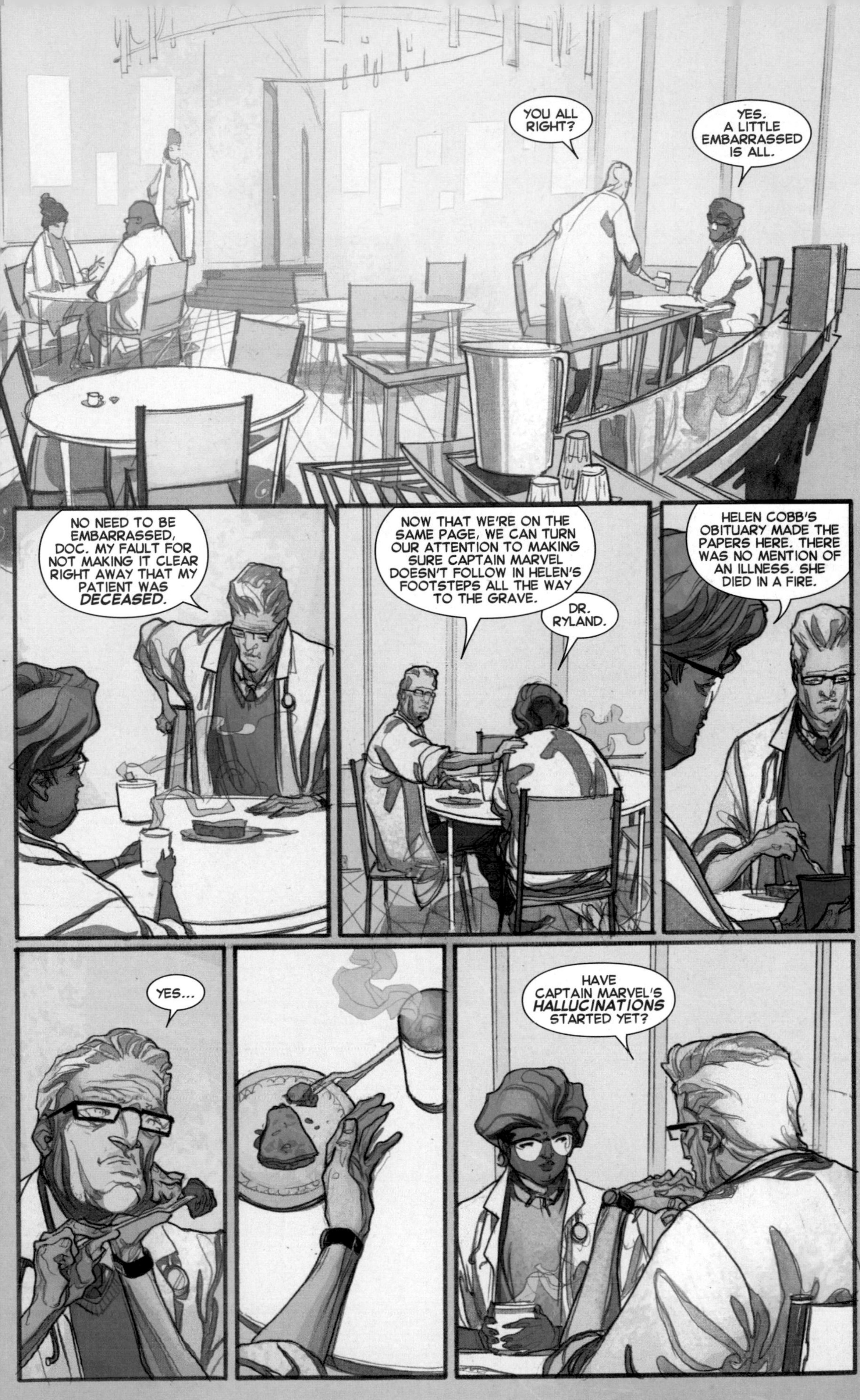
YOU ALL RIGHT?
YES. A LITTLE EMBARRASSED IS ALL.
NO NEED TO BE EMBARRASSED, DOC. MY FAULT FOR NOT MAKING IT CLEAR RIGHT AWAY THAT MY PATIENT WAS DECEASED.
NOW THAT WE'RE ON THE SAME PAGE, WE CAN TURN OUR ATTENTION TO MAKING SURE CAPTAIN MARVEL DOESN'T FOLLOW IN HELEN'S FOOTSTEPS ALL THE WAY TO THE GRAVE.
DR. RYLAND.
HELEN COBB'S OBITUARY MADE THE PAPERS HERE. THERE WAS NO MENTION OF AN ILLNESS. SHE DIED IN A FIRE.
YES...
HAVE CAPTAIN MARVEL'S HALLUCINATIONS STARTED YET?

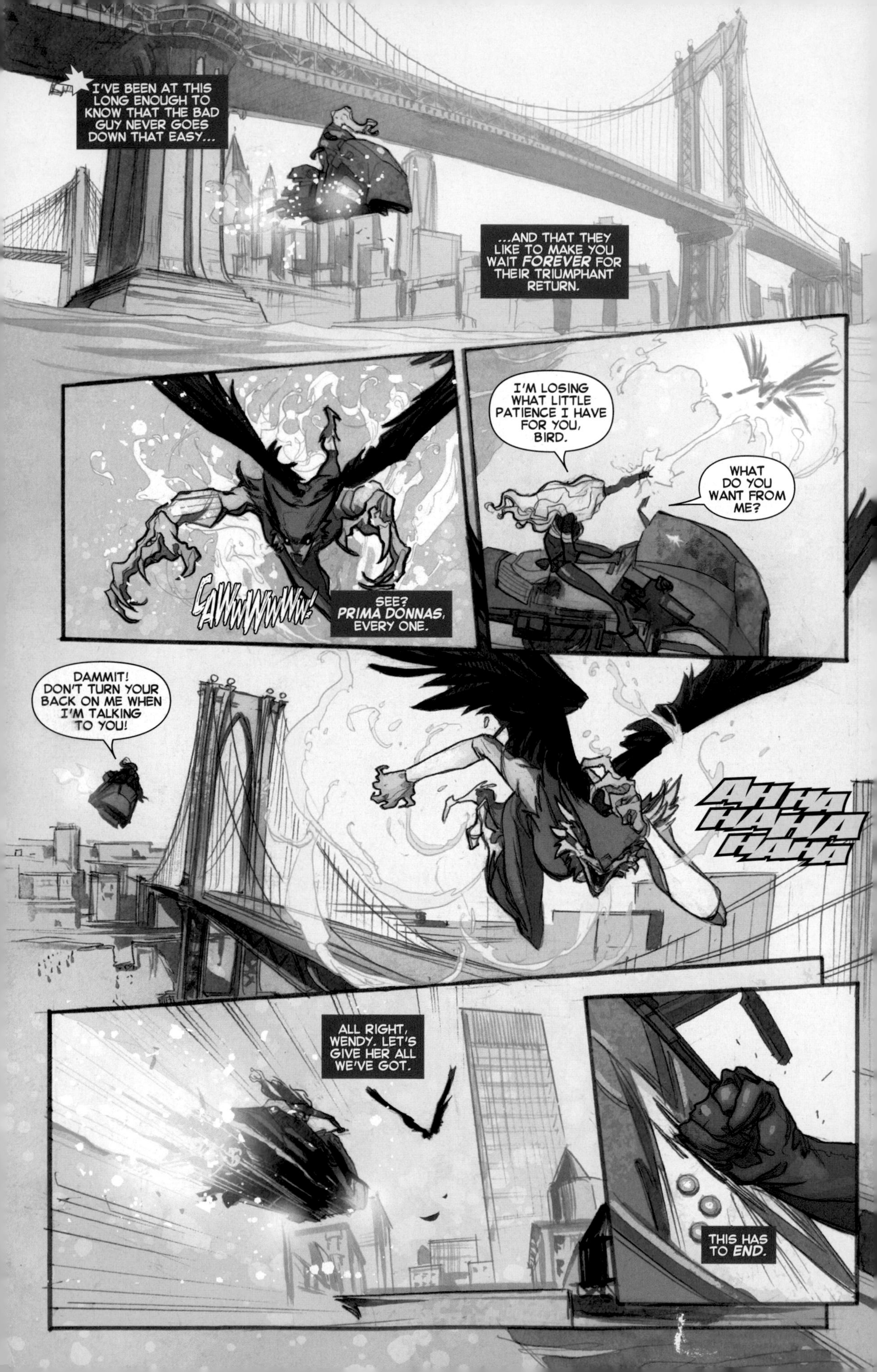
I'VE BEEN AT THIS LONG ENOUGH TO KNOW THAT THE BAD GUY NEVER GOES DOWN THAT EASY...
...AND THAT THEY LIKE TO MAKE YOU WAIT FOREVER FOR THEIR TRIUMPHANT RETURN.
CAWWWWWW!
SEE? PRIMA DONNAS, EVERY ONE.
I'M LOSING WHAT LITTLE PATIENCE I HAVE FOR YOU, BIRD.
WHAT DO YOU WANT FROM ME?
DAMMIT! DON'T TURN YOUR BACK ON ME WHEN I'M TALKING TO YOU!
AH HA HAHA HAHA
ALL RIGHT, WENDY. LET'S GIVE HER ALL WE'VE GOT.
THIS HAS TO END.

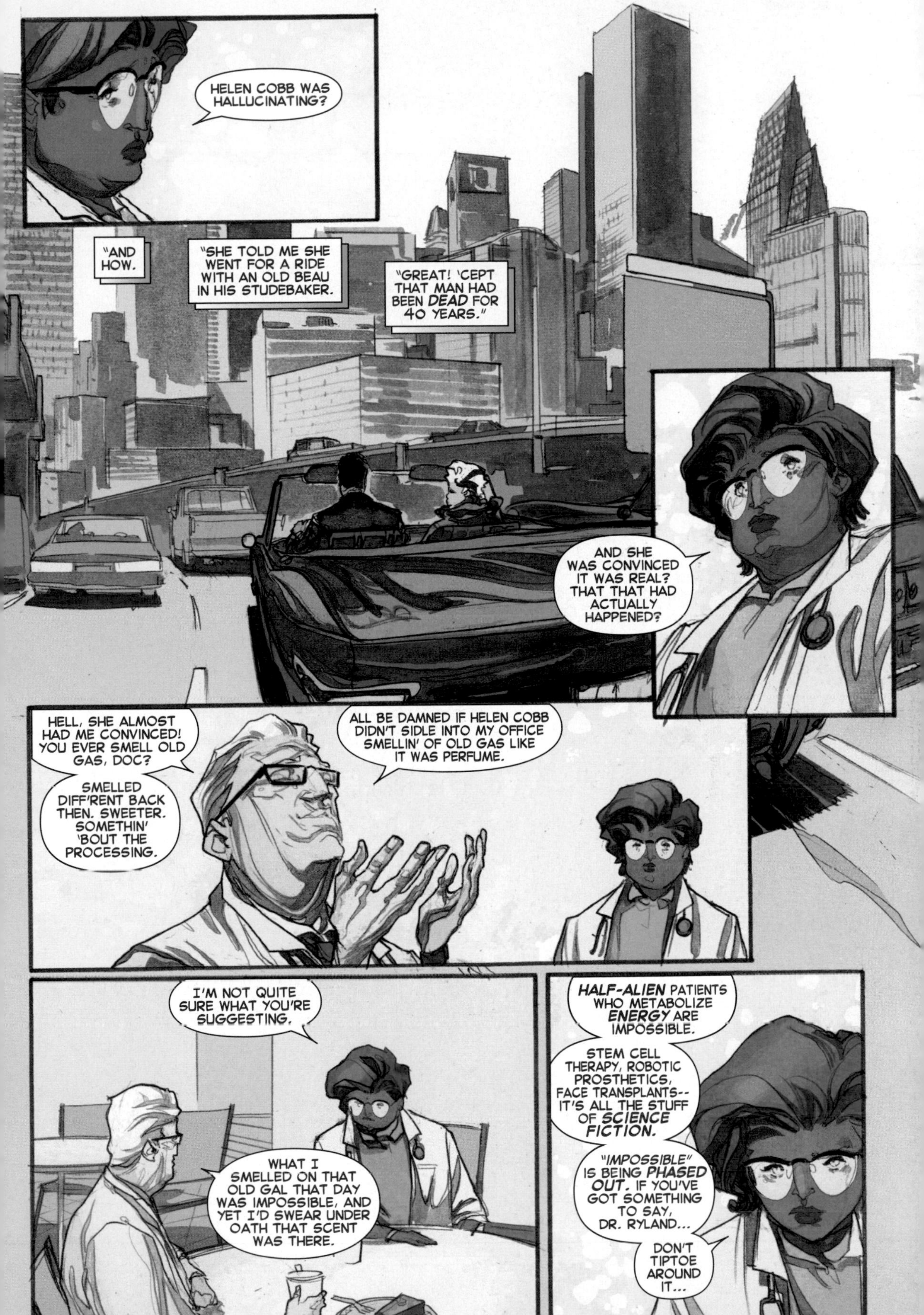
HELEN COBB WAS HALLUCINATING?
"AND HOW.
"SHE TOLD ME SHE WENT FOR A RIDE WITH AN OLD BEAU IN HIS STUDEBAKER.
"GREAT! 'CEPT THAT MAN HAD BEEN DEAD FOR 40 YEARS."
AND SHE WAS CONVINCED IT WAS REAL? THAT THAT HAD ACTUALLY HAPPENED?
HELL, SHE ALMOST HAD ME CONVINCED! YOU EVER SMELL OLD GAS, DOC?
SMELLED DIFF'RENT BACK THEN. SWEETER. SOMETHIN' 'BOUT THE PROCESSING.
ALL BE DAMNED IF HELEN COBB DIDN'T SIDLE INTO MY OFFICE SMELLIN' OF OLD GAS LIKE IT WAS PERFUME.
I'M NOT QUITE SURE WHAT YOU'RE SUGGESTING.
WHAT I SMELLED ON THAT OLD GAL THAT DAY WAS IMPOSSIBLE, AND YET I'D SWEAR UNDER OATH THAT SCENT WAS THERE.
HALF-ALIEN PATIENTS WHO METABOLIZE ENERGY ARE IMPOSSIBLE.
STEM CELL THERAPY, ROBOTIC PROSTHETICS, FACE TRANSPLANTS-- IT'S ALL THE STUFF OF SCIENCE FICTION.
"IMPOSSIBLE" IS BEING PHASED OUT. IF YOU'VE GOT SOMETHING TO SAY, DR. RYLAND...
DON'T TIPTOE AROUND IT...

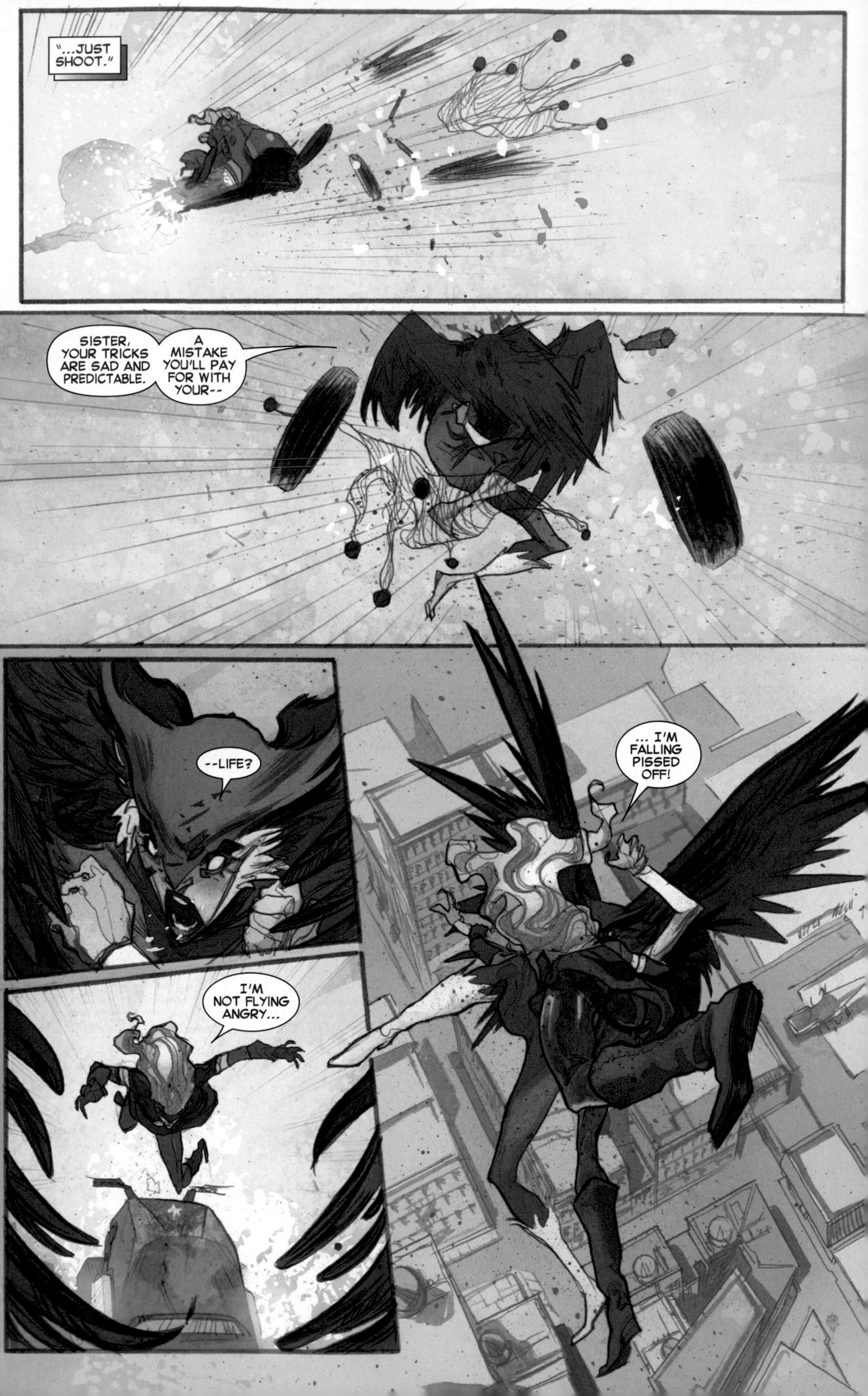
"...JUST SHOOT."
SISTER, YOUR TRICKS ARE SAD AND PREDICTABLE.
A MISTAKE YOU'LL PAY FOR WITH YOUR--
--LIFE?
I'M NOT FLYING ANGRY...
... I'M FALLING PISSED OFF!

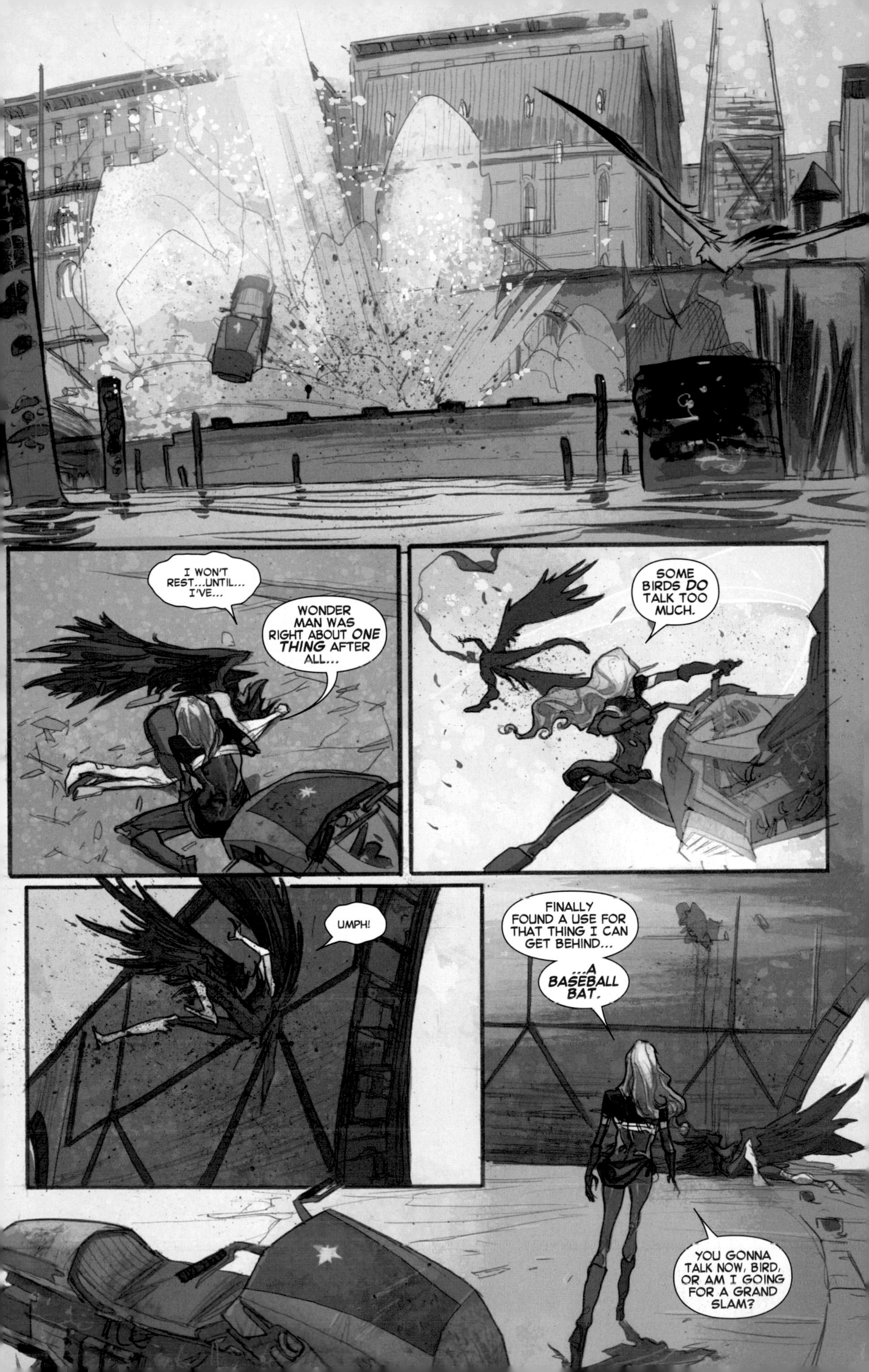
I WON'T REST...UNTIL... I'VE...
WONDER MAN WAS RIGHT ABOUT ONE THING AFTER ALL...
SOME BIRDS DO TALK TOO MUCH.
UMPH!
FINALLY FOUND A USE FOR THAT THING I CAN GET BEHIND...
...A BASEBALL BAT.
YOU GONNA TALK NOW, BIRD, OR AM I GOING FOR A GRAND SLAM?

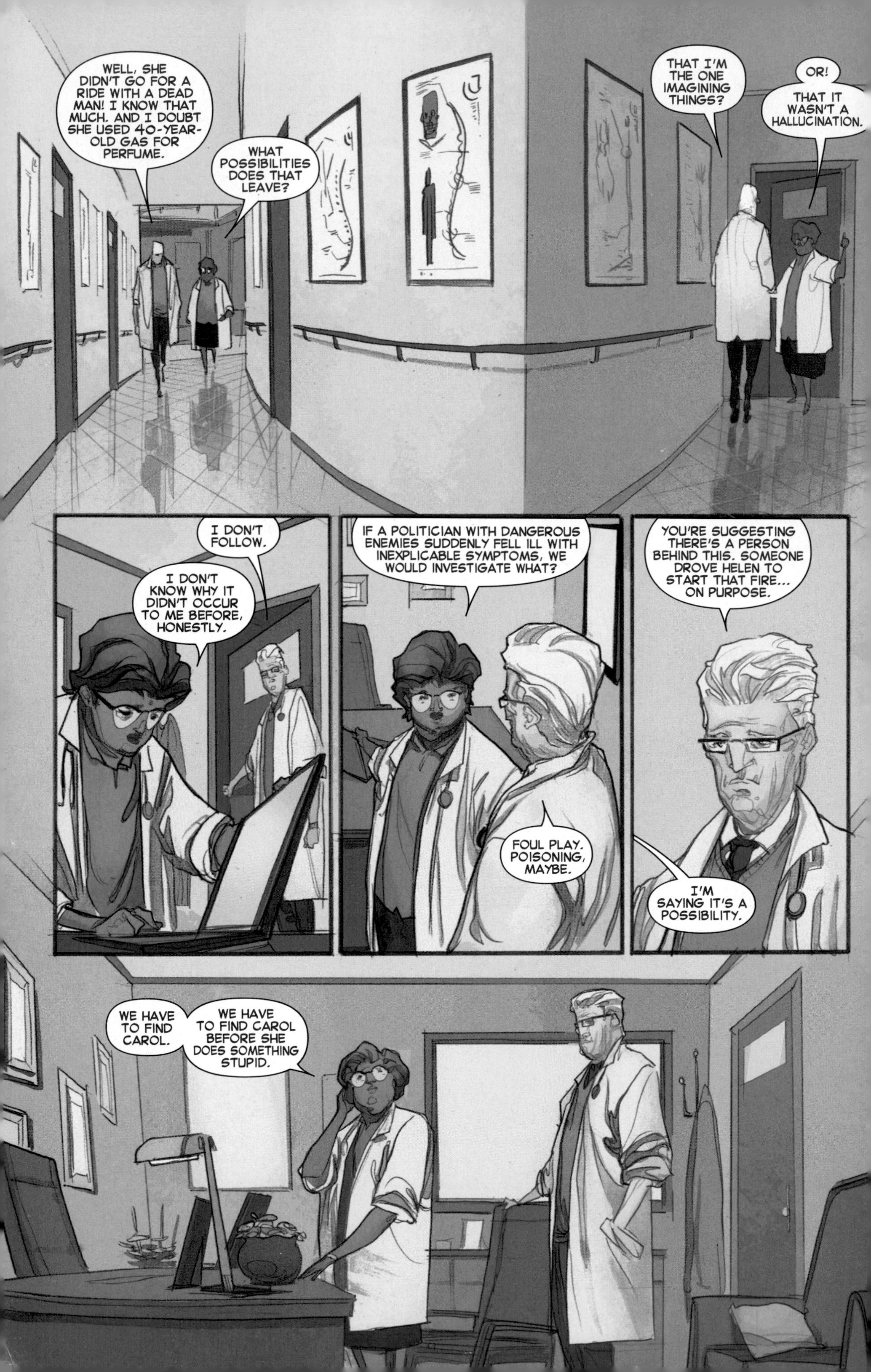
WELL, SHE DIDN'T GO FOR A RIDE WITH A DEAD MAN! I KNOW THAT MUCH. AND I DOUBT SHE USED 40-YEAR-OLD GAS FOR PERFUME.
WHAT POSSIBILITIES DOES THAT LEAVE?
THAT I'M THE ONE IMAGINING THINGS?
OR!
THAT IT WASN'T A HALLUCINATION.
I DON'T FOLLOW.
I DON'T KNOW WHY IT DIDN'T OCCUR TO ME BEFORE, HONESTLY.
IF A POLITICIAN WITH DANGEROUS ENEMIES SUDDENLY FELL ILL WITH INEXPLICABLE SYMPTOMS, WE WOULD INVESTIGATE WHAT?
FOUL PLAY. POISONING, MAYBE.
YOU'RE SUGGESTING THERE'S A PERSON BEHIND THIS. SOMEONE DROVE HELEN TO START THAT FIRE... ON PURPOSE.
I'M SAYING IT'S A POSSIBILITY.
WE HAVE TO FIND CAROL.
WE HAVE TO FIND CAROL BEFORE SHE DOES SOMETHING STUPID.

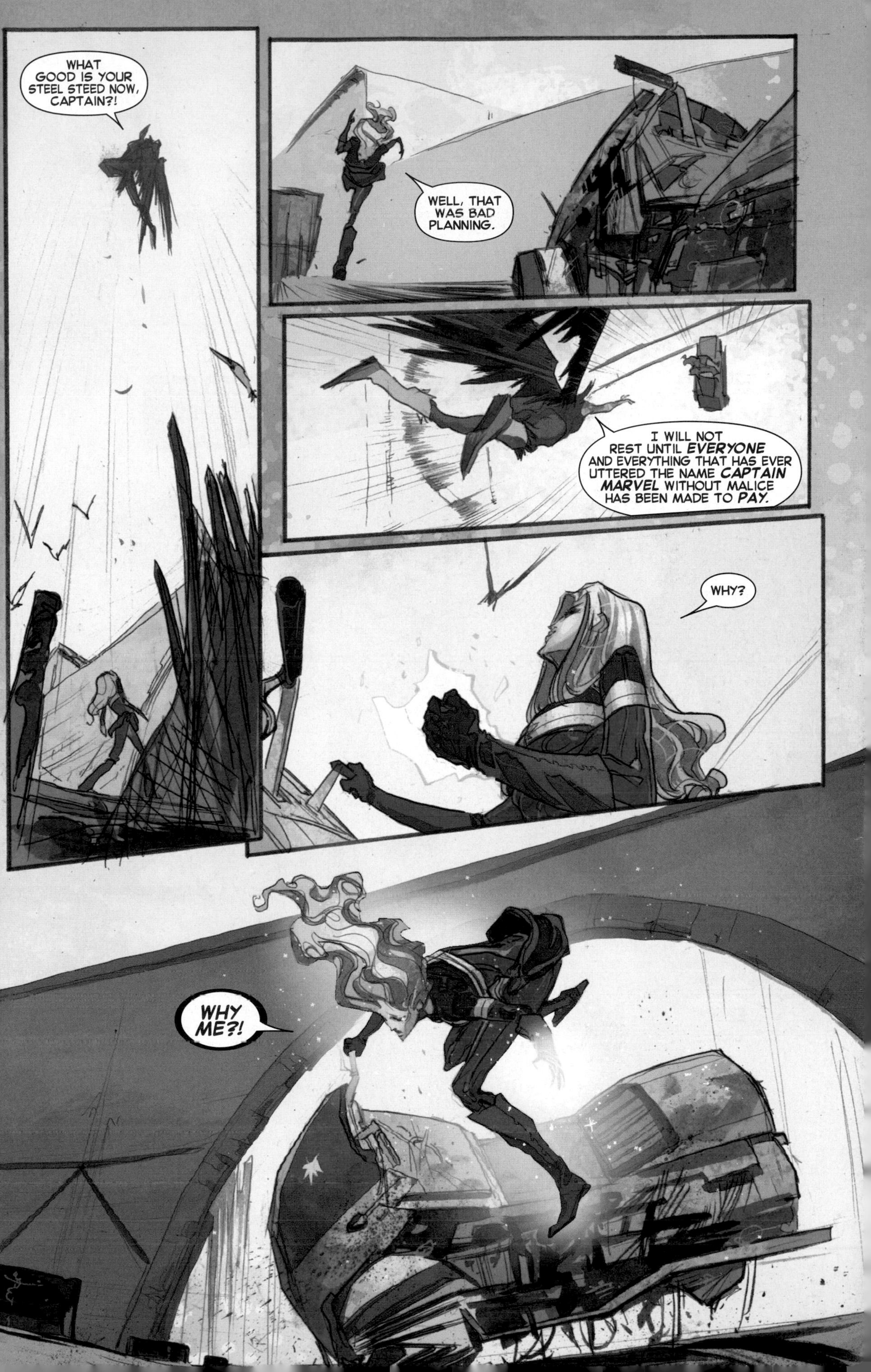
WHAT GOOD IS YOUR STEEL STEED NOW, CAPTAIN?!
WELL, THAT WAS BAD PLANNING.
I WILL NOT REST UNTIL *EVERYONE* AND EVERYTHING THAT HAS EVER UTTERED THE NAME *CAPTAIN MARVEL* WITHOUT MALICE HAS BEEN MADE TO *PAY.*
WHY?
WHY ME?!

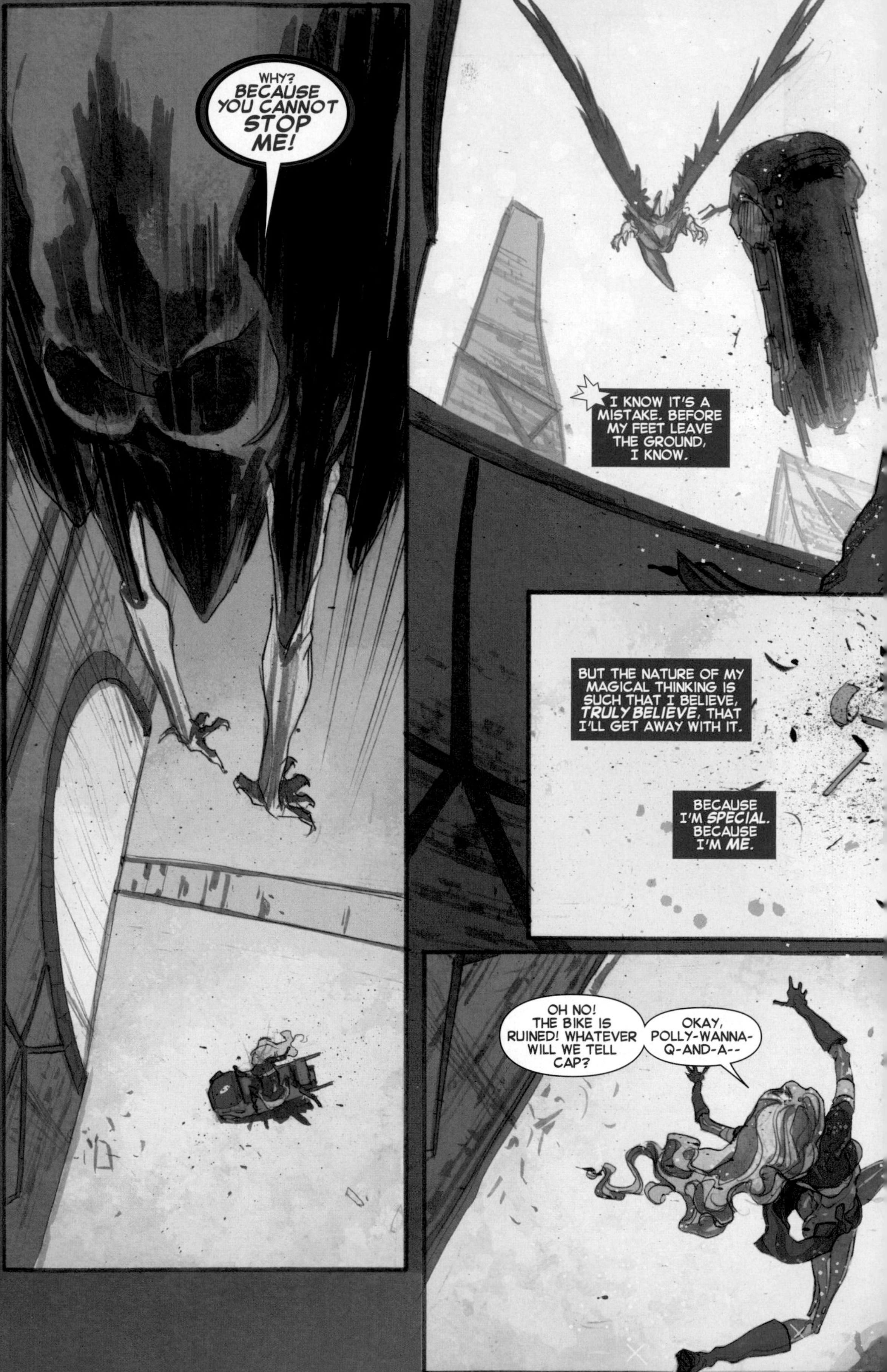
WHY? BECAUSE YOU CANNOT STOP ME!
I KNOW IT'S A MISTAKE. BEFORE MY FEET LEAVE THE GROUND, I KNOW.
BUT THE NATURE OF MY MAGICAL THINKING IS SUCH THAT I BELIEVE, TRULY BELIEVE, THAT I'LL GET AWAY WITH IT.
BECAUSE I'M SPECIAL. BECAUSE I'M ME.
OH NO! THE BIKE IS RUINED! WHATEVER WILL WE TELL CAP?
OKAY, POLLY-WANNA-Q-AND-A--

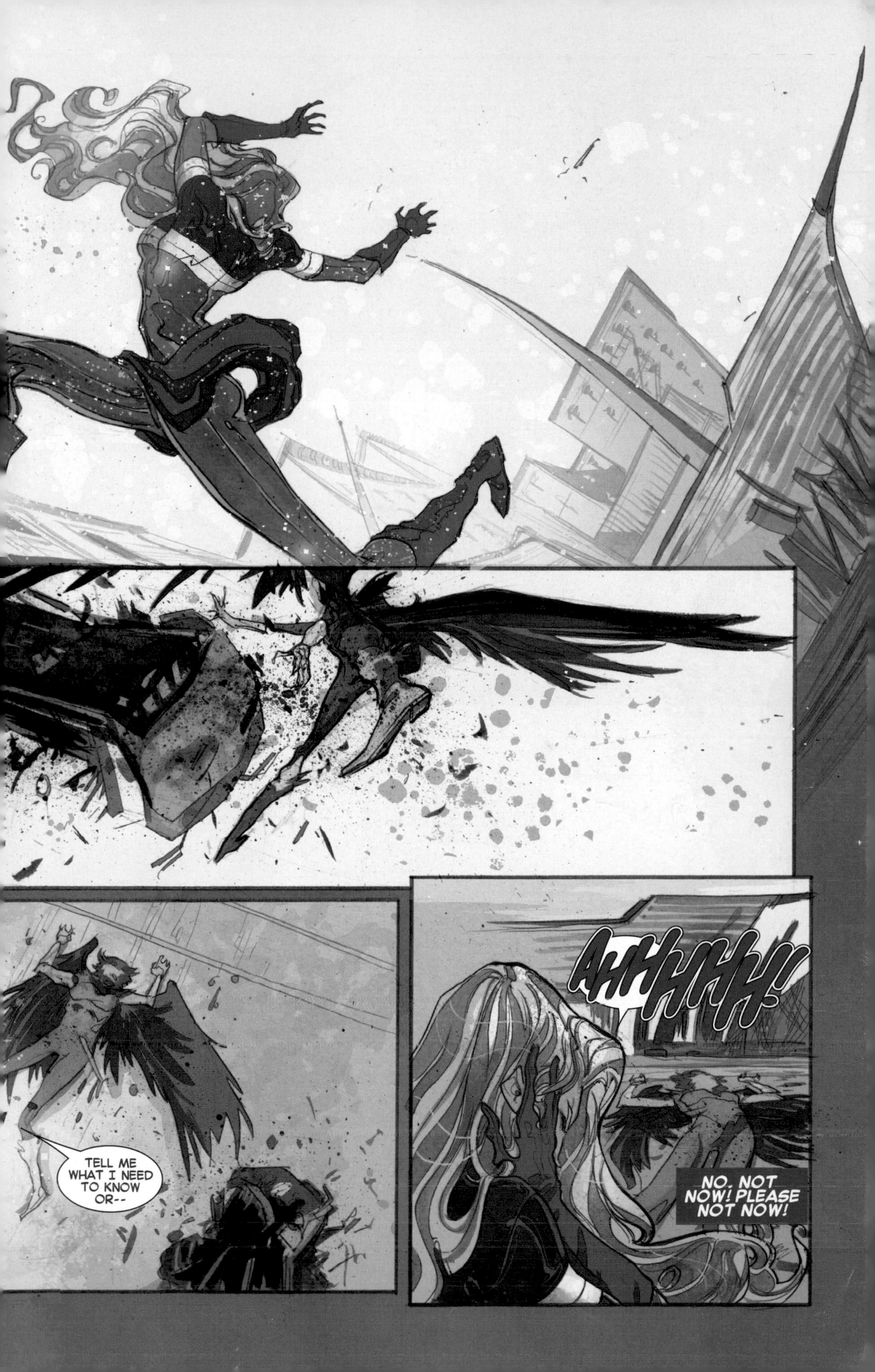
TELL ME WHAT I NEED TO KNOW OR--
AHHHHHH!
NO. NOT NOW! PLEASE NOT NOW!

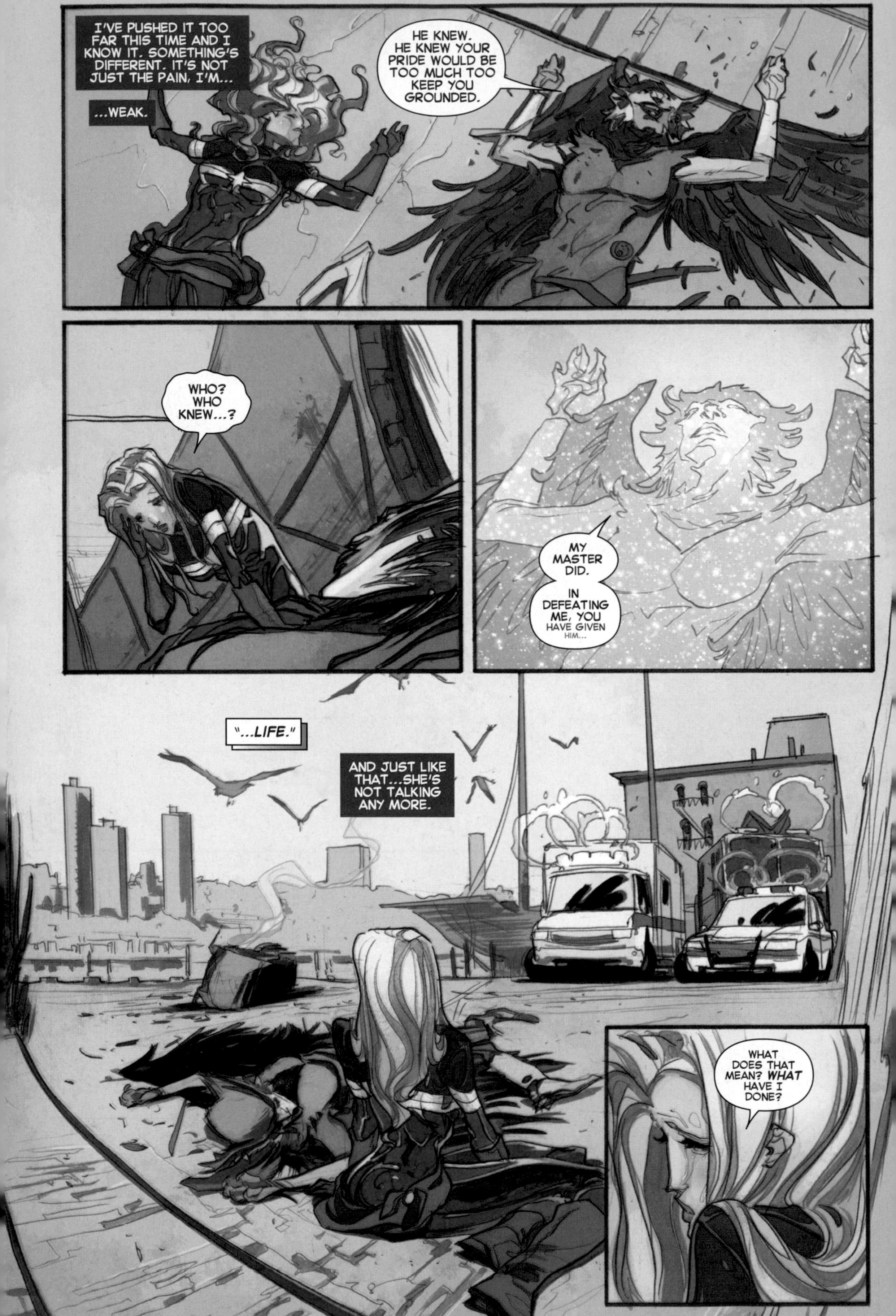

I'VE PUSHED IT TOO FAR THIS TIME AND I KNOW IT. SOMETHING'S DIFFERENT. IT'S NOT JUST THE PAIN, I'M...
...WEAK.
HE KNEW. HE KNEW YOUR PRIDE WOULD BE TOO MUCH TOO KEEP YOU GROUNDED.
WHO? WHO KNEW...?
MY MASTER DID.
IN DEFEATING ME, YOU HAVE GIVEN HIM...
"...LIFE."
AND JUST LIKE THAT...SHE'S NOT TALKING ANY MORE.
WHAT DOES THAT MEAN? WHAT HAVE I DONE?

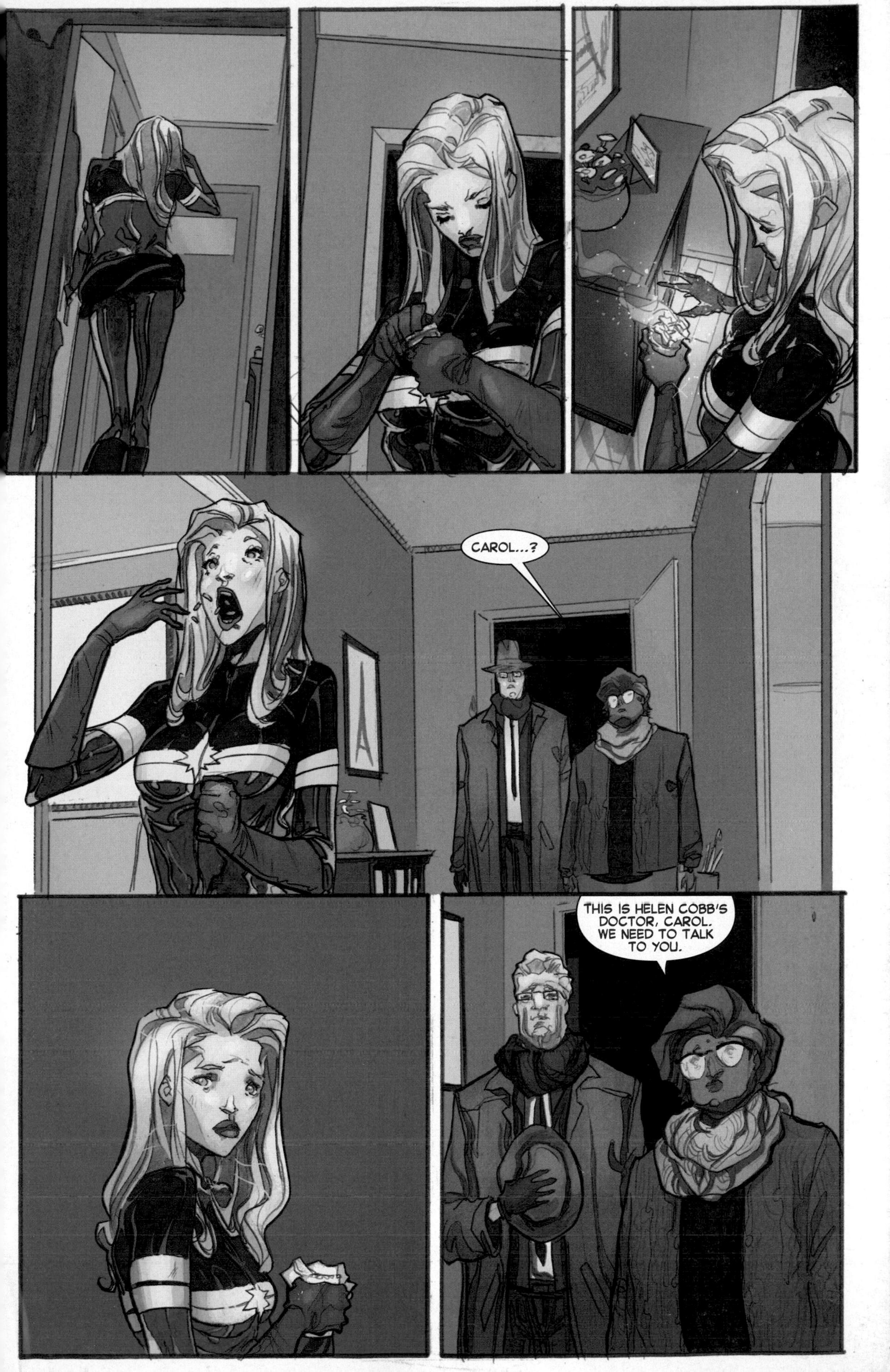
CAROL...?
THIS IS HELEN COBB'S DOCTOR, CAROL. WE NEED TO TALK TO YOU.

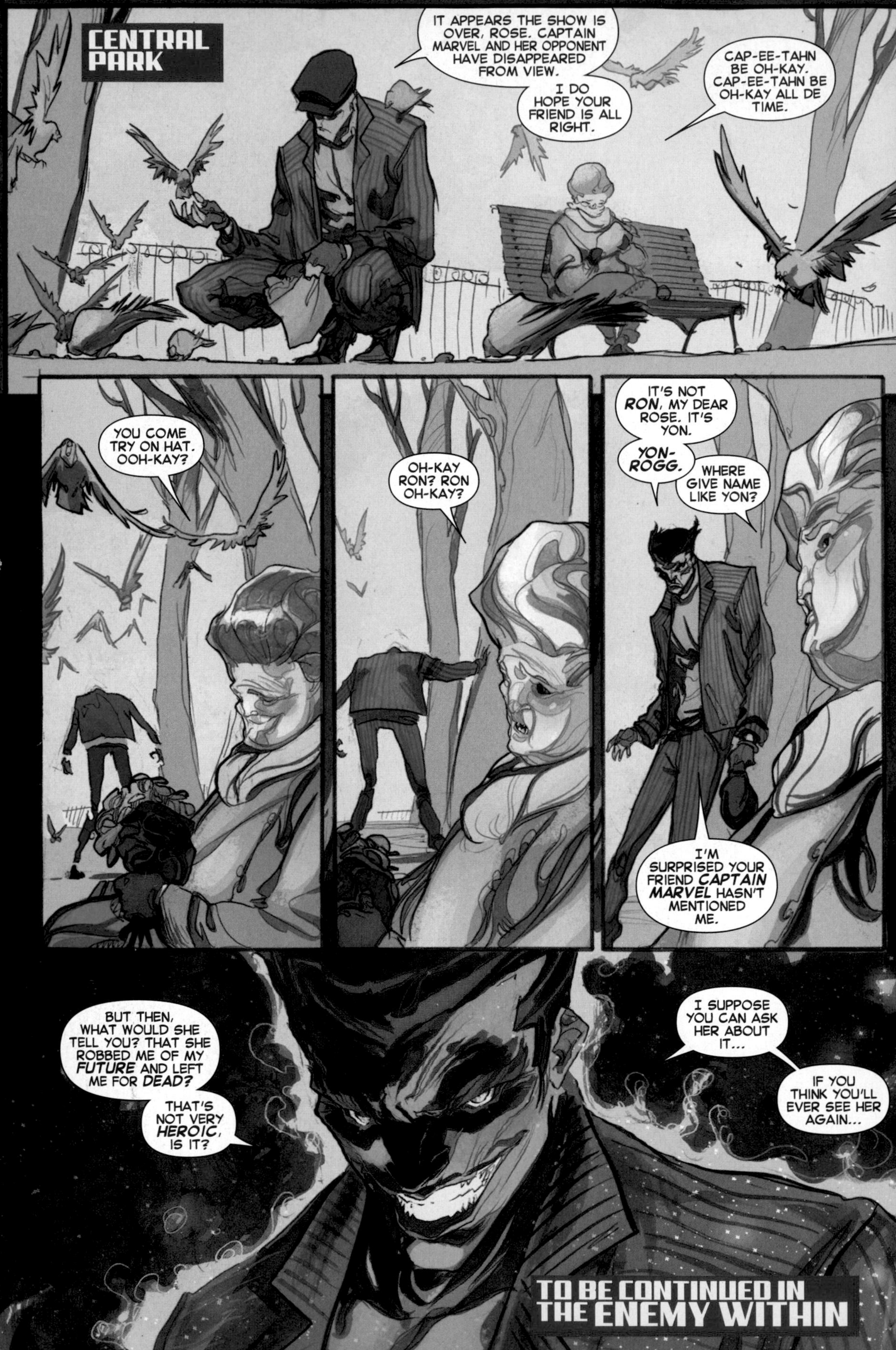
CENTRAL PARK
IT APPEARS THE SHOW IS OVER, ROSE. CAPTAIN MARVEL AND HER OPPONENT HAVE DISAPPEARED FROM VIEW.
I DO HOPE YOUR FRIEND IS ALL RIGHT.
CAP-EE-TAHN BE OH-KAY. CAP-EE-TAHN BE OH-KAY ALL DE TIME.
YOU COME TRY ON HAT. OOH-KAY?
OH-KAY RON? RON OH-KAY?
IT'S NOT RON, MY DEAR ROSE. IT'S YON.
YON-ROGG.
WHERE GIVE NAME LIKE YON?
I'M SURPRISED YOUR FRIEND CAPTAIN MARVEL HASN'T MENTIONED ME.
BUT THEN, WHAT WOULD SHE TELL YOU? THAT SHE ROBBED ME OF MY FUTURE AND LEFT ME FOR DEAD?
THAT'S NOT VERY HEROIC, IS IT?
I SUPPOSE YOU CAN ASK HER ABOUT IT...
IF YOU THINK YOU'LL EVER SEE HER AGAIN...
TO BE CONTINUED IN THE ENEMY WITHIN

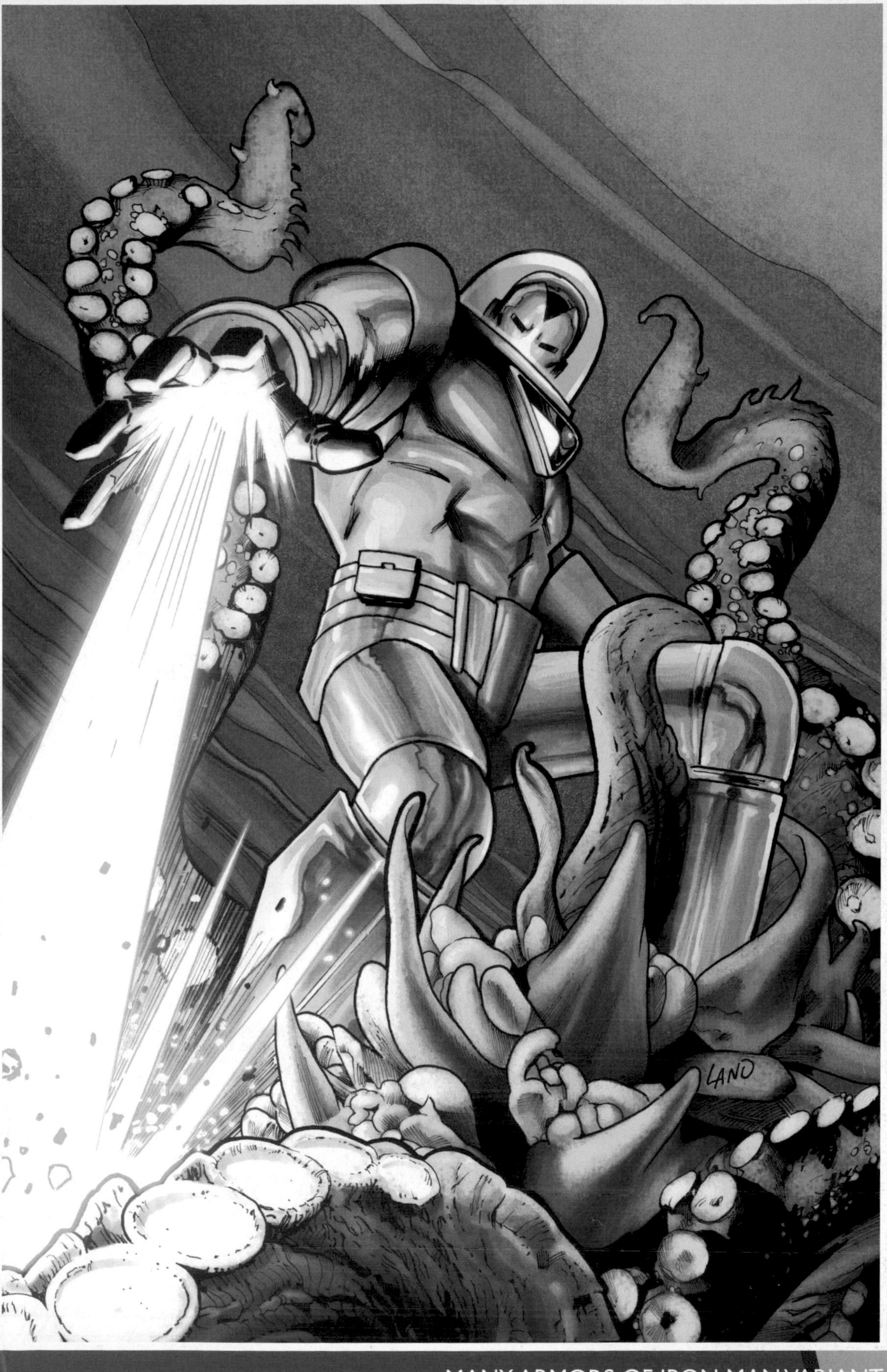
LAND

TWELVE MANY ARMORS OF IRON MAN VARIANT
BY GREG LAND & MORRY HOLLOWELL

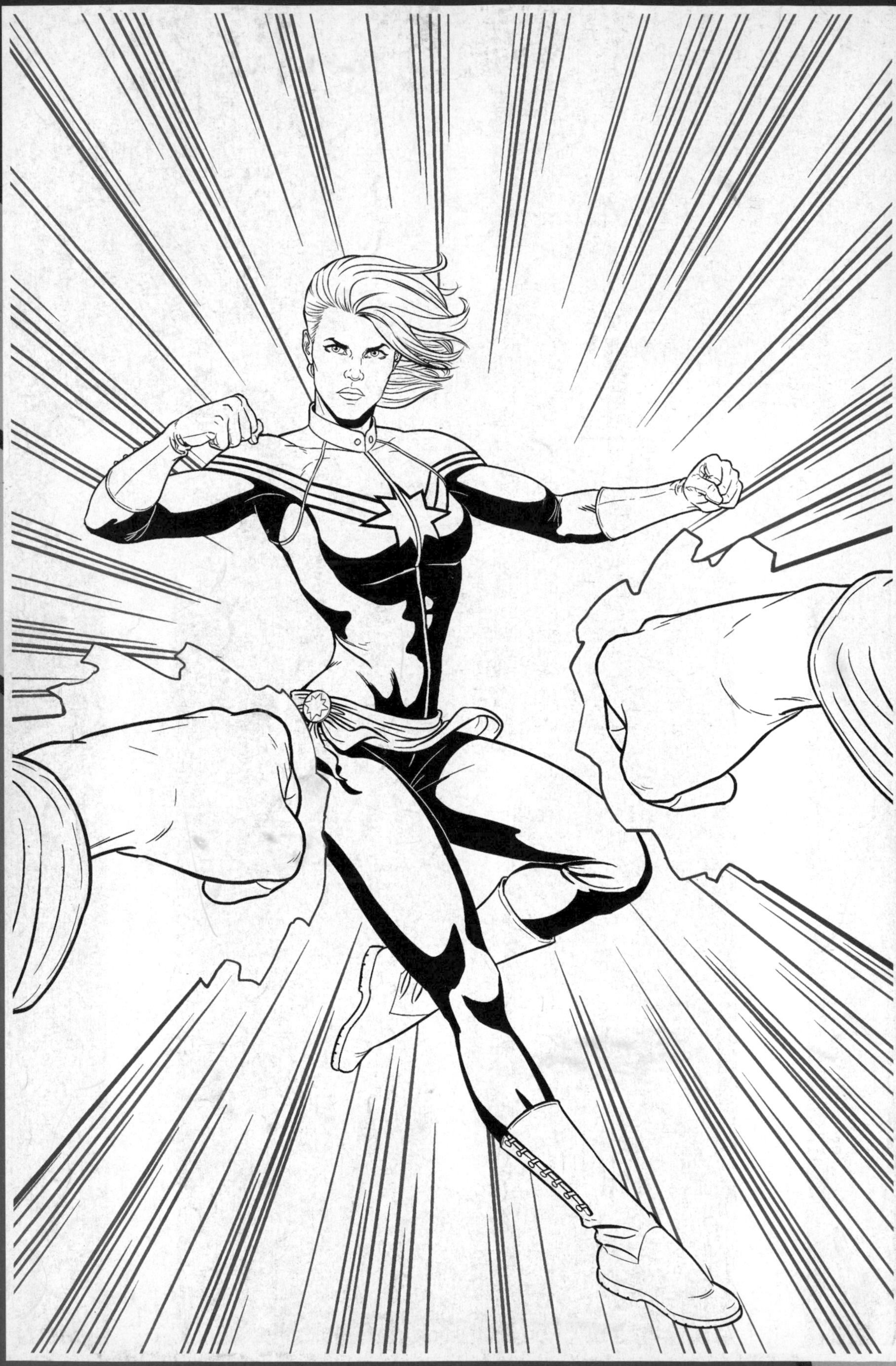

SEVEN COVER INKS BY JAMIE McKELVIE

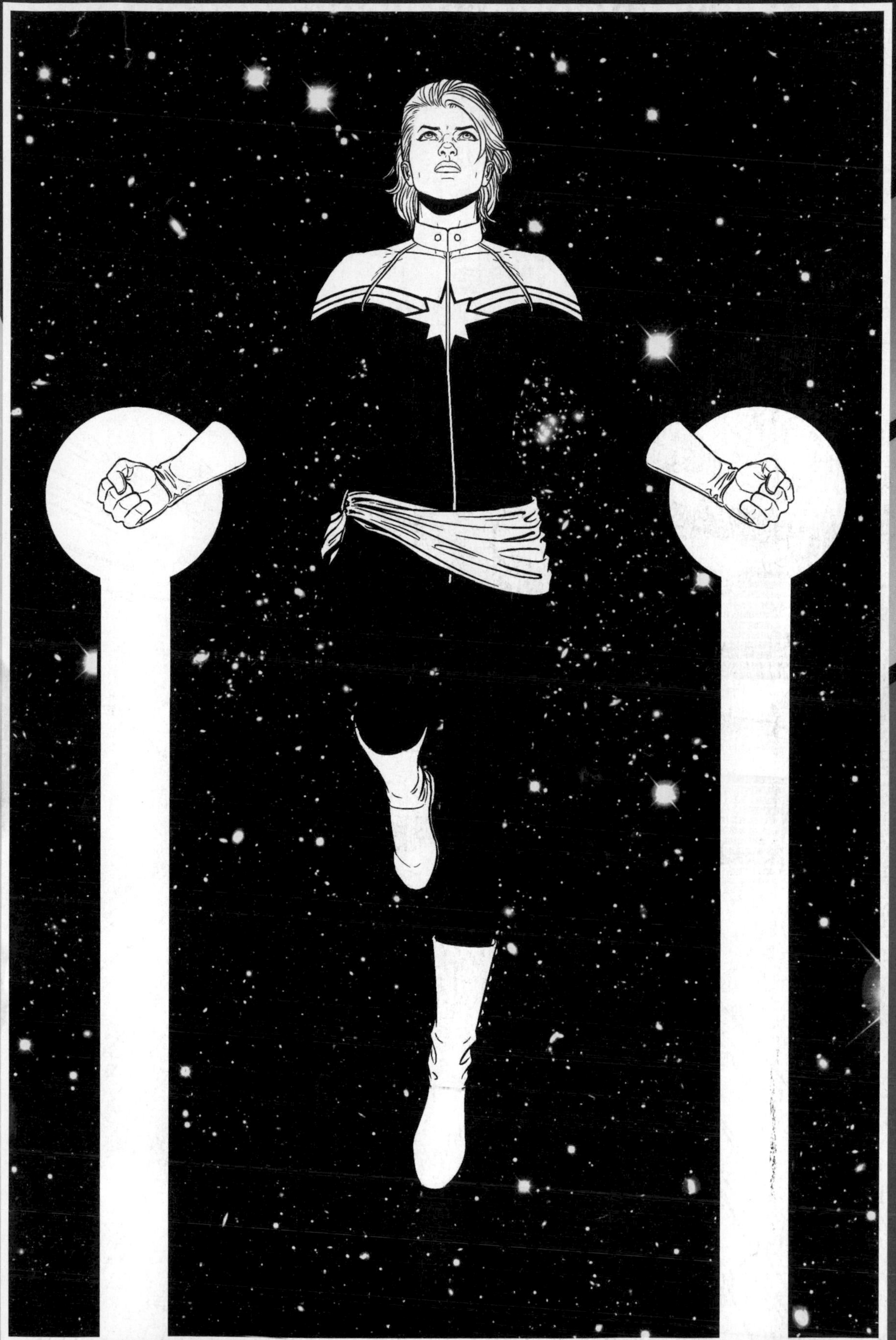

NINE COVER INKS BY JAMIE McKELVIE

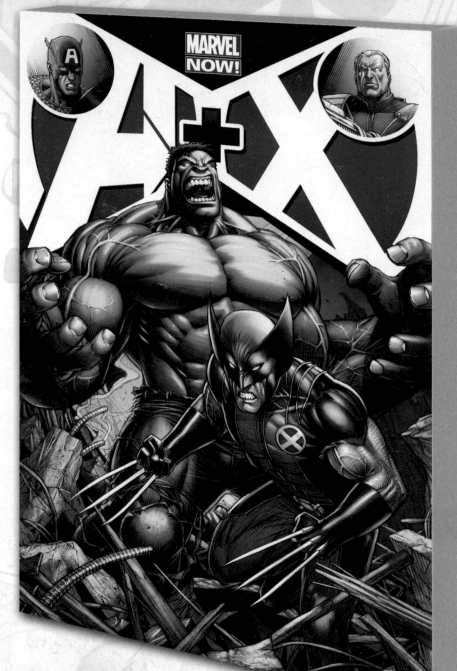